# Poetry Report

## *Books For Life Foundation*

Nancy —

all the best,

Mark Shaw

---

**JIM WALKER &**
**MARK SHAW**

# Books By Mark Shaw

Book Report

Grammar Report

Poetry Report

No Peace For The Wicked

Let The Good Times Roll

From Birdies To Bunkers

Code Of Silence

Miscarriage of Justice,
The Jonathan Pollard Story

Larry Legend

Testament To Courage

Forever Flying

Bury Me In A Pot Bunker

Jack Nicklaus, Golf's Greatest Champion

The Perfect Yankee

Diamonds In The Rough

Down For The Count

# Poetry Report

**Creative Ideas and Publishing
Strategies For Aspiring Poets**

*JIM WALKER and
MARK SHAW*

*Publisher's Cataloging—In—Publication Data*

*Jim Walker 1968 —*

*Mark Shaw 1945—*

> *Book Report, Publishing Strategies, Writing Tips, and 101 Literary Ideas For Aspiring Authors and Poets by Mark Shaw*

> *p.      cm.*

*ISBN 0-9717596-5-0*

> *1. Shaw, Mark 1945—*
> *2. Jim Walker 1968 —*
> *3. Book Publishing*
> *4. Poets*
> *5. Writing Skills*
> *6.  I. Shaw, Mark II. Title*

*10 9 8 7 6 5 4 3 2 1*

*Printed in the United States of America*

# Contents

# Acknowledgments

Without the assistance of many people, *Poetry Report* would not be possible.

Author Jim Walker wishes to thank his wife, Shauta, and children, Vivien and Max. Their love, affection, and support are a vital artery in his life. He also thanks poets Karen Kovacik, Robert Bly, and Li-Young Lee for lending their professionalism to this book. Their interviews and works of poetry will serve to inspire many aspiring poets.

Mr. Walker's fellow teachers and students at Indiana University-Purdue University at Indianapolis and Warren Wilson College are also thanked for their words of wisdom. The generous editors of *NUVO* magazine receive thanks for permitting the re-printing of interviews with Lee and Bly and for their ongoing support.

Author Mark Shaw wishes to thank Christina Williams, a gifted poet and wordsmith with a love for the literary arts for her contribution to this book. Editor Heidi Newman's expertise is also most appreciated as is that of Sara Charette for her layout of the book.

Mr. Shaw also thanks his family; brother Jack, and sisters Anne and Debbie for their support. And his canine companion, Black Sox, for his friendship at 5:00 a.m.

The authors are most appreciative of the support provided by Books For Life Foundation founding benefactor Jack Lupton. He is a man of few words with a passion for one of them. His financial wizard Dave Gonzenbach, and his sidekicks Audrey and Debbie are also thanked for their assistance with the foundation.

Above all, the authors thank the Good Lord for his blessings. Without him, they are nothing.

Jim Walker
Mark Shaw

Poetry is unlike any other form of writing. It is unique, both in form and substance. Restricted by space, words are kept to a minimum, but poetry nonetheless generates excitement, changes minds, stimulates alternative viewpoints, inspires, educates, informs—all of this and more. Poetry is full of life, full of messages, subject to differing interpretations to any who cross its path.

Poets too, are a separate breed. Unlike their brethren, fiction and non-fiction writers, they weave a magic spell using their talents despite the unlikelihood that they will ever become rich or famous. Some do—the Frosts and Whitmans of the world—but for the most part the poet writes because he or she loves the craft, not the ultimate reward. Some gather at writer's meetings or conferences, but most are the lone wolves writing their gems longhand or at the computer in the dead of night when silence is their best friend.

Many poems are seen or heard by no one but the poet, or a few loved ones, but this makes no difference since the poet has succeeded in composing a symphony of words straight from the heart. Their passion is embedded in the few stanzas or lines, their ideas and thoughts cast out of their minds onto paper for history's sake or simply for pleasure. Dedication is the poet's credo, but dedication to the message, not the almighty dollar.

To these diehards of the written word—these lovers of the written word—*Poetry Report* is dedicated. Together the authors hope their collective thoughts about the creative process and the potential to become published will assist the efforts of those who decide to take pen to paper and let their brain deposit its matter in whatever form of poetry is chosen. Practical advice is the byword of the book – there is no theory or "you should do it this way" marching orders to complicate the simple guideposts featured.

Instead, the authors present a simple game plan designed to stimulate the imaginative process. Using a proven method of creative thinking, several exercises, and knowledge gained from interviews with three successful poets, you will learn how to tackle the challenge of drafting lines of poetry in sync with the message you wish to convey. As time passes, and you gain more experience, the method will become second nature.

To assist your efforts, the Appendix includes a section recommending poets and poetry books for reference. There is also a list of poetry guides, textbooks, and essay collections you may want to consider.

Once you have crafted poetry you believe worthy of publication, the book provides a well-grounded strategy for those who wish the world to know of their writings through traditional publishing. No advice is given regarding the potential to engage a literary agent, a necessary element for the aspiring author who desires a traditional publishing contract, since most literary agents are not interested in representing poets. This is not because of any lack of appreciation for the craft, but a fact of life based on potential earning power, or lack thereof, for the aspiring poet. Literary agents may love books, but earning a living is paramount and requires their representing very few poets.

Those poets who dream of publication will embark on a journey to attract interest in their works through selected magazines and other outlets. This provides good exposure and builds credentials that will impress book publishers. The formula for success then becomes a simple one: a terrific poetry book idea, a well-conceived strategy, and hard work. Once this has been formulated, it is only a matter of time until you, the poet, will shout to the world, "I am published!"

Since writing and/or publishing poetry is a terrific training ground for writing fiction and non-fiction, the Appendix features information regarding the publishing industry in general. Text also provides information regarding copyright procedures designed to protect your writings, a sample publishing agreement, a sample book proposal, and an analysis of a *Poet's Market* publishers' listing.

This all said – let's begin your sojourn into the world of poetry. You are about to join a respected group of individuals who respect the written word and are, in turn, respected by those who appreciate the poet as a wordsmith in the true sense of the word.


Jim Walker
Mark Shaw

# **Creative Thinking**

# Chapter One
## The Budding Poet

Poetry doesn't begin with writing. It begins with recognizing. It begins with seeing the poems that dance and sing and shout and bawl their eyes out all around you. It begins with knowing a poem when you see one.

When a photographer walks through a city with her trained eye searching the faces of people on the street, the steel buildings rising above the sidewalks and the cement landscapes surrounding her, she sees pictures. Even without a camera to her eye, she will begin to zoom in on details. She will crop and frame photographs in her mind. She may or may not take her camera out of her bag to snap these pictures. Either way, they were recorded.

For our photographer, the world is full of pictures the rest of us may never see. This is what makes the photographer an artist. She is using the available materials of the world to create something new and specific to her vision.

To be certain, we can all push a button and take a picture. But we won't all arrive at the same details in the same composition. We won't capture the same pieces of the world that only she sees.

Poets work this way as they walk down the street. Like the photographer, they capture images with their eyes. By noticing what they experience and writing it down, poets capture images frozen in time like moving, talking, feeling pictures. They could be actions or interactions – perhaps a man shouting to himself on the corner, a baby bouncing on his mother's lap, or a dove ascending in front of a war monument.

Poets have an advantage over our photographer because they can do more than capture what is recorded with **sight**. Poets also harness the other senses: **sound** – an overheard conversation between mother and daughter, saxophone music from an apartment window; **smells** – onions and hamburgers frying in grease on a diner grill, an elderly woman's rose-scented perfume; **touch** – warm sunlight on the back of the neck, a stranger's damp skin brushing softly against yours as you pass; and **taste** – a pink, cold lemonade from a corner store, the sweet breath of your lover as you kiss hello, having arrived at your meeting place.

Beyond those five senses, the poet has an even more important advantage. Poets can record the sixth sense, the feelings of emotion, intuition and spirit. **Poetry, at its best, is a blending of the physical and emotional.** It's a leaping from the beautiful and ugly concrete realities of the world into the unknown and abstract world of dreams and emotions inside of all of us.

Poems allow us to "stand on the earth" in between our attempts to climb to heaven or dig to hell. As a poet, you will face the challenge of relaying an experience that is both tangible – something we can hold in our hands, something that we can physically feel – and something that happens beyond the everyday realities of our world.

This may sound like a daunting challenge, but if we return to our walk through the city, we already have a starting point that will work for everyone. You don't have to wait on a birth or death or marriage for a poem to arrive. The world doesn't need to be at war and you don't need to travel to Paris or the Grand Canyon to find poems. **To begin, you need only turn on your observational skills and take a walk in your world, looking around you and inside you.**

## Getting Started

While our photographer spent hundreds of dollars on her camera gear, film and processing, as a starting poet, you need only invest in a notebook and pen. While inexpensive, your choices are important. Your notebook should be small enough to fit into your pocket, purse or a bag carried with you at all times.

Portability is crucial. Your notebook will be with you while attending church, while at dinner with friends, when you slip into bed at night. **Your life will become one long observational walk though the cityscape that is your day.**

Some small, spiral-bound notebooks include pockets inside, perfect for saving love notes dropped on the street, ticket stubs, museum maps, flyers from art galleries, etc. Try to find a notebook with a pocket. Most discount or office-supply stores sell a variety of these.

Choose a notebook in a color that you like, that best represents you. Decorate your notebook with pictures or stickers if you wish. Make it your own. Be sure to write your name and telephone number inside in case you misplace it. As close as you will soon become with your notebook, losing it would be like leaving a child behind.

Spend a little time, likewise, choosing a pen that feels comfortable in your hand, that makes you feel good as you pick it up. Consider purchasing a special poetry pen – one dedicated to your notebook. Use pens that remind you of where you bought or found them – maybe an Elvis pen from Graceland, a cheap pen from a motel in Florida where you stayed on your honeymoon. Find one that will fit in the notebook's binding so that it is always there when you need it.

At this point, you don't need to worry about computers or typing. You are going to generate your raw material in your notebook. Nearly every poet working today starts out by hand writing his or her poems. The first step of revising and honing the raw material into poems, explained later, occurs at the keyboard.

**With a notebook and pen chosen and comfortably placed in your pocket, satchel or purse, you are ready to take a walk and write your first commentary on the observations you notice in your world.**


## Exercise One

Choose a place you like where you can walk or sit and visit, notebook in hand. If you live in a city, stroll though a busy downtown area or a blighted side street. Visit a church or café. If you live in a small town or suburb, stroll through a park or neighborhood where people are mowing their lawns, walking their dogs, or where children play. Visit a farm near your home. If you want to further escape the city, hike a forest trail or sit by a body of water.

The key factor for choosing the location for your walk or visit is to find a place that is somewhat unfamiliar to you, a place you can examine objectively. Set out with a fresh perspective and be ready to discover. At this point, don't try to write about a place that you love or hate.

Make a list of the senses on separate pages of your notebook. List: See, Hear, Smell, Taste, Touch and Feel (emotion). Allow two or three pages for each sense, depending on the size of your notebook. If you fill one page, you can add more. Then begin your walk or find your observation spot at the location of your choice.

Resist the urge to write a poem. List the sensory details you observe on the appropriate pages, being sure to fill the pages for all of the senses. If you discover you aren't hearing enough sounds, stop looking around, close your eyes, and listen. Even if you have chosen to walk, you can stop and sit down (especially if you are closing your eyes). This also makes writing a little easier. Don't worry about writing neatly in your book.

Don't edit anything at this point. Leave it all there. Don't re-read what you are writing. Let the words flow freely and automatically. Don't force anything. Don't concern yourself with the structure or form of the content. Don't try to write in rhyme. **Just write what you sense.**

Be sure to write about whatever you observe concretely. Remember the photographer. She was creating art because her pictures were her own distinct vision of the world. The pictures were taken from a perspective that was only hers.

If you walk by a pond filled with ducks floating and simply jot in your notebook: "pretty pond with ducks quacking," you haven't captured anything distinct or specific. This observation says nothing about you or about the reality you observed. It is too broad, too abstract. It would force anyone reading it to fill in all of the details. You need to do that.

Instead, zoom your imagination lens in on the specific details. What does the pond look like? What does it smell like? Can you taste the water in the air, feel heat or cool rising off of it? Does it remind you of anything else? Does it make you feel a certain way as you look at it? What size and shape is it? Is it mossy? What color is the water? Are other people around it? What are they doing? What color are the ducks? How many ducks? Are there other creatures living in or around the pond? What did the ducks' quacking sound like? What would you compare it to? Were they talking to you? What do you think they were saying?

As you fill in the details, the pond becomes a concrete scene that could make readers feel like they are really there. The pond could even move from reality to something more as you begin to examine the way it makes you feel and what the ducks – and maybe the bugs and fish and frogs – might be saying to you. While hundreds of other people may walk by the pond every day and think "oh, a pond," you will eventually increase its sway with your poem.

This example is not intended to limit you to only writing about a nature walk. All of these same questions can be answered and these sensory details found in city neighborhoods, at salvage yards, in art museums or in your grandfather's garage. Go where you want to go and fill the first several pages of your notebook with detailed pictures full of sights and sounds and smells and feelings that only you could interpret in this exact way.

# Chapter Two
## Ah, Poetry

Having generated several notebook pages of raw material, you are ready to craft that material into a first draft of a poem. **But those notebook pages and the roughed-out images, ideas and emotions contained within them, are like wooden beams cut fresh from the forest.** They remain green and wet. You need to give these beams time to cure. While you pause to consider some practical poetic principles, stick the notebook in a drawer and try to wait patiently. We will return to your poem soon.

Some experienced poets habitually draft notes for their poems and leave them in the desk drawer until they've forgotten the original impulse that led them to jot the notes. Sometimes, they'll pick up the drafts and forget even writing the words on the page. This is all by design. The wait allows them to step back and look at the raw materials as just that.

More objective about the work, they are less in love with their lines and more apt to move into the drafting and revising steps with less worry about all those shavings whittled on the workshop floor. By waiting to move to drafting and then revising, the poet is almost self-collaborating, giving the material a second set of eyes. We are all different people inside from one week, or month, to the next.

While you are in your holding pattern writing-wise, let's answer a few major questions about poetry before you continue with your work.

## What Is (or Isn't) Poetry?

**Ultimately, poetry is about truth. It is about focus and pattern. It is about emotion and sensation. It is about precision of language: choosing the right words in the right order with no unnecessary padding.**

Sometimes, poetry is about rules, about form and structure. Sometimes, it can utilize fancy literary devices. Sometimes it can be difficult to write and difficult to read. Sometimes it can be elusive and puzzling both in its creation and reception. Other times it can pour right from the pen. It can be read as straightforward, simple and clear.

Whatever method a poet uses, the goal needs to be to take a small slice of life – an epiphany, a key moment, a particularly revealing experience – and allow that slice to expand in the mind of the reader. Poetry differs from prose most in the way it starts small and grows. It is a vitamin that contains the nutrients of an entire meal minus the fat and bulk.

**Think about this way: the poem is a pill, a short story is lunch, a novella is supper and a novel is Thanksgiving dinner.** The idea of the poem, and the language used to convey this idea, are tightly wound, condensed. With prose, the idea can remain big and sprawling through thousands of pages. The language doesn't have to be so dense because a novel or non-fiction book must build a gentler, easier pace for the reader to sustain over the long haul. **Think of poetry as a funnel with the big part open, taking everything in, grinding it up, and spitting it out into one tiny, powerful pill.** The reader, then, allows that pill to expand again in his mind, nourishing it.

**You may wonder: What's this business about *truth*?** Does that mean all poetry must be confessional, autobiographical or journalistic? No. It means the poem must be written in a way true to its purpose, its emotional intention, its impulse. A poem shouldn't be self-censored, dumbed-down, or shrouded in hocus-pocus mystery for the sake of hiding this impulse, this original truth. It must come from your brain and heart, your thoughts and feelings.

What makes poetry bad, you may ask, what makes it flat, lifeless and pointless? The world needs no more poems full of dishonest sentimentality and cliché. Sentimentality is an overindulgence of emotion that rings false. Like a stage actor overplaying his part in an emotional scene, these poems can turn sadly comical.

We know the actor is only aping the lines. He doesn't know what to really say, thus he pretends. In a sentimental, clichéd poem, we know the writer is afraid to say what he or she really feels and is just repeating what other people have already written on the subject. These are somebody else's bad lines not worth repeating. The reader of these poems, if he or she isn't afraid to see the truth himself, will know this is the stuff of bad acting.

**Examples of sentimental and dishonest poetry can be discovered at your local greeting card store.** The words inside these cards, by design, must be sentimental, dishonest. The anonymous writers – professing love, congratulating marriage, consoling death, celebrating birth – doubtlessly feel nothing when they write these words. They certainly can't include true and telling details from their own lives, from their own loves or losses. Instead, they are penning vague and generic poems that fit most everyone, most every occasion, like a baggy sweatshirt. Often written in first person, these poems say little, in detail, about how anyone really feels. The "I" is all of us and nobody at the same time. Greeting card poems draw on the sentiments of society at large and try to say what we might feel.

When emotions are true, they shine through clearly and easily in the poem. This is not to say you won't have to work hard on the poem. The ease comes most for the reader. Untrue, sentimental poems are a breeze to write. This is because you can draw on the bad writing that drifts over our society like a fog. One need only to turn on the local television news, watch an action movie or listen to a boy band on the radio to hear shovels full of sentimentality and cliché. The same goes for text found in newspapers, magazines and on Internet sites. You must work hard to avoid using these public domain phrases bouncing around in your head.

If you are writing about a moment when an important idea became clear in your mind, you will find yourself immediately wanting to write that it was suddenly "clear as day" or "clear as a bell" or "crystal clear." The sarcastic cliché "clear as mud" probably also pops into your mind. But where did these similes – comparisons using like or as – come from? You didn't create them. You remembered them from lines in a sitcom, from your mother saying them when you were a kid, from a romance novel you read.

**If a phrase stems from recall instead of your creativity, then it is probably a cliché. It will probably ring false.** Do you see anything when you imagine "clear as day?" A day can be cloudy and dark or bright and sunny. With the other two, you just see a vague bell and an even more vague crystal. Since we are already writing about something abstract – an idea becoming clear – we want to compare it to something concrete and tangible. If this moment of clarity is worth writing about, worth comparing to something, shouldn't we be more precise about that comparison and make it our own?

What else is clear? Water from a Canadian mountain lake. Fish scales. Cut glass. Vegetable oil. Aqua Velva cologne. By choosing one of these non-cliché comparisons, we are opening the poem to all kinds of possibilities. If the moment of clarity concerned your father and he was a fisherman, then maybe the fish scales or Canadian water similes would fit well. If the moment of clarity had to do with death, then cut glass takes on a much different connotation or meaning beyond itself. Do you see how "clear as cut glass" resonates in a way that "clear as a bell" does not? The simile's image is fresh, requires imagining the cut glass, and the alliteration (or sound repetition) of "clear" and "cut" makes nice music.

## Exercise Two

Retrieve your notebook (don't look at your other notes) and turn to a blank page. Make a list of several things you love and several things you dislike. Be specific: Your best friend's laugh, your favorite pair of shoes, your mother's apple pie, your commute to work or school, the illness afflicting a relative, and so forth.

Now compare all of these things using "like" or "as" to create several similes. Write down the very first thought that comes to mind. Don't worry if it is sentimental or clichéd. Just write it down.

Move through the list and create a simile for each. Then go back through all of them and ask yourself if the comparison is coming from your creative mind. Is it true and specific and telling? Does it carry a fitting connotation? If so, you are on the right track.

If you have any doubt, draw a line through that simile and think a bit more. Take your own "clear as a bell" cliché and turn it into something more interesting like "clear as cut glass" or "clear as the flash of a northern pike in Canadian lake water."

Detective writer Raymond Chandler, who began his career as a poet, collected similes in his notebooks even before he knew how he'd use them. These would later appear in novels like *The Big Sleep*. Here are a few examples:

> The light had an unreal greenish color, like the light filtered through and aquarium tank.

> The plants filled the place, a forest of them, with nasty meaty leaves like the newly washed fingers of dead men.

> They smelled as overpowering as boiling alcohol under a blanket.

The General spoke again, slowly, using his strength as carefully as an out-of-work showgirl uses her last pair of stockings.

Here are a few more examples from Chandler's notebooks:

As noiseless as a finger in a glove

Lower than a badger's belly

A face like a collapsed lung

As clean as an angel's neck

**Ultimately, the best of human creations, from a poem to a well-designed building, are born of necessity.** How can a poem be necessary? First, it is important for poets to fulfill their individual drive to create. For many, writing becomes necessary for mental – even physical – wellbeing.

Beyond the personal reasons for poetry, these creations are necessary because each hard-working poet contributes something unique, something nobody else could have created the same way. This is why everybody who writes a truthful poem becomes another voice joining the choir of poets in singing the hymns and blues of human life.

# Chapter Three
## Learning From Others

Just as minor league ballplayers learn from those in the majors, beginning poets should learn from established poets. You may have favorites, but read as varied a field of poetry as possible. Soak up the ambiance of the poetry, the word usage, the style, the way the experience unfolds.

The Appendix lists several excellent resources regarding poets, books of poetry, poetry guides, anthologies, textbooks, and essay collections. Consider referring to them further your education about poetry.

To provide additional thoughts about the craft, here are interviews of three highly- regarded poets who have weathered the creative and publishing processes.

## Robert Bly: Translating his way to Jerusalem

Known in the 1990s for his involvement with the men's movement that peaked with the nonfiction prose best seller "Iron John," Robert Bly has written, translated and edited dozens of books, magazines and anthologies. Some of his best work has come late in his career. *Morning Poems* (1997) and *The Night Abraham Called to the Stars* (2001), a book of poems written in an ancient Islamic ghazal form, are both exceptional. His anti-war book *The Light Around the Body* won the National Book Award in 1968, and his first book, *Silence in the Snowy Fields*, is regarded as a classic of free verse poetry.

A poet who constantly translates work from other languages, Bly first learned to speak German, Norwegian, Swedish and Danish. He also knows how to read and speak Spanish. When he translates work from the Middle East or Asia, he depends on others who know the language. Either way, as learned through the following interview, he sees translating as "a fantastic discipline for a poet – better than going to a poetry workshop."

**Jim Walker: As a writer working in the Midwest, what do you think of it as a home for poetry?**

Bly: People tend to get lonely in the Middle West because they don't meet enough people who are enthusiastic about art and literature. That can be solved. I solved it myself, by starting a magazine. Then I met all kinds of people.

**Walker: Some people think a person must live somewhere "exciting" or "romantic" to become a writer. How do you feel about this?**

Bly: It isn't that you need you need to go somewhere else to learn how to write or to find what to write about. It's the question of what we have inherited in our immediate literary descent. I stayed in Minnesota. But I learned a lot about writing about fields from the Spanish poets. And now, there are poets learning to write about the events in Minnesota from the Islamic poets. And James Wright learned a fantastic amount from Pablo Neruda from Chile. It's not a matter of where you live. It's how wide your reading is.

**Walker: Through your translations, you've helped introduce many writers from around the world to American audiences. Many remain overlooked and underappreciated. Do you think that is a mistake?**

Bly: It gives us something to do. There will always be holes. Someone else will come along and see everything else I and the other translators haven't done and do that. Just thank God there's a huge amount of great literature coming into us now because we have contacts with so many countries. It's a huge blessing.

**Walker: Has technology helped make the world smaller and make translating easier for you? Do computers make much difference for you as a poet today?**

Bly: I don't think the technology and computers are adding anything to that. It enables you to find material a little more quickly. But I don't know any poet who writes on the computer. Sometimes I get wonderful ideas by being unable to read my own handwriting. Technology makes things too clear. Our emotions are extremely confused. And there are huge gaps of ignorance and greediness in everything. All poetry is a kind of commentary on the mess. And the computer is too neat. Most technology is too neat.

**Walker: How were you able to make a living as a poet without teaching full time?**

**Bly:** At one time I supported the children by doing poetry readings – 12 or so a month – instead of teaching, which he was afraid he liked too much. Now, I take one airplane trip a month. And I'll try to put two or three readings into one trip. If some one else wants me in another part of the country, forget it, I'm not going that way.

**Walker: When you conduct readings, do you enjoy the performance aspect of poetry or the public connection?**

**Bly:** I don't call it a performance. It's a matter of finishing the poem by giving it to other human beings. And one tries to do that by publishing, which is helpful. But, in order to decipher language (as a reader), the rational part of the brain has to take it over. And then, if you're lucky, it communicates it to your emotions. But that's a very awkward way of doing it. Poetry, through the ancient times, was always given directly from the mouth to the heart of the person listening. The poetry reading is not a performance. It's returning to the origin of poetry, which the voice of the poet – man or woman – speaks without the intrusion of the written language.

**Walker: Do you find poetry readings very well received in America today?**

**Bly:** In the European-American world, we are the leaders of this kind of poetry reading. Recently we had the Dodge Poetry Festival in western New Jersey. There were 20 poets there and 20,000 people came to that. They drove all night from Oklahoma and places like this. It's astounding. It was a three-day thing with nothing but poetry. If they did that in France, they'd have 115 people, period. In England you would have 20 people and 42 critics who would attack it. There are a lot of bad things about the United States and our cultural habits, which are getting worse. But the willingness of normal human beings to be moved by listening to poets, that's amazing.

**Walker: For some people, their writing changes drastically through their careers. Yours, when collected together from decade to decade, fits pretty seamlessly. Can you explain this?**

**Bly:** From the Chinese poets, from whom I learned to do the first book, "Silence in the Snowy Fields," one immediately notices a distinction between vertical poetry on one hand and horizontal on the other. Now, horizontal poetry is the type in which a poet describes everything he has done today. And maybe everything his mother did and his father did and so on. It's sort of like driving around town. It's interesting in its own way. But literature has usually been connected with the vertical. Like somebody like Dostoyevsky who goes straight up to God and then down to the demons. So this tradition is also powerful in Buddhism, in Daoism, it's true in St. John of the Cross, and especially in Muslim poetry. It's very vertical. So therefore I hitched onto that a little bit in studying the old Chinese poets in "Silence in the Snowy Fields." So my attempt has simply been to write a kind of vertical poetry with different subject matters and different view of the world and my own life.

**Walker: Where do the ideas of surrealism fit into your views of the horizontal and the vertical? You've said that the Spanish surrealists were more horizontal.**
**Bly:** The French tried to be surrealistic, but they were too horizontal. They thought if you put a sewing machine next to an autopsy table it would be a big deal. It wasn't. It wasn't anything."

**Walker: What do you think of the surrealist notion of approaching art with the attitude of a child?**
**Bly:** I believe that poetry comes deeply out of childhood and, especially, out of those days in childhood in which we weren't doing anything.

**Walker: What's your typical workday like as a poet?**
**Bly:** I get up and try to write a poem before I do anything else in the morning. So I just got up at six or so and I had three hours in bed working on some new poems. Once I finish that, my day is really over. Then it's time to cook a little bit. And then, if I have any time left over in the afternoon, then I'll get to work on some project I had. I'm working on a book of selected translations. And then I need to put together a collection of literary essays and I promised someone a collection of interviews. So that's the sort of thing that happens.

**Walker: Is writing these morning poems an idea you adopted from your friend William Stafford? Is it something you'd recommend to other writers?**

**Bly:** I like tremendously the whole idea that Stafford brought out that, when you sit down to write a poem, you don't decide what you're going to talk about. That's not your job. So, what he would do, was lie down on his sofa at five o'clock in the morning and see what occurred to him. It could be the steps of a jogger going past the window. It could be a dream pressing in from the night before. Or it could be what his wife or one of his children said the day before.

So, he considers that the end of a string. Then, the job of writing poetry is to follow that string, to see where it wants to go. And, it's only your mind who knows where that thing came from or where it's going to. So he said the most important thing is, when you're writing, put down whatever comes. And don't allow your standards to come in and say: "oh, that doesn't make any sense, how did an alligator get in this line." He said: "lower your standards." That was great. And then he said: "If you continue to follow this thread, it will lead you to the center of the universe." Amazing. Astounding. He uses (William) Blake's line: "I give you the end of a golden string/ only wind it into a ball/ it will lead you in at heaven's gate / built into Jerusalem's wall." And I said: "Whoa, Bill, you get to Jerusalem every day?" He said: "Oh no, the suburbs are good enough for me. That's great. You talk about vertical poetry. Just to get to the suburbs would be great.

## Five Poems by Robert Bly

### Driving to Town Late to Mail a Letter

It is a cold and snowy night. The main street is deserted.
The only things moving are swirls of snow.
As I lift the mailbox door, I feel its cold iron.
There is a privacy I love in this snowy night.
Driving around, I will waste more time.

### The Russian

"The Russians had few doctors on the front line.
My father's job was this: After the battle

Was over, he'd walk among the met hit,
Sit down and ask: 'Would you like to die on your
Own in a few hours, or should I finish it?'
Most said, 'Don't leave me." The two would have
A cigarette. He'd take out his small notebook –
We had no dog tags, you know – and write the man's
Name down, his wife's, his children, his address, and what
He wanted to say. When the cigarette was done,
The soldier would turn his head to the side. My father
Finished off four hundred men that way during the war.
He never went crazy. They were his people.

"He came to Toronto. My father in the summers
Would stand on the lawn with a hose, watering
The grass that way. It took him a long time. He'd talk
To the moon, to the wind. 'I can hear you growing' –
He'd say to the grass. 'We come and go.
We're no different from each other. We are all
Part of something. We have a home.' When I was thirteen,
I said, 'Dad, do you know they've invented sprinklers
Now? He went on watering the grass.
'This is my life. Just shut up if you don't understand it.'"


**The Face In The Toyota**

Suppose you see a face in a Toyota
One day, and you fall in love with that face,
And it is Her, and the world rushes by
Like dust blown down a Montana street.

And you fall upward into some deep hole,
And you can't tell God from a grain of sand.
And your life is changed, except that now you
Overlook even more than you did before;

And these ignored things come to bury you,
And you are crushed, and your parents
Can't help anymore, and the woman in the Toyota
Becomes a part of the world that you don't see.

And now the grain of sand becomes sand again,
And you stand on some mountain road weeping.
**Rembrandt's Portrait of Titus with a Red Hat**

It's enough for light to fall on one half of a face.
Let the other half belong to the restful shadow,
The shadow the bowl of bread throws on the altar.

Some paintings are like a horse's eating place
At the back of the barn where a single beam
Of light comes down from a crack in the ceiling.

Painting bright colors may lie about the world.
Too many windows can cause an artist to hide.
Too many well-lit necks call for the axe.

Beneath his red hat, Titus's eyes hint to us
How puzzled he is by the sweetness of the world –
The way the dragonfly hurries to its death.

So many forces want to kill the young
Male who has been blessed. The Holy Family
Has to hide many times on the way to Egypt.

Titus receives a scattering of darkness.
He's baptized by water soaked in onions;
The father protects his son by washing him in the night.


**The Difficult Word**

The oaks reluctantly let their leaves fall,
And hesitatingly allow their branches to be bare;
And the bear spends all winter in separation.

The beauty of marriage is such that it dissolves
All earlier unions, and leads man and wife
To walk together on the road of separation.

*Jim Walker & Mark Shaw*     27

It's a difficult word. The thought frightens us
That this planet with all its darkening geese
Was created not for union but for separation.

Suppose there were a dragon curled inside each drop
Of water, defending its gold. It's possible
That abundance has the same effect as separation.

We all knew nothing of this when we floated
In the joy of the womb; but when our lips touched
Our mother's breast, we said, "This is separation."

It is my longing to smooth the feathers
Of brown birds, and to touch the sides of horses
That has led me to spend my life in separation.


## Karen Kovacik: When a writer enters a family

Karen Kovacik is a writing professor with a doctorate degree. But her poetry isn't the sort of parched work one might expect from an "academic" poet. Instead, she writes passionately about the people and things she loves in her life.

Born in East Chicago, Indiana, Kovacik's work is often influenced by her Polish heritage and her stay in Warsaw, Poland from 1985 to 1987. She has published translations of contemporary Polish poetry in *American Poetry Review* and *Poetry East.* In 1998, her chapbook *Nixon and I* appeared from Kent State University Press, and a full-length collection, *Beyond the Velvet Curtain,* winner of the Stan and Tom Wick Poetry Prize, was issued by Kent State in 1999.

Kovacik, also an award-winning short fiction writer, has had poems and stories appear in many journals, including *Salmagundi, Chelsea, Glimmer Train, Massachusetts Review, Indiana Review,* and *Crab Orchard Review.* She is Associate Professor of English and Director of Creative Writing at Indiana University-Purdue University of Indianapolis.

Karen's views about poetry, as noted in the following interview, provide much insight regarding the craft.

**Walker: How do you get started with poems? Where do they come from for you?**

Kovacik: The process is pretty various for me. Sometimes a political event will trigger something. Sometimes a photograph or painting. Sometimes something from my own life, an experience of foreignness. But usually there's something language based in all that where whatever it is gets converted to a first line or an idea of how things could unfold.

**Walker: The starting point could be different each time?**

Kovacik: Yes. And I also I do a lot of assignments with my students. Ones that I give them I'll also do. I get a lot of poems that way.

**Walker: Do you feel that as you have become a more experienced poet, you need prompts more often than you did at first?**

Kovacik: When I first started writing, I struggled with what part of what I write is really the poem. And so I'd do these really long things and I'd have to chop them way back. Where as now, if anything, I have the opposite problem. I chop too much, too prematurely and I already have a much more limited notion of what the poem is – for better or for worse.

**Walker: Are you editing and revising in you head as you write your first draft?**

Kovacik: Usually, I try to be very free initially and I'll write out a sloppy prose passage, kind of free writing. And then, when I make a first draft, I always write it by hand. Then I'll type it up. Usually when I get to the first typed draft I'll start editing massively. I try not to do too much right at the beginning so as not to freeze.

**Walker: You compose everything handwritten at first?**

Kovacik: Prose no. Poetry yes.

**Walker: Prose goes into the computer straight out of your head?**

Kovacik: If I'm starting a short story, for example, I will make notes in my journal about the character or whatever. Maybe "what if this" and "what if that." But, because prose depends so much on the rhythm of the sentence, I'm not good at just writing sentences any more longhand. I just can't write fast enough. But I can type really fast. It helps me because, typing, I can keep up.

**Walker: Did you have any trouble converting to a computer from a typewriter?**
Kovacik: Once the first Macintoshes came out they were so easy. So, in many ways, it was a relief. But I had one thing I was afraid of, so I tried to work against this. I was seeing a lot of archival manuscripts by writers, like Sylvia Plath at the Lilly Library (in Indianapolis), and there you will see a whole sequence of drafts. And, sometimes, that process can get lost when you are just realizing on the computer. Now, when I'm working on poems, I just staple the printed drafts into my journal. That way I can just mark them up. I still have a little bit of that process where I can grapple, hands on, with the text.

**Walker: To see those early drafts and learn what the poets crossed out or moved can prove very interesting.**
Kovacik: I love seeing that. Once, one of my classes and I went to the Lilly. We were studying Plath. And we came up with a writing assignment where we had to use, in one of our poems, a line that Plath crossed out. That was fun.

**Walker: When it comes to revision, do you jump in right away after you've drafted the poem longhand or do you wait a while?**
Kovacik: It depends on the poem. I find that, if I'm struggling and I can't find the solution, I will wait. For me, the finishing of it is important, but not at the cost of something else. I know Elizabeth Bishop would wait famously, or infamously, seven or more yours before she found a solution. She would have blanks in her poems and just kind of fill them in as something came to here. I'm not really capable of doing that. But I'm capable of putting something aside for a while.

**Walker: How do you know when something is done?**
Kovacik: When I don't wince at anything anymore. When I don't have a nagging doubt about a single word. Sometimes I'll send things out if I have a nagging doubt about two or three words. Sometimes I'll send things out for a while and more nagging doubts will arise and I'll have to change something. Sometimes after something is published I'll have nagging doubts.

**Walker: How do you find the motivation to send out your work? There's not always much of return for the effort.**

**Kovacik:** Having had a certain amount of success hasn't hurt. There was a time when I sent things out for a couple of years and I hardly got anything published. I know that it was more difficult to motivate myself then. As soon as I get something rejected I'm pretty good about either revising the stuff or immediately sending it back out if I don't think it needs revision. I've had things rejected, as has everyone, X number of times and then accepted. It's a matter of sending it to the right place. Using the Internet to preview journals without totally going bankrupt has helped me a little bit. It sort of motivates me. I can kind of see this greater community of work out there and it makes me feel like I want to participate in that conversation.

**Walker: Do you subscribe to many journals?**

**Kovacik:** About six or ten. In addition to *Poetry* and *American Poetry Review*, I subscribe to *Crab Orchard*, *Nimrod* and *Missouri Review* and a few others.

**Walker: Do you submit to online publications?**

**Kovacik:** No. I assume I will eventually. But I do like the artifact of the book. But maybe that will change as more things become electronic. Some journals, like Glimmer Train, do take submissions online. So I do take advantage of that. I like reading things online. Some of my poems that have been published in print are also online. A lot more people can see it that way. And that's nice.

**Walker: You first worked toward publishing chapbooks and then a full book of your poems. How did that process work for you?**

**Kovacik:** When I did my master's degree, it was a 100-page manuscript of translations from Polish poetry and some of my own poems. I took out the translated poems and had a quasi book manuscript. It was called *Old and New Testaments*. That just kept evolving into what became *Beyond the Velvet Curtain*. That was a nine-year process. In that time, I published two chapbooks and published a lot in journals.

**Walker: Did you submit *Beyond the Velvet Curtain* to competitions?**
Kovacik: It was a finalist in a lot of contests. I knew it was getting closer. It had been a bridesmaid many times. And then it won the Stan and Tom Wick Poetry Prize from Kent State and was published the following year.

**Walker: In terms of content, would you agree that many of your poems focus on family and people you care about?**
Kovacik: Yes. As well as art, history and politics.

**Walker: How do you approach writing poems about family and other people you care about?**
Kovacik: Whenever you care about someone, there's always conflict. And what do you do with that? Ceslav Milos said: "When a writer a writer enters a family, that family is finished." With that in mind, I try to be mindful of my family's fragilities. That doesn't mean that, at times, I haven't written rather harsh things about family members. It's just that, if I'm going to put them in a book, I feel it's the ethical thing to do to show the manuscript to my family and let them have veto power on things. In magazines, just because probably so few magazines really get read, I don't have that same compunction. And I'm not above or beneath writing some things purely for myself, for whatever therapeutic value. What I'd caution against is absolutely censoring things from your self. The more that you can bring into the light of awareness, the better it is for you as an integrated being.

**Walker: You mean it is good for you even if you don't send your poetry anywhere?**
Kovacik: Yes.

**Walker: Have you ever had a poem vetoed by a family member?**
Kovacik: I had a situation with my sister when my chapbook, *Nixon and I*, came out where she was deeply hurt by one of the poems in the book. It only alluded very obliquely to her. Who was right, who was wrong in that situation? That isn't even for me to talk about or think about. But I don't want to provoke that kind a reaction in people I love. So, when I was coming up with *Beyond the Velvet Curtain*, any poems I thought my parents might have a problem with, I read out loud to them. One is called "What My Father Told Me About Sex." I

read it both to him and my mother and my mother said: "That's how your father is." And, also, there was a poem in there about watching my father pray and I refer to him as a boy in boxer shorts too big to be on his knees. And he was very gracious. And he just said: "this is your version of reality." They've really come to be quite accepting and to be able to make that distinction between how I see things versus some sort of objective truth. There's another one in there in *Beyond the Velvet Curtain* about not giving birth with kind of a difficult image of my mother post-birth. I was afraid that would be painful or insulting. But she didn't seem to have a problem with that. My family, with that last book anyway, was pretty open. I can't really complain.

**Walker: In your writing, how close is the speaker of the poem to the real you?**
**Kovacik:** There's always mediation. Whenever you're dealing with language, you are mediating "experience." If you are using any kind of form – not even traditional form, but a form that you made up – that's another remove from whatever it is. Kenneth Burke said: "Any every reflection of reality is about the selection and a deflection." And so it is.

**Walker: What is your attraction to writing about sexuality, about the erotic?**
**Kovacik:** Sex is one of the great mysteries of life. From it, life can result. In many cases, death can result, of course, now. It's a huge topic. I'm interested in how it reveals aspects of us differently than other kinds of experiences do because of the vulnerability of it, because of the nakedness of it. In terms of advice to people who would write about or it maybe be afraid to write about it, there's a wonderful book called *The Joy of Writing Sex* (Elizabeth Benedict). It's more for fiction writers, but there's plenty that's applicable for poets too. One piece of advice is to be as specific as possible. Whenever you write generally about sex, it tends to either run to bad pornography or euphemism. Another one is to keep body parts to a minimum so it isn't "insert Tab A into Slot B" sort of thing. The mystery really lies in the specificity. To be really present to another person, you are really noticing what is one-of-a-kind, what is idiosyncratic.

**Walker: Most poets have to have a full-time job to pay the bills. Do you find it difficult to juggle your writing and teaching during the school year?**

Kovacik: I do write during the school year. If I'm dealing with a huge grief while trying to teach and deal with my administrative work, maybe then I will write less. I always do something. This semester I wrote a couple of poems and finished a story and a half and also worked on some translations of Polish poetry. That isn't very much, but it's enough. I'm not a super prolific writer anyway. I don't know that if I weren't teaching I would necessarily write any more. Maybe I would. But teaching also motivates me. I love teaching. I love interacting with the students. Teaching has made me less controlled, less rigid. That's been a good thing as an artist too.

**Walker: People often knock "academic poetry" these days. But, without universities, we'd have very few poetry presses and, without teaching jobs, many poets would be struggling financially. Do you think that the concern about "academic poetry" is legitimate?**

Kovacik: I am attracted to lots of different kinds of poetry: from a slam or performance poetry to poetry that is complex and layered on the page. Not that no performance poetry is layered and complex. Of course, sometimes it is. But there are different aesthetics. I think poetry can be appreciated within an aesthetic frame, no matter what that frame is. I have gone to readings by people who have been in the academy for decades. Because things like tenure and promotion can be tied to one's publishing success, the danger for poets can become a narrow careerism. That could be absolutely soul denying. In my own life, while having to be somewhat practical and mindful of publication for those career ends, I try to the best of my ability to still make it a vocation rather than a career. I also suspect that some of the bad reputation that "academic poetry" has is inflated. A lot of good things have come from the academy. And not all poets from the academy are intolerant or stuffy or narrowly formal – whatever the stereotypes are. A lot of teaching poets, if they are at all awake and alive, are awake and alive to different ways a poem can be made and try to engage with different kinds of aesthetics in the classroom.

**Walker: Besides education, do you think there's a way to bring poetry to more people?**

**Kovacik:** We're basically in a culture where people hardly read anything, let alone poetry. I'm fairly optimistic that, in part because of performance poetry, there's a greater interest in learning about it and reading it. As teachers, we can do a certain amount to excite people about what's being written today, about supporting poetry. We can take people to readings, let them hear great poets. We can sort of instill this love of both the spoken and written word. I've had so many students who have never been to a poetry reading. You take them once and they want to go all of the time. They are just blown away by how magical it is.

**Walker: People unfamiliar with poetry often struggle to understand it. But, once they get to know it, people can really fall in love with it. Why is it so hard to bring people to poetry?**

**Kovacik:** In many high schools and grade schools, poetry isn't taught that much. And contemporary poetry isn't taught at all. In my creative writing classes, I have students do a lot of reading and, sometimes, imitating poets just to help them become intimately familiar with how different poets do things.

**Walker: Why is poetry the art form for you?**

**Kovacik:** I made visual art for many years and got a certificate from the Art Institute of Chicago and was making paper cutouts with origami paper – kind of witty, very colorful, small format kind of work. I worked a little bit in computer media as well. Reading poetry when I was an undergrad – I was a Spanish-English double major – was important. I read a lot of Latin American poetry and a lot of metaphysical English poets. The sort of distillation of idea and experience and emotion appealed to me enormously. I wanted to be able to do that too.

It took me a long time before I could make anything I was remotely satisfied with. But, now, I can't imagine living without it. Because, in a country with so many pressures to be devoid of an inner life, any sort of art making – poetry for me – is a way to have some sort of record of the inner life. So it doesn't just disappear. It doesn't vanish into consumer culture. It doesn't vanish period.

# Five Poems by Karen Kovacik

## What My Father Taught Me About Sex

That mother and he never "had relations"
before the wedding, that even now when she sits on his lap
he squirms, turns red and tells her she's fat
and she kisses his neck and pretends he's Clark Gable.
Yet he loves to move her around the dance floor,
his left palm tucked into the trough of her back.

That I should play poker instead, or read a book,
that I shouldn't give away the milk for free, for who would want
the cow, that I should wait till I marry and if I never marry
to keep myself chaste as a saint, to cultivate vegetables
or a musical life, to touch only the skin
of the piano, for he had always wanted to play.

## Nixon on the Pleasures of Undressing a Woman

With us, it is easy: a tug on the tie, the ubiquitous zipper.
But with a woman, you can never be certain how deep
the layers go. First, perhaps, a jacket of mink, gloves

lapping up the greedy length of the arm, shoes
like airy Eiffels for the feet. Then the untethering
of beads and bracelets, the slow dismantling

of those hanging gardens of skirt
crashing around foundations of lace and bone.
And right when the patience has died in your fingers,

and your tongue has gone cool and dry with desire,
you are suddenly faced with that blinding symmetry
both spherical and isosceles, the twin raptures

of Sinai and Everest. Some mornings I linger
in Pat's closet, among all the incompatible species
of fox and alligator, ostrich and lamb,

where I'm reminded of my Russian stacking dolls:
how the smallest is absolutely empty
but for silence, longing, a residue of perfume.


## Herman Kafka's Dinnertime Pantoum

When father says it's time, it's time!
Come, the table is for eating, not for chatter.
Why the long face, my skeleton-son?
It's jellied carp – my favorite!

The table is for eating not for chatter –
Our dear cook has prepared us a feast.
It's jellied carp – my favorite!
Now, don't crack the bones with your teeth.

Our dear cook has prepared us a feast,
But sip the vinegar, please, without slurping
And don't' crack the bones with your teeth.
Manners, for a Kafka, are everything.

Franz, sip the vinegar, please, without slurping
And take care not to scatter any scraps.
Manners, for a Kafka, are everything.
When I was a boy I wasted nothing

And took care not to scatter any scraps.
But, son, must you eat like a shadow?
When I was a boy I wasted nothing,
Never once did I languish on the sofa.

Son, must you eat like a shadow?
You are slow in all but the will to marry.
Never once did I languish on the sofa
Dreaming of love and grievances.

You are slow in all but the will to marry:
She parades before you in a lacy blouse,

Dreaming of love and grievances,
And right off you decide to marry her!

She parades before you in a lacy blouse,
Smiling, quoting your silly stories,
And right off you decide to marry her –
Will you ever grow up?

Smiling, quoting your silly stories,
You're always scribbling in that notebook.
Will you ever grow up?
A man needs manly work to be content.

You're always scribbling in that notebook –
Why the long face, my skeleton-son?
A man needs manly work to be content
And when Father says it's time, it's time!


## Jankowice, Poland

A black veil hangs from my hat: I am learning bees –
the incest, the swoop of them, their love
of tunnels, silky buzzing under blankets–
all this I want to learn because I am thirty
and restless and noticing the finch-colored
clothespins flying on the line or the sunflowers
six feet tall, coveted by the village elite
to hedge their stuccoed homes, I am thirty
and every inch of my body feels unloved
but awake, the electricity on but no glow
in my belly, in my bony arms, no lamplit
wings to thrust me over the cups of flowers
to sip their sweet milk, all this I grasp
from my uncle's coalmining hands,
his nails tiny shafts of ore, the palms educated
in sickle and drill, fingers that speak anthracite
or clover, that have been stung by a hundred bees
but survive to twirl my aunt on linoleum
then summon the small of my back out of stiffness,

sweet wheezing accordion in 3/4 time.
I'm the waltz, I'm the polka, I'm honey
still warm from the hive, loudness
that will not let him sleep, nectar-flavored
vodka on his capable tongue, and yes, friend,
a black veil hangs from my hat, but I am no widow:
I am learning bees.


## Come as You Are

She drives all night through the bovine dark,
drinking pop from the can, fumbling for change
to feed the insatiable booths, their bellies full of mesh.
Red light, green light: *Pay Toll! Thank You!*
How did she end up this desperate
for familiarity, the sound of someone else's
breathing in sleep? Surely, she thinks,
we are not meant to live alone.

Her ancestors, who herded sheep
in the High Tatras, lived three generations
to a house. They had, if nothing else, dull uncles
to annoy. Living alone is too polite,
too Romantic. She feels like the Rousseau
of house pets and aggressive ferns. While suppering
on chicken from a jar, brussel sprouts
from a box, she has time to get anxious about

all of those thing the herd dwellers don't,
not the least of which is dying alone.
It's easy to feel immortal at a Cubs game,
or in her friend's kitchen strung with oregano
and chiles, or in her lover's bed
when she hears the sea in his ears.
Not so, alone. She hears what eternity
will sound like: quiet

but for the summertime swoosh of cars.
Quiet has become so much the habit

that when she finally arrives, when he pulls back
the blanket to make room, when she smells his hair, hears
the hoarse morningness of his voice, she feels
shivery as a veal calf suddenly sprung
from his narrow box. How to live in this unexpected
abundance? How, later, to fit back in the box?


## Li-Young Lee: Poetry at the tip of the iceberg

Chicago poet Li-Young Lee writes as a rare bird among modern poetry's flock of poets more focused on building pretty word nests than soaring the sky to God. Now forty-six, Lee has published three books of poetry *Book of My Nights* (2001), *The City in Which I love You* (1990) and *Rose* (1986). His stream-of-consciousness autobiography, *The Winged Seed* (1994), was written from start to finish with the computer screen turned off.

While working as a poet, Lee has helped raise two college-age sons while working at a Chicago warehouse for twenty years. "As the years have gone by and I started publishing books, my supervisor has all of my books in his office," Lee says. "And he says 'I don't read that crap.' But he's real proud of me."

His supervisor, though, wonders why he spends his time "hiding" at the warehouse instead of writing. "He will ask me 'why aren't you doing more?' I feel as if I'm doing the most that I can. I'm writing poems. I feel that the most a human being can try to do is make art of some sort. But I have to say I'm lazy too. I'm really lazy. If I spend all day doing nothing and writing one line and taking a walk with my kids or whispering in bed with my wife, that was a good day."

Lee's passion for poetry, as noted in the following interview, stems from a love for the written word.

**Walker: You left the University of Arizona's MFA writing program, in part, because you heard no discussion of God and the spiritual there in the context of poetry. Talk about your views on the importance of those things in your writing and in poetry in general.**

Lee: I sometimes think that if the making of art doesn't make us more complete people then what are we doing? We're just making knickknacks. I don't understand the point of it. The practice of art is a viable yoga. I think that the practice of any art form is the highest yoga there is. The Sanskrit word yoga means "yoke, link or connection." And the exact equivalent in Latin is the word "religio" and we get the word "religion" from it. Religio means "link or bond or connection." First of all we have to ask bond to what? Connection to what? We could theorize on that. And it seems to me that something is yogic if it links us or connects us or binds us to our complete nature. Not some narrow bandwidth of our nature like we function as only a husband or only a father or only a working person. But all of who we are: dark and light, male and female, eternal and temporal, spirit and matter. Whatever puts us in touch with our whole nature seems to me is yogic or religious. And art does this by its very nature. A good poem is a condition of language which accounts of all of who we are. When I read a really really great poem by Emily Dickinson or Robert Frost I have this feeling that the feeling function is working, the thinking function is also present, the spiritual function is present, the erotic function is present. So a poem is an instance of that wholeness. And that wholeness is religious. Unless we're making doilies I don't understand another purpose to practicing art. Am I making any sense?

**Walker: What you are talking about is vertical poetry, something spiritual and universal that reaches somewhere beyond the day-to-day horizontal surface of life.**
Lee: Yes. I have this feeling that all horizontal paradigms are somehow paradigms of scarcity. The vertical paradigms are paradigms of abundance. We live in a world that really emphasizes the horizontal paradigms where we compare ourselves to others. Even if it is comparing ourselves to others in history, it's still horizontal. And somehow, there's a kind of scarcity there in seeing ourselves as only social units. That seems to me those are models of scarcity because there are only so many resources in those kinds of models. In vertical models there is infinitude and abundance. And it seems to me that poetry has to access that somehow. And I experience that when I read the poems that I love. The practice of art is to affirm these models of abundance of being and personhood. Our persons aren't just defined by our social conditions.

**Walker: Do you think the poetry that is vertical asks the reader to feel more than the horizontal? And maybe, as an audience, people are more used to having a passive role?**

**Lee:** Feeling is the biggest challenge. I think feeling disallowed in the culture. It's not really promoted. We're pretty undeveloped, maybe as a species, about feeling. But there are such fine degrees of difference, for instance, between love and desire. When you really go into it you find out, wow, ultimately they are different. But we hardly know the difference. So feeling is the area where we really need to begin integrating more and, at the same time, differentiating more one feeling from another. There's probably a lot of feeling that we leave out in our literature. And I get the feeling that there's a lot of poetry and literature that reproduces agony in the reader and I wonder about the value of that, ultimately. Somehow we think that agony is a more authentic feeling that joy or ecstasy or something like that. I've been reading Robert Lowell and John Berryman and I feel like all that work just really reproduces agony in me and I walk around thinking "why is he doing this to me?" If I walked into a party and there was a group of people having this conversation I would walk past it. Why am I made to believe that this is somehow valuable. I can't help but think that it trivializes the practice of poetry unless we tie it to some sort of transcendent function. I can't see any way past the transcendent. We have to come to terms with feeling and transcendence. Otherwise, we're locating human value in the social world alone. And we know that it doesn't exist in the social world. Human value is rooted necessarily in transcendence. Even ideas of equality on exist in the transcendent world. If I look around, we're not equal in wealth, there are people who are cripples and people whose bodies are not crippled. We're not equal that way. So where does the equality lie unless it lies in some transcendent idea? If poetry doesn't ultimately come to terms with that it seems to me we're defining everything in social paradigms and that seems bankrupt to me. So that's why I think it's important to see the religious, the yogic capacities of art and practice it with full knowledge of that.

**Walker: It seems that many people are afraid to write that kind of poetry and create that kind of art today because of the stigma of cliché and sentimentality connected with it. It's sort of a risk to approach something like that.**
**Lee:** It is a risk. And we do risk sentimentality. But it just means that our craft has to get better. The better our craft is the greater the chance that we can deal with sentimentality, negotiate it better. I don't think the answer is just backing off. That would be like you're falling in love

and saying "I'm afraid so I won't ever fall in love." That's not the way to deal with it. The way to deal with it is to go ahead and make your mistakes and learn and keep going. It doesn't seem to me that backing away from feeling is a way to deal with feeling.

**Walker: There's a whole different level between confessional poetry, which is about personal feeling, and then poetry that is universal and personal at the same time. Is this the line that poets walk that you find yourself dealing with when you approach what you want to write about?**
Lee: For me, the poems I'm trying to write are poems that somehow enact a temporal personality. All speech is a portrait of the speaker. When we hear speech we can kind of intuit the countenance of the speaker. The speaker that I'm trying to make a portrait of is a temporal, personal self imbedded in a larger, transpersonal context. If I could enact that the speech, the imbeddedness of the personal in the impersonal, the bigger, the universal I feel like the poem is successful. That's what I get out of the poems that I love reading. I always get the feeling of solitary personal speakers speaking in the context of the universe.

A poem is the instance of the totality of causes. If we look hard at any particular thing – like I'm holding a pen in my hand – if we look how this pen came to be, I would have to account for the person who made it in the factory and the person who put it together, and I'd also have to account for the person who invented plastic and the person who invented ink. Just for to figure out how this pen came to be there's an infinite myriad of causes that made it come into being. I don't always see that. I just pick up the pen and use it. But it seems to me that a poem is an instance of that kind of vision. And I think we can read poems that are successful and experience something like the totality of causes. Aside from just experiencing the narrative and the subject of the poem – which I think is one level of enjoyment – there's something about the sound value, the sonic value of the poem that makes you feel like all of the causes are present that brought this poem to being. Am I making any sense?

**Walker: Yes. To use a cliché, it's the tip of the iceberg. Everything else is there, but it's beyond your sight.**
Lee: That's right. Exactly. Everything is somehow present when you are reading that poem but you can't put your finger on it. There you

have Frost talking about picking apples. Somehow, his language is doing something that you feel the rest of the iceberg present. He's making you feel that, experience it viscerally in your body, and you don't even know how you are experiencing that because the subject is just apple picking. And that is the miracle and the yoga that poetry does.

It's just like somebody talking you through the steps of putting your ankle behind your head and breathing deeply. And, after a while, you begin to feel access to greater power that's beyond language. I think that's what the poem does. Reading the poem is a form of yoga. It's the highest form of yoga there is.

**Walker: It seems to me that one of the things that you do in your work is take big, abstract ideas and place them in a tangible thing, in a body in food. And much of that seems to be repeated as obsessions. Do you have personal symbols and personal obsessions that are always there for you when you write?**

Lee: I guess I do have obsessions. Probably to a fault. I try to free myself of them, detach myself from them, but they I feel haunted or visited by them. At the same time, the process for me is that I keep discovering the universal or the abstract in these little things, these mundane things. It isn't so much that I have the abstraction in my head and I try to find a figure for it. It's more like that as I'm writing about eating I discover "wow, it's present there." Or if I'm writing a poem about combing my wife's hair, I discover that the universal is there too.

I keep discovering that the universal is everywhere. The whole universe is in every part of the universe. But I guess a physicist would say: "what else is new, we've discovered that already." And the Chinese philosophers knew it 2,500 years ago.

**Walker: For someone so obsessed with perfection in his art, writing *The Winged Seed* in a surrealist's fashion, with the screen turned off, must have been a challenge for you.**

Lee: I'm so ashamed of that book. I'm confused by it. I was experimenting. I feel like the book is a mess because of the way I wrote it. I want to go back and redo it and I don't know how. When I read through it there are passages that I actually like and I think 'that came about because the computer screen was turned off.' How do I redo something like that? It's exactly what it is. It's as close as I can get to my naked mind without any editor. It's just raw on the page without any corrections. I'm not even sure there are sentences in there. It was very difficult for me to tell myself 'you're not allowed to go back.' It was so scary for me. Some days I would sit down and I would begin and I would think 'I think I wrote this already.' But then I'd tell myself 'you're not allowed to look back.' So there are repetitions in there I'm told. I haven't even read the whole thing. I'm terrified of it. It was just so scary to do it.

**Walker: You write a great deal about cities and your settings aren't always so typically "poetic." Do you find it difficult to write spiritually about the city because it's so human?**
Lee: For me, a city is basically our inner reality projected into brick. Somebody had a vision in him or her first. They projected it and manifested it. So when I look at the city I see a manifestation of my own soul. I know that my soul is full of side streets and little areas and unlit alleys and bigger, well-lit places. I just feel that everything that we see that's human made existed first in our minds or in our hearts or in our souls and we projected it out into the world. That can be a problem because there are all kinds of psychological or emotional dysfunctions. And that's what gets projected into the world. I happen to agree with William Blake. What he says is if we can perfect the inner city, the inner Jerusalem, then the outer Jerusalem of harmony and richness can come to pass. But as long as our inner Jerusalem is a mess, it is disharmonious and confused and in conflict and that's the nature of human community that we keep projecting out into the world. So the city, for me, is a symbol of the condition of the soul.

**Walker: Do you find your poems or do they find you?**
Lee: When it comes to writing, I feel like a slave. When it says: "write," I put everything down. When it says: "I'm going to be quiet a while," I sit down and suffer. It tells me when. I don't even know what it is. The poem comes from I don't know where and I don't know when. I work on it until the poem is beyond me somehow. I just stop and say "that's as much as I know." Even working on the poem, the revision is a deep, deep form of yoga. I don't always love doing it but I know the importance of doing it. And I know that somehow making the poem is making myself. I have to face my own imprecisions, my own dysfunctions, my own faulty assumptions when I'm working on the poem. And I discover a lot about myself. The opus or the grail isn't

even the poem. It isn't even a book of poems or a prize. It's self-knowledge. And making poetry seems to be a very viable yoga toward self-knowledge.

**Walker: Where does the audience fit into that?**
Lee: It's a triaxial relationship. There's the poet. Then there's the poet's inspiration or obsession. And then there's the audience. My sense is that if any part of that triaxial relationship is missing then there's something wrong, the poem isn't full. The audience is a witness to the poet's demonization, the poet's being possessed by these transcendent powers, whether they're dark or light. The audience is a witness to that. They watch it going on. But the poet has to be a demonized speaker. There might be a kind of poetry that is just between the poet and the audience and there's no demon involved. That's not as rich. There's also the kind of poetry where there's just the poet and the demon and there's no audience. And, somehow, that seems incomplete to me. Then don't send it out, don't publish it. The moment we publish it, we enter into a very important dialogue. Publication isn't a shallow thing. It's not about fame or anything like that. It should be honored and it should be practiced as a dialogue. As we do, we could practice it as a shallow, stupid, meaningless thing or we could practice it as a deep, meaningful thing. If that's what we do, then that's what it becomes. If enough of us practice it as a necessary dialogue that is going on in the culture, then it becomes that. It becomes more profound. If it's just fame seeking, then that's what it becomes. That's what we get.

**Walker: There are other art forms that could help you find the yoga that you speak of. Why did you choose poetry or did it choose you?**
Lee: I used to sculpt and paint and my brothers are both painters. I think maybe laziness. I see the amount of work that goes into what my brothers do. It's just a lot of materials and a lot of work. I could write a poem on a bus on the back of my hand if I wanted to. And it's because I love poetry the most. In your own house, you pull it down from the shelf and you read. There you are all alone. Reading itself is an archetypal situation. The book itself is a gift of the gods. The whole thing feels magical to me.

# Five poems by Li-Young Lee

## Persimmons

In sixth grade Mrs. Walker
slapped the back of my head
and made me stand in the corner
for not knowing the difference
between *persimmon* and precision.
How to choose

persimmons. This is precision.
Ripe ones are soft and brown-spotted.
Sniff the bottoms. The sweet one
will be fragrant. How to eat:
put the knife away, lay down the newspaper.
Peel the skin tenderly, not to tear the meat.
Chew on the skin, suck it,
and swallow. Now, eat
the meat of the fruit,
so sweet
all of it, to the heart.

Donna undresses, her stomach is white.
In the yard, dewy and shivering
with crickets, we lie naked,
face-up, face-down,
I teach her Chinese. Crickets: *chiu chiu*. Dew: I've forgotten.
Naked: I've forgotten.
*Ni, wo:* you me.
I part her legs,
remember to tell her
she is beautiful as the moon.

Other words
that got me into trouble were
*fight* and *fright*, *wren* and *yarn*.
Fight was what I did when I was frightened,
fright was what I felt when I was fighting.
Wrens are small, plain birds,
yarn is what one knits with.

Wrens are soft as yarn.
My mother made birds out of yarn.
I loved to watch her tie the stuff;
a bird, a rabbit, a wee man.

Mrs. Walker brought a persimmon to class
and cut it up
so everyone could taste
a *Chinese apple*. Knowing
it wasn't ripe or sweet, I didn't eat
but watched the other faces.

My mother said every persimmon has a sun
inside, something golden, glowing,
warm as my face.

Once, in the cellar, I found two wrapped in newspaper
forgotten and not yet ripe.
I took them and set them both on my bedroom windowsill,
where each morning a cardinal
sang. *The sun, the sun.*

Finally understanding
he was going blind,
my father would stay up all one night
waiting for a song, a ghost.
I gave him the persimmons, swelled, heavy as sadness,
and sweet as love.

This year, in the muddy lighting
of my parents' cellar, I rummage, looking
for something I lost.
My father sits on the tired, wooden stairs,
black cane between his knees,
hand over hand, gripping the handle.

He's so happy that I've come home.
I ask how his eyes are, a stupid question.
*All gone*, he answers.

Under some blankets, I find three scrolls.
I sit beside him and untie
three paintings by my father:
Hibiscus leaf and a white flower.
Two cats preening.
Two persimmons, so full they want to drop from the cloth.

He raises both hands to touch the cloth,
asks, *Which is this?*

*This is persimmons, Father.*

*Oh, the feel of the wolftail on the silk,*
*the strength, the tense*
*precision in the wrist.*
*I painted them hundreds of times*
*eyes closed. These I painted blind.*
*Some things never leave a person:*
*scent of the hair of one you love,*
*the texture of persimmons,*
*in your palm, the ripe weight.*

## Early in the Morning

While the long grain is softening
in the water, gurgling
over a low stove flame, before
the salted Winter Vegetable is sliced
for breakfast, before the birds,
my mother glides an ivory comb
through her hair, heavy
and black as calligrapher's ink.

She sits at the foot of the bed.
My father watches, listens for
the music of comb
against hair.

My mother combs,
pulls her hair back
tight, rolls it
around two fingers, pins it
in a bun to the back of her head.
For half a hundred years she has done this.
My father likes to see it like this.
He says it is kempt.

But I know
it is because of the way
my mother's hair falls
when he pulls the pins out.
Easily, like the curtains
when they untie them in the evening.


## Eating Alone

I've pulled the last of the year's young onions.
The garden is bare now. The ground is cold,
brown and old. What is left of the day flames'
in the maples at the corner of my
eye. I turn, a cardinal vanishes.
By the cellar door, I wash the onions,
then drink from the icy metal spigot.

Once, years back, I walked beside my father
among the windfall pears. I can't recall
our words. We may have strolled in silence. But
I still see him bend that way-left hand braced
on knee, creaky-to lift and hold to my
eye a rotten pear. In it, a hornet
spun crazily, glazed in slow, glistening juice.

It was my father I saw this morning
waving to me from the trees. I almost
called to him, until I came close enough
to see the shovel, leaning where I had
left it, in the flickering, deep green shade.

White rice steaming, almost done.  Sweet green peas
fried in onions.  Shrimp braised in sesame
oil and garlic.  And my own loneliness.
What more could 1, a young man, want.


## Eating Together

In the steamer is the trout
seasoned with slivers of ginger,
two sprigs of green onion, and sesame oil.
We shall eat it with rice for lunch,
brothers, sister, my mother who will
taste the sweetest meat of the head,
holding it between her fingers
deftly, the way my father did
weeks ago. Then he lay down
to sleep like a snow-covered road
winding through pines older than him,
without any travelers, and lonely for no one.


## A Story

Sad is the man who is asked for a story
and can't come up with one.

His five-year-old son waits in his lap.
*Not the same story, Baba. A new one.*
The man rubs his chin, scratches his ear.

In a room full of books in a world
of stories, he can recall
not one, and soon, he thinks, the boy
will give up on his father.

Already the man lives far ahead, he sees
the day this boy will go. *Don't go!*
*Hear the alligator story! The angel story once more!*

*Jim Walker & Mark Shaw*          51

*You love the spider story. You laugh at the spider.*
*Let me tell it!*

But the boy is packing his shirts,
he is looking for his keys. *Are you a god,*
the man screams, *that I sit mute before you?*
*Am I a god that I should never disappoint?*

But the boy is here. *Please, Baba, a story?*
It is an emotional rather than logical equation,
an earthly rather than heavenly one,
which posits that a boy's supplications
and a father's love add up to silence.


By reading the words of wisdom and the poetry of writers such as
Robert Bly, Karen Kovacik and Li-Young Lee, a wide spectrum of
ideas can emerge for you as a beginning poet.

Reading allows you to soak up craft ideas and techniques you can
begin to apply to your own work. You may also think of subject matter
for your own poems prompted by the words, stories and emotions
expressed in what you read. **Think of exploring and studying the
world of poetry as an endeavor just as important as writing your
own poems.**

# Chapter Four
## Creating a Poem

**You have permitted your raw materials to cure while spending time thinking about poetry and reading various examples. You are ready to revisit your original notes and begin drafting a poem.**

For the sake of ease in discussing the process, examine some sample material specifically created by the exercise you completed earlier. Don't think of this as a definitive example of subject matter or style. And don't feel the need to copy or imitate the material you will soon see. It is just one way of doing things.

Use this step-by-step example as a dry run through the drafting process. Later, you'll be able to apply these same steps to your own work, launched with the walk assigned in Chapter One.

If you discover your work lacks the type of sensory detail you see in the sample included in this chapter and leans toward the sentimental and cliché, revisit Chapter Two. Then continue with the information presented below.

To begin, imagine the below text is the typed version of your notes from the exercise in Chapter One. You sat in a car in Chicago, stuck in the rain, waiting for a haircut appointment. Instead of letting the storm and situation become an irritant, you seized this as an opportunity to take notes for a poem. Here are the original jottings from your notebook:

**Who, what, when, where:** Sitting in my idling blue Hyundai on Michigan Street, a busy thoroughfare in downtown Chicago, waiting ten minutes until it is time for a $25 hair appointment at Just Hair with Jenni. She wears pigtails. She dyed her hair red this month. It is 3:20 and my appointment is at 3:30. I just got done getting my car out of the impound lot where it had been towed to after I left it in a meter spot all morning. I'm wearing a blue and orange all-weather running coat. **Smell:** rain, French fries, Osco all-in-one shampoo in my hair; **Taste:** Pepsi, the fries; **Hear:** "Fell on Black Days" by Soundgarden from a cassette tape in the car radio, bus passing, rain blowing on the windshield, a big black and gray Chevy Blazer with loud exhaust; **See:** another blue Hyundai like mine passes - windows not tinted blue, a man walks by in a brown Russian fur hat and yellow Sony Sport radio headphones. A big sky blue Ford LTD. Three buses in a row. They have signs on them: "Recharge your batteries" and "Touch a life." One says "Innovation." It's going to Wrigley Field via Lake Shore Drive. A man in a clean white shirt and brown slacks smoking a cigarette in front of the building; **Feel:** warm, the car is still running. Legs sore from playing basketball at noon. The car is shaking and that makes me nervous.

All of this information is now at your disposal since you wrote it down in your notebook. You then worked on something else while forgetting exactly what you had wanted to say, if anything, while you were sitting in the car outside the hair salon. But now you are excited to tackle your notes and possibly create a poem from them.

A resulting poem is not a certainty at this point because notes will often fail to materialize into anything but notes. They may contain a line or phrase or simile you can use later in a different poem. This is why it is important to keep all of these notes, even if they don't become poems, in one easy-to-find location – your notebook.

Your first step from ideas to poem is to type all of the notes in your computer verbatim. If you created these notes in list form, the second step is to remove the headings from the lists and let everything merge together. Then think about how and where you want to start and end the poem.

With the example, begin by establishing a sense of place: we are inside the car. You might make the speaker of the poem (the "I" talking to the reader) a character with a little personality and tone to his voice. At this point, don't worry about linebreaks, the poet's conscious choice to limit the length of the free verse line for a variety of sound and content effects.

Instead, leave the lines in prose form and just let the margins end the line. We'll come back to linebreaks soon. Here's a first try at revising the beginning of the poem:

It's 3:20 p.m. and my hair appointment with Jenni is at 3:30. I was just at Just Hair Tuesday afternoon, but Jenni didn't quite get it right. She needs to fix this spot on the side of my head that keeps flipping out too far.
Jenni's probably about 24, cute with her hair just dyed red — I think it was blonde last time — and put up in pony tails like my little sister used to do in sixth grade. She likes U2 the most. Didn't care for the REM show this summer at Grant Park.

I look through HEO6190 hand-written on my windshield, and all I see is rain and the $117 I just spent to get my Hyundai out of the impound lot. I had a few parking tickets. I'm in a good meter spot along Michigan Avenue; I don't have any change. The radio blares out "Fell on Black Days" by Soundgarden. It's warm in here. I can smell the Finesse all-in-one shampoo in my hair. I just took a shower before I came out in the rain. That was after I played basketball. I'm a little achy from basketball. Maybe it's the rain.

**In these lines, you answer the key narrative questions: Who, what, when, where, why and how.** You offer some information about the speaker. And, hopefully, the reader will want to know more.

The pattern of the poem is beginning to be shaped. It begins from the perspective of being inside the car and looking out. The reader may figure out that some of the information, like all of the music references, distract from the rest of what has been created. A future revision will push our pattern further along while eliminating details that are not necessary.

Leave the extras around in case these fit in other ways – like the sound and music of the poem. This will rise to the surface when we insert linebreaks. It is most important to make sure you are creating a broad vision for the poem. This one, so far, is rather cinematic, asking the reader to follow along as if watching a motion picture. Because of this, everything will seem somehow pertinent. **The reader will think: If the camera is taking the time to focus on something, it must be part of the picture for some reason. You need to keep this expectation in mind as you continue to revise.**

Here's more:

A big Chevy Blazer rumbles by. A bus pulls up to the stop with a sign: "Recharge Your Batteries in Florida." There's a girl in a red bathing suit under those words.

A man in a brown Russian hat stumbles into the slushy street on his way to the bus. He's wearing yellow headphones. He looks drunk. A bright blue LTD – long as a city block – stops for the man. The ancient lady inside is pissed, her thin hair covered with a plastic rain hat. The man makes it past the stop. This isn't his bus. He stands too close to a younger guy in a big black ski jacket and stocking cap.

The man in the Russian hat pulls out a wad of paper and looks it over in the rain. Most of the others at the stop are crammed into the covered clear Plexiglas shelters. When the bus to Wrigley Field via Lake Shore Drive pulls up, the man gets on. The sign on this bus says: "Touch a Life."

I notice another man standing outside the granite building next to my car. He's wearing a clean white shirt and brown pants, smoking a cigarette — raindrops working to put it out. His glasses are tinted brown.

We see images and details outside on the street. The speaker of the poem is limited to what he sees and hears (or doesn't hear) through the car's window glass. Likewise, the reader receives a somewhat muffled and clipped picture of the scene. But the clips are still as detailed and specific as the speaker could observe from his place in the car. When he looks, he doesn't just see a hat worn by the man stumbling through the street, he sees a "brown Russian hat." Other minor players in the scene are described in less detail. The speaker had no reason to notice them.

Pretend that you really did sit in the car and observe these things. But, after letting the poem sit for a while, the "I" is no longer you. It becomes a more a flexible version of you writing about events and emotions that can also be flexible and even fictitious. If you decide the Russian hat should be gray to better fit the scene, it can be gray.

**The poem's pattern, thus far, began with a small, interior perspective and moved out.** Circular patterns often make people feel safe and comfortable. Bringing a poem back to its starting point can give the reader a sense of closure, an understanding of being somewhere, venturing from that place, and returning home – even if the home, in this instance, is the front seat of a Hyundai Elantra.

The continued draft reveals:

My blue car is warm, running, shaking slightly. That's starting to make me nervous. I look at the digital clock. It's 3:30. I put up the hood on my Nike All-Condition Gear jacket, get out, lock the door, put an old parking ticket under a wiper blade and walk along Michigan Avenue in the January rain with everyone else. Jenni is getting her scissors sharp and ready, sweeping off the blonde curls cut from her last appointment. Jenni's probably about 24, is cute with, I'll soon find out, her hair just dyed red — I think it was blonde last time — and put up in pony tails like my little sister used to do in sixth grade.

In these three blocks of text, we have a first draft for a poem. It has a pattern – in, out, in – and it is off to a good beginning in terms of setting, perspective and voice. At first glance, a couple of themes or central ideas begin to emerge. The speaker is concerned about money, appearance and generally superficial things.

Meanwhile, the people waiting on the bus are dealing with a more difficult version of life. The well-dressed man by the building is more like the speaker, bringing him back to himself. In the third part, he is, once again, looking at things superficially – even to the point of mentioning the brand of jacket he wears. But, in the last line, he is worried about money again (no change for the meter - he places an old ticket under the wiper). Finally, he must walk in the rain like everyone else. He isn't any better or any different.

The poem, while about the speaker, could be about all of us. We all think we are different. We all concern ourselves with unimportant, tiny things while others deal with larger, even life-and-death issues.

**The key to creating an autobiographical poem like this one work is to make it both about you and about all of us.** If readers can't enter the poem, can't feel like they are there, can't identify with the speaker or know her, then this kind of poem will fail miserably.

The success or failure of this example poem remains to be seen. **But you are ready to move to the next step in the process: shaping the drafts into a poem.**


## Exercise Three

Keeping in mind the drafting steps just demonstrated, type your revised notes into a computer. Do not worry about breaking the lines. Let them run from margin to margin at this point. Do not try to make them rhyme or fit into some kind of pattern.

We are writing a narrative (or story-based) free-verse poem. While there is no rhyme, this doesn't mean there is no reason behind what we're doing. We've already established a host of poetic possibilities in our example. Free verse simply releases us from the restraints of end rhyme that often results in forced, clichéd poetry only written to make the rhyme scheme work.

This is not to say rhymed poetry is impossible to write well. People have crafted beautiful rhymed poetry for centuries. But, as a beginning poet, focus on mastering the craft on other levels before dealing with the difficulty of creating something new and original and beautiful within the confines of a traditional form. Structured verse will be discussed later.

The "free" in free verse poetry should not make your feel you are free of any kind of structure or guidelines for the way the poem's lines are shaped. As the poet Robert Wallace wrote: "All verse, even free verse, has some kind of measure – some rationale or system by which the poet breaks or ends lines. The choice of the measure may be intuitive or trained, but the nature of verse demands that the poet have a clear perception of the identity of each line, even if he or she cannot articulate the reason."

During this next step in the process, type your own notes into the computer. This will be beneficial since you will find alter, add, and delete text almost automatically. Follow your instincts. Don't trim out any details that may wind up fitting into the poem later. As you type your notes, you may have no idea what the poem's theme is. You may have no idea about pattern or perspective. This will become clearer after you type everything and stand back to take a look.

If you do not own a computer, find one in your community where you can type your work and save it on a disk. Public libraries and colleges offer open computer labs where you can type your poems, print them out, and save them on disks.

**If you use a library or school lab, create an inexpensive email account through Hotmail or Yahoo and send your poems and drafts to yourself.** This is an insurance policy that will allow you to locate poems that might otherwise be lost if your disk becomes cranky passing from one computer to another.

If your budget allows, purchase a computer. A working poet will often have the urge to work on poems in the middle of the night and will want ready access to works-in-progress at any moment. This is why a laptop computer can be a great tool for a poet. A poet only needs a PC or Mac laptop with Microsoft Word installed, a good filing system created on the hard drive, and a printer. When we discuss publishing, you'll learn why Internet access is also beneficial.

No matter where or how you type your poem into the computer, always print out a hard copy of each draft and save it in a real file folder. Mark each copy with its draft, or version, number.

When you finish typing your notes for the poem we are creating, print out three copies, writing the number "one" on each copy in pen.

There is no need to avoid writing on this pretty, clean sheet of paper. We will soon make dozens of notes and scratches all over it and it won't be pretty anymore.

# Chapter Five
## Continuing the Creative Process

Now that your notes are typed into a working draft for a poem and you have a printout in hand, you are ready to move to a major revision bringing you closer to the eventual shape of the poem. The challenge: to decide what your poem is really trying to say, what its truth really is, and then shape everything toward that truth.

**A poem's message is carried in two distinct ways: through its content and through its structure.** We learn much about a poem by reading it closely. We find out its story, its emotional core. We imagine its images. We follow its comparisons with our minds. We enjoy the sensations the poem presents. We trace the pattern of what happens in the poem. We hear the voice of the speaker. These are all messages delivered through content.

Unlike most prose, the structure of a poem can also deliver additional messages. Most often, you want these messages to complement the ones presented in the content. But, if the structure of the poem seems to counter the tone of the content, then it can send a powerful signal of conflict to the reader.

**Poetry's structural messages are delivered, primarily, through line and stanza breaks.** A stanza, or group of single-spaced lines separated from another group by two spaces, works much like a paragraph in prose.

A stanza break can show a shift from one idea to another. A stanza break also serves as an extended pause between the music of the lines. Pretending that a poem's line is a musical note, the stanza break serves as a rest for the reader before resuming another set of notes. The white space can also indicate a passage of time or a gap in the narrative.

The dominant impact of a stanza break is a slowing down of the experience of the poem – both as to how it is read aloud and how its content is unveiled. **Often, what's left out of a poem – what happens in the white space between stanzas – is almost as important as the words included on the page.**

**Linebreaks, meanwhile, help create pace, rhythm and music in a poem.** A long line, as presented in a Walt Whitman (*Leaves of Grass*) or Allen Ginsberg (*Howl*) poem, keeps a poem fluid and flowing forward. A short line, like those in William Carlos Williams's "Red Wheel Barrow" creates a cut and clipped poem.

## The Red Wheelbarrow

so much depends
upon

a red wheel
barrow

glazed with rain
water

beside the white
chickens


Instead of steaming ahead with a long, prose-like line, we must pause, start and stop, as we read Williams. This gives us a clear message as readers: Take your time to look at what you are seeing here. Each line break – the spot where the line ends and returns to the left margin – works like a full-note of pause in music. This means you hold on for a full-note's pause between reading "wheel" and "barrow" – both when you read the poem aloud and when you read it silently. Your eyes must pause as they move to a new line. This pause is part of the creation of music and pacing in free verse poetry like "The Red Wheel Barrow."

In this image-based poem, the pauses where the lines end encourage the reader to slow down and examine the detailed pictures ("glazed with rain water") instead of rushing through the short poem.

**In free verse poetry, lines are broken in two ways: end stopped and enjambed.** Most often, poems contain a blending of the two methods. An end-stopped line follows the natural patterns of speech with its linebreaks, ending the lines where phrases break with punctuation or natural spoken pauses. An enjambed line breaks less naturally – forcing the reader to halt mid-phrase and move quickly to the next word. Enjambed lines can be jarring and disconcerting. But this discomfort relays a rich message.

In her poem, "I Go Back to May 1937," Sharon Olds hints at the perilous future of her parents' relationship as she describes a picture of them at college. Here's a stanza from that poem:

I see them standing at the formal gates of their colleges,
I see my father strolling out
under the ochre sandstone arch, the
red tiles glinting like bent
plates of blood behind his head, I
see my mother with a few light books at her hip
standing at the pillar made of tiny bricks with the
wrought-iron gate still open behind her, its
sword-tips black in the May air,
they are about to graduate, they are about to get married,
they are kids, they are dumb, all they know is they are
innocent, they would never hurt anybody.

While the linebreaks work to strong effect in this portion of Olds's poem, this sort of herky-jerkiness – like the imagery she selected – would not make sense in a poem about a couple that enjoyed a wonderfully peaceful marriage.

To check your progress, place your three printed-out drafts in front of you on your desk or table. **As you consider your first draft, use a pen to mark possible line and stanza breaks. On the first copy, break it with natural, end-stopped pauses.** The lines will probably be medium length to longer. If your phrases and sentences are short, feel free to allow the lines to follow that path.

The easiest way to discover the natural pauses in a poem is to read it aloud several times. You may also try reading your first-draft notes into a tape recorder before making any linebreak choices and then play the tape and mark what pauses you make by inserting a slash (/) where the linebreaks will be positioned.

Look at the draft you created and break it in an end-stopped style. As you begin to break the lines, you'll see words to cut or text to change. Do this as you mark up your poem. Draw lines through the words or circle them and indicate where they should be moved.

Let's attempt this exercise with our poem in progress. Here is a first stab at line and stanza breaks:

My hair appointment is in 10 minutes.
Jenni didn't quite get it right yesterday,
needs to fix this spot on the side of my head
that keeps flipping out.

Jenni with her hair just dyed red
— was blonde last time — has it up in pigtails
like my little sister in sixth grade.

I look through HEO6190 grease-penciled
on my windshield, and all I see is rain
and the $117 I just spent to get my car back.
I had a few parking tickets.

I'm in a good meter spot now on Michigan Avenue,
I don't have any change.

As you see, several lines have been cut and others rearranged. Compare this draft to the section as it appeared as a prose block in Chapter Four. When placed in lines, the weaknesses and excesses began to stand out. The first draft was far too loose, too airy, too much like bad prose. But the tightening process is underway thanks, in part, to the process of creating lines of verse. It is beginning to sound and look more like a poem.

**With this example in mind, take your marked-up poem and revise it on the computer with all of the lines end stopped. Is your work starting to take the shape of a poem?**

Next, take the second copy of your poem you printed and mark the linebreaks as enjambed. Read these out loud as well.

Look for interesting images and ideas that occur from ending the lines at particular words. Some may take on double meanings that contribute to the poem. Others may be distracting and laughable. In any line of enjambed poetry, the first and last lines carry extra weight. Leave them there for now.

Let's attempt this approach with the second section of the poem in progress. Here, most of the lines are enjambed:

A Chevy Blazer rumbles by. A bus
pulls up to the stop with a sign:
"Recharge Your Batteries in Florida."
A girl in a red bathing suit

under those words. A man in a brown Russian hat
stumbles in the slushy street on his way

to the bus. He wears yellow headphones. He
looks drunk. A bright blue LTD – long
as a city block – stops for the man. The ancient lady
inside is pissed, her thin hair covered
with a plastic rain hat. The man makes it over
to the stop. This isn't his bus. He stands too close

to younger guy in a big black ski jacket
and stocking cap. The man in the Russian hat
pulls out a wad of paper and looks
it over in the rain. Most of the others at the stop
are crammed into Plexiglas shelters. When the bus
to Fort Harrison via 56th Street pulls up, the man
gets on. The sign on this bus says: "Touch a Life."

Looking back at the earlier draft in Chapter Four, notice the
difference in what we snipped here and what we highlighted. Fewer
words wound up on the cutting-room floor in the second part.

The enjambed lines work well in certain lines to create double
meaning and amplify the images. For example, "A Chevy Blazer
rumbles by. A bus/" allows us to get rid of the adjective "big" in
describing the Blazer because the line reads, in one way, that the
Blazer is "a bus" and thus even bigger than "big." The image of the
Russian Hat man standing too close to the others receives extra
emphasis by appearing before an enjambed stanza break – one that
splits the line not only across the pause of a linebreak but also across
the extended pause of a stanza break.

To continue, take the third printout and mark the poem for
linebreaks with a combination of end stopped and enjambed lines that
worked especially well in our first two attempts. Take the printouts
with all your marks and give the poem a good content revision. Open
the file on your computer and begin by breaking the lines as you have
indicated on the three printouts. As you insert these linebreaks, you
will begin to notice lifeless lines – like many of the ones slashed from
the example poem.

Delete any unnecessary lines. Then do this with a focus on words.
**The key is to examine the poem asking every line and every word
"what are you doing here?"** If the word answers "just hanging out, I
guess," then give it the boot. If it says: "I might be doing this," tell it
"there's no room for "mights" in my poem," and delete it. Each word –

from the biggest adverb to the tiniest article – needs to be performing a specific and crucial role. If not, the word will stand in the way of the truth of the poem.

**A poem's truth is like a ghost.** It is transparent and invisible. As a poet, you are attempting to give physical form to this ghost. You start by piling sheets and blankets on the ghost to make sure we can all see it. But what we see is a big block of bedding. It's your job to pull off the blankets and sheets, one by one, until all that's left is the sheerest sheet. That last one will fit close to the contours of the ghost, allowing us to see her.

All of the extra words and phrases are extra blankets and sheets. As we begin our content revision, we will need to mark out all the unnecessary material in our draft. Sometimes it is hard to let it go.

**The decision is about focus.** We had no idea of the focus of the example poem when we began the exercise. We soon narrowed it down to an atmospheric meditation (or poem of thought) on being part of the city, about being a person with problems – probably smaller than everyone else's – in the middle of a sea of people with problems. Entire lines or stanzas just didn't fit into the poem. **We often need several lines to write ourselves into a poem and several more at the end to write ourselves back out.**

Watch for this. It is a very common problem. While these extra lines help us write our way to the ghost of the poem, they often stop the reader from being able to see the ghost. Once we delete this padding – often found at the beginning and ending of poems – we bring the reader directly into the thick of the poem and leave them there. Unlike a short story, novel or film, a poem – especially an emotion-driven lyrical poem (the counterpart to a narrative poem) – doesn't need to begin or end on a timeline. Human feelings aren't linear. And poems work wonderfully to represent this satisfying experience of timelessness.

One benefit of revising poetry on the computer is the opportunity to cut and paste entire lines and stanzas, moving them around and dropping them into place at will. While our example poem contained the beginnings of a clear pattern, it drifted away at times. After marking possible moves with arrows, place your notes next to your computer. Revise for content and structure at the same time by referring to notes from all three pages. Look for major issues, including shifts in tense (from present to past), good and bad uses of repetition, awkward sentence structure, and poor word choice. Begin looking for smaller details like spelling and grammar errors. **Work one word at a time, then one line at a time, then one stanza at a time.**

Here's a revision of the first draft:

## With Everyone Else

I look through *HEO6190* grease penciled on my windshield,
and all I see is gray January rain and the $117 I just spent
to get my car back. I had a few parking tickets.

Jenni didn't get my hair right yesterday,
A clump on the side of my head keeps flipping out.
She's going to fix it in 10 minutes. I wait.
My car is warm and running, shaking slightly.

Jenni safe inside with her hair dyed red. Was blonde
up in pigtails last time like my little sister in sixth grade.
Jenni safe inside sharpening her scissors,
sweeping up curls cut from the last appointment.

I'm in a good meter spot. I don't have any change.

A Chevy Blazer rumbles by. A bus
pulls up to the stop with a sign: "Recharge Your Batteries."
A girl in a red bathing suit reclines under those words.
A man in a brown Russian hat stumbles in the slushy street. He
looks drunk. A long blue LTD skids to stop for him.

The lady inside is angry, her thin hair lined with a plastic rain net.
The man makes it to the stop. It isn't his bus. He stands too close

to a young man in a ski jacket and stocking cap.
Russian Hat pulls out a wad of paper and looks it over in the rain.
The others wait in a Plexiglas shelter. When his bus arrives,
the sign on it says: "Touch a Life."

Another man outside the granite building next to my car
in a white shirt and tan pants, smokes a cigarette that raindrops

work to put out. His glasses tinted brown. I put an old parking ticket under my wiper blade and walk into the rain.

The poem, still a work in progress, is closer to its ghost. Originally a 518-word first draft, it has been trimmed by more than a third down to 291 words. Some items from the last portion of the first draft appear in the first stanza. Much of the original information at the start of the first draft has disappeared.

Each draft has been saved in the computer. If you decide you have cut too much, retrieve it from an earlier file. Little was lost in tightening this poem; quite the opposite. We now have a clear focus on what images, what sensory experiences, were crucial to presenting this scene, to telling this slice of life story.

**As you consider your poem and continue revising, remember that poets don't create finished products with their first drafts.** It is a step-by-step process taking as much work and creativity as the discovery of the poem in the first place. With each poem, no matter how it begins, work through these major drafting and revision steps to create the best possible final product.

**During the revision process, keep these ideas in mind:**

## Eleven Tips for New Poets

**1. Left Justify All Poems, Don't Center Them.** Poems are read left to right and may move from the left-hand margin. But the pacing of the poem – the length of the pauses created by the linebreaks – depends on the page's left margin serving as the place where the line starts.

Consider our example poem. Notice that only the right side of the poem is uneven. If we center a stanza instead of leaving it left-justified, it looks like this, giving us unclear direction about what the linebreaks are doing. It also places heavy emphasis on the word "he" – something we don't want:

A Chevy Blazer rumbles by. A bus
pulls up to the stop with a sign: "Recharge Your Batteries."
A girl in a red bathing suit reclines under those words.
A man in a brown Russian hat stumbles in the slushy street. He
looks drunk. A long blue LTD skids to stop for him.

When reading a poem aloud or to yourself, the voice pauses slightly at line-ends (about as long as a period in a sentence), as if acknowledging the slight muscular movement of the eye shifting back to the left margin for the next line. If the next line starts halfway back to the left margin, the pause is shorter, and so on. **Linebreaks always indicate a pause. Don't read through them.**

Linebreaks may coincide with sentence phrases or the natural pauses created by punctuation. This kind of linebreak choice emphasizes normal speech pauses. Linebreaks also may occur between grammatical or syntactical units – this is called enjambment, remember – creating pauses and introducing unexpected emphasis.

White space can indicate pauses. If white space entirely surrounds a word or phrase or line, then that portion of the poem takes special emphasis. The last word on a line receives extra attention; that's where your eye stops before it returns to the beginning of the next line. Then, the first word in a new line is also emphasized.

Some people expect that short-lined free verse reads quicker than long lines, but that's not usually the case. Short lines invite pauses at the ends of the lines, and the fewer words in each line receive more prominence than the many words in long lines. Enjambment may quicken the pace of end-stopping – but not always.

## 2. Avoid Adverbs, Passive Verbs and Excessive Adjectives.
Pick the right verb instead of making it right with an adverb. Don't write: "she said hysterically" when "she screamed" will do the job much more efficiently. No need to write: "the sky was getting dark" when you can write "the sky darkened" or the equivalent. Don't deflate the imagistic action of your verbs. Likewise, resist the temptation to use multiple descriptive words prior to a noun. Example: "The awkwardly lettered, hand-built, black and white lunch menu sign hung over the counter." Instead, try: "The black and white lunch menu sign hung above the counter. Long ago, someone built and lettered it with awkward hands."

## 3. Avoid Using a Big Word When a Smaller One is Better.
Use words that are easily understood, ones that you know. Even a slightly misused "big word" sounds pretentious and undermines an otherwise terrific piece of writing. Be cautious of the connotations certain words carry with them. For example, "strolled" and "sauntered" both mean to walk at an unhurried place. But

"strolling" feels much more innocent, and less intentional than "sauntering." These subtle differences aren't found in the dictionary.

## 4. Avoid Repeating For No Positive Effect ("Doubling").
Unless you are establishing a musical or functional pattern of repetition, don't say the same thing twice – especially back to back in a poem. Example: "He was funny, hilarious, the kind of person who made you laugh all of the time." Instead, write: "he was hilarious."

## 5. Don't Introduce a First-Person "I" Speaker or Second-Person "You" Auditor Late in the Poem. If a poem
begins in third person (like "The Red Wheel Barrow"), with no "I" speaking and no "you" addressed, a sudden switch can be jarring. The reader will wonder where the speaker came from or why the speaker is suddenly speaking to a "you" in the poem. "I love you" is a sentence with both a speaker ("I") and a second person auditor ("you"). If those three words suddenly appeared in an otherwise third-person poem, the reader would have to figure out whom this "I" is and who the "you" is. It's best for readers to have those important bearings straight early in the experience of the poem.

## 6. Avoid Clichés. There is no need to use commonplace catch
phrases, similes or metaphors in a poem. Nothing takes the power out of a poem quicker than a cliché. Many people find clichés comforting, just as they might enjoy laugh tracks and predictable happy-ending story lines on television sitcoms. This doesn't make clichés valuable or make it right to pander to the laziness of readers who only want the safe and familiar because they are afraid to experience anything new.

## 7. While Emotion-Driven Lyrical Poems Can Survive in the Realm of the Abstract, Narrative Poems Need
**Details.** Storytelling is important. The reader should have a good sense of *who* the main characters are, *where* and *when* the story is set, *what* is happening in the story and *how* and *why* the characters are affected by the situation or conflict, the rising action, the climax and the resolution of the story (if there is a resolution). Be certain that a narrative poem, in most cases, has a good beginning, middle and end.

## 8. Avoid Overusing the Poetic "This of That"
**Construction.** It usually contributes to clutter and an awkward elevation of the language. Example: "I walked past a **building of red brick**." Why not: "I walked past **a red brick building**"? The second version sounds better musically and eliminates the useless word "of."

## 9. Write in a Real Voice, Not a Poetspeak of Archaic Words No Longer Used in Real Speech. Typical "poetic" words to avoid include: "alas," "perchance," "amongst," "shall," "thou" and the rest of the Elizabethan ilk.

## 10. Title Every Poem. Titles introduce a poem's subject, provide background information, set a mood for the poem, or create mystery. Don't give too much away in the title and avoid using the best or final line of the poem as the title.

## 11. Avoid Using CAPS, Funny Fonts, Boldface or Excessive Punctuation !!! to Indicate the Impact of a Statement in a Poem. Let the words speak your message. You are working on a poem not a textbook or magazine ad. If you need to add emphasis, you are using the wrong words. Trust the intelligence of the reader. Note: Italics designate a spoken line in a poem – a quote or sound that comes from a voice other than the speaker's. Quotation marks can be used for this as well. But italics rarely indicate emphasis in poetry.


## Exercise Four

Rewriting a poem backwards can be an excellent way to dissect and rediscover what you have written during the revision process.

For this exercise, choose another poem you have written or a short, more lyrical portion of our first poem – maybe a section you cut out and broke into a mixture of end-stopped and enjambed lines.

Rewrite it in reverse, taking the last line and making it the first, and rearranging others as well. This can create interesting possibilities for the poem, making it completely different than the original – and sometimes much better.

When you reverse the poem's order you will be forced to revise along the way, cutting, adding or moving words and lines around to make the poem follow some kind of logic – even if it is an entirely different logic than the poem followed when going its original direction.

This technique works best with lyrical and surreal or associative poems – something discussed in an upcoming chapter. Narrative poems can become surreal through this technique since the original story will be lost in this kind of shuffling. Here's an example from an unfinished poem that is going nowhere as a narrative:

**My Real Dad**

I am eloping with my boyfriend
to Las Vegas because of Elvis. He'll
be there, Elvis I mean. We thought
about eloping to Memphis but
there's no way. He would be spotted
too easy. Las Vegas is full of
imposters. It is full of people
who look like him. So many
that I won't even know which one
he is. But he'll be there. Even if he can't
make it to my wedding he'll pass me
in the street. He'll know his daughter
is getting married. Not like the man
who raised me, the one who doesn't approve
of it. Elvis will sing to us instead
of slapping my face hard and complaining
because Todd doesn't have a job and Todd
has Navy tattoos and Todd drives a loud Trans Am.
Elvis understands and I know Mom lies
that it wasn't him who put me in there. She was
backstage once. She was.

Reversed and revised, the poem provides new meaning:

**Backstage once**

Mom is saying it wasn't him who put me in there.

She is as understanding as Elvis. I know Mom lies,
has Navy tattoos and drives a loud Trans Am.
She doesn't have a job, slaps my face, complains.

Elvis will sing to us instead of the one who raised me.
The one who doesn't approve of us getting married
in the street. He'll know his daughter made it
to the wedding. He'll pass me. He'll be there.

Las Vegas is full of imposters. It is too easy. It is
full of "there's no way." He'll be spotted
if we elope to Memphis. We thought of Vegas
because of Elvis. He'll know.


Reversing your poems may work well for you. It may not. But, whatever the technique, revision will only come when you can release the words and lines in your early drafts and allow yourself to improve them. **You can certainly revise a poem too much, but this is usually better than not revising it enough.**

With all of these dos and don'ts and revision steps to think about, focus first on finding your poem and then let the revision, the honing of the product proceed gradually. Revision should be fun. Like the experience of escaping into the world of discovery with creating a first draft, poets long for the vacuum of time and energy that opens up for them as they dig into revising their poems.

# Chapter Six
## Writing Prompts

Congratulations. You have completed the major first steps of writing poetry: Generating raw material, shaping it into a poem and revising it.

Before you share your work with an audience through public readings or publishing, consider honing your skills through helpful prompts designed to generate a variety of poems.

The prompts, or exercises, collected here are listed in a suggested order. Skip around and try ones that appeal to you, but complete Steps One and Two before proceeding further. These are important building blocks for the other exercises that follow.

Some prompts refer to poems in Chapter Three for examples. More include sample poems produced by these prompts. These examples are only included to show one possible outcome from one poet. Don't feel any pressure to mirror the style or subject matter of these examples in your own work.

## Prompts for Generating Great Poems
## Your Obsessions and Accompanying Personal Symbols

Begin by making a list of your obsessions. These are the things you see when you close your eyes at night, the things you are unable to get out of your mind as much as you try, the things that appear in recurring dreams. You have obsessions that you embrace and despise. Both are excellent sources to tap for poetry.

Your list can include significant obsessions such as a passionate love, a failed relationship, an intense fear of death—to "less important" matters such as fixations with baseball, a particular Hollywood actor, spiders, or a color. Some of the most gifted artists and writers have been afflicted or blessed with obsessive personalities. Even if you don't consider yourself an obsessive person, draft a list of your strongest obsessions. Start with the dominant ones and then move down to the smaller, stranger ones. Your first handwritten list may fill every line on a full page of notebook paper.

Many obsessions, like those of surrealist artist Rene Magritte, are hatched in childhood and live on in the adult's creative mind. Magritte's haunting paintings frequently featured trains, hot-air balloons, water, a woman covered by a white sheet. These oft-repeated obsessions can be linked to his growing up near a train line, to a hot-air balloon crashing into his house, and to his mother drowning herself in the river, a white nightgown covering her face.

Once you've made a list of obsessions, assign a symbol for each. Some may stand as symbols for themselves. If you are obsessed with toasters, then the toaster is the thing. If you are obsessed with death, think of what object symbolizes this obsession for you. You are not listing universal symbols; you are listing personal and specific ones. A gravestone doesn't fit. But your grandmother's gravestone might symbolize death for you.

If you think about the person you love, you don't think of vague things. You focus on specific things you've done together, places you've been. You think about the person's eyes, their ankles, the smell of their clothes, the skin on their wrist. Do the same thing in your poetry. The key is to be as concrete and detailed as possible with your symbol list.

Personal symbols can be strange and arrive at strange times. A poet might see a tick as a symbol for his wife if he proposed to her on a forest trail where a tick with a red heart shape on its back dropped from the trees onto her white shirt. This scene is the stuff of poetry

Examples of obsessions and personal symbols are featured in the poems by Robert Bly, Karen Kovacik and Li-Young Lee in Chapter Three. Review them.

## An Annotated Timeline of the Key Moments of Your Life

If you began dating someone, made a new friend, or visited a psychotherapist for the first time, what moments would you share? What would people need to know to know you? What were your turning points? What are your fondest memories? What are your most painful? What small moments say the most about you, about your life so far? When do you experience epiphanies? When did you experience a side of life or a side of yourself you never knew was there? When did you surprise, thrill or disappoint yourself? With these questions in mind, prepare a list starting at childhood (what is your first memory?) and move through adolescence (when was your first kiss) to high school days (what was your first car like?) to young adulthood (when did you realize you weren't a kid anymore?).

All of these points on your timeline are fodder for great poems. One of the benefits of creating the above list is that these key moments were already bouncing around your head in search of escape as poems. You've released them.

There is no need to begin working through timeline moment in any kind of project order. Release the poems when they are ready. Remember that one poem about these things may be just the start. Like Magritte's painting the veiled woman repeatedly throughout his life, your central symbols and key moments should be allowed to keep returning in your poems.

## Looking Inward: Poems About You and Yours

The above lists will lead to related poems about you and the people important to you. Focus on your family and family history (see Sam Shepard's plays for inspiration). Your ancestors, distant and recent, make great subjects for poetry.

The same is true for legends and stories from within your family. Did any relative do anything exceptionally important or strange? Who are the interesting characters in your family? What are your family secrets?

A great place to begin writing about you comes with a first or third person self-portrait. Who are you? Consider yourself in terms of metaphor. What is a fitting metaphor for you? Write an "I am a …" poem. You can compare yourself to anything: an animal, a mountain, a stalk of field corn. This is a great way to begin thinking about yourself as a poet. Consider your dreams and write about them. The symbols in dreams say much about you.

Consider the high and low points of your life and condense them into an all-encompassing mini-autobiography. A variation of this involves dividing yourself into two or more characters and voices within the same poem.

A little at a time, take each moment and a write separate poems about each. Focus on childhood memories, first kisses or first crushes. Focus on the monumental moments and the small things that stick with you. Write poems about the great loves of your life – relationships past and present. Write personal poems of spiritual ecstasy.

When, in your life, have you felt connected with the universe? Link varied moments and obsessions into poems that tell the reader who you are. Write poems about your greatest fears. Why are you afraid? How did it all start? What are your biggest secrets? Write poems about what you hope to accomplish in your life, what you haven't done as well as what you have done. Write poems about your political and social viewpoints. Open yourself up honestly and the reader will connect.

The options are endless. Everyone has families, dreams and ambitions, childhood memories, loves and losses, joys and pains, secrets and spiritual experiences, intense fears and political opinions. **Be sure to write about yourself in a way that invites the reader into the poem and allows the reader to feel that the poem is about them as well as you.**

The poets featured in Chapter Three offer extensive examples of this kind of poetry.


## Automatic Writing or Free Writing

The best way to focus on these poems about you and yours is to clear your mind of all pre-planned ideas and sit down with a pen and paper and no agenda. This exercise in "automatic" or "free writing" is simple. Take pen to paper for a pre-planned amount of time and don't allow yourself to stop writing until the time is up. Don't edit or cross out anything along the way. Don't even stop to read what you have written. Once you are finished, go back and revise the raw material as much as you desire.

**Listening to music is a good way to encourage automatic writing.** Try music without lyrics, something with varying musical moods, for inspiration. While classical music is inviting, it can be emotionally manipulative in a clichéd way and can produce sentimental work. Listen to electronic or ambient music by artists such as Brian Eno and Vangelis or soundtracks to films directed by David Lynch and Alfred Hitchcock.

When free writing to music, let go of yourself and slip inside the sounds. Look around at the images you see, the colors, the textures. Don't force a narrative onto the music. Just feel it. If it takes you to a story, fine. If it takes you to an emotion, to images that represent that emotion, great. When the mood of the music shifts, reflect it in your writing.

The music, if you choose to listen while free writing, should not hide in the background of the process of generating the poem. Allow it to influence your words by helping you build song into your first draft.

Here is a poem drafted while free writing to a song on the instrumental album "El Greco" by Vangelis. The song – like many on this album by the musician best know for his soundtracks to "Chariots of Fire" and "Blade Runner" – begins with a haunting wind sound that might put a listener in the mind of a snowy day.

### Winters

A snowplow rolling along, blade down,
on a hilly gravel road in Hancock County, Indiana.

I sat in the passenger seat, taking pictures for the newspaper.
The man offered to let me drive it but I said "no thanks"
– afraid of shifting so many gears, smashing into stranded cars.

At that moment I was struck by how I should have
learned to paint, sing from my guts instead of turning nervous
and tinny, instead of shifting and slipping back.

I think about this again as it storms today. I'm ready for a nap,
for sleeping myself away from heavy snow, for swallowing it all
in my dreams, the plow, the gravel, the fear.
Then, it all becomes mine. Flat and manageable.

– Jim Walker


## Question and Answer of the Day

A great way to begin working on your list of obsessions is to consider questions that arise from the list or are part of the list. What aspect of yourself do you want to better understand? Are there things you always wonder, things you'd like to ask somebody, but can't? What do you want to know about the world, about another person?

For this prompt, write the question on a small index card and carry it around in your pocket. Look for the answer in what happens to you that day, in what people say to you, in signs alongside the road. Let the world answer your question.

Write down all of the possible answers that come to you from the world and from yourself. Blend them together into the raw materials for a poem. Often, it may take longer than a day to find answers. Keep the questions with you until you've discovered them.

One variation of this exercise is to look around the world and into your mind for questions you can assemble into a list that develops into poems.

There may be no answers to some questions and that's fine. Wonderful questions are all you'll find in Pablo Neruda's excellent *Book of Questions*.

Some examples:

If I have died and don't know it
of whom do I ask the time?

Tell me, is the rose naked
or is that her only dress?

If you prefer answers to questions, then Neruda's book offers hundreds of opportunities for you to write poems as answers to his questions. These could even serve as the questions you carry with you each day.

Another variation: use your imagination to conduct Q and A interviews with objects that can't talk. Consider what a tree, a street sign, a taxicab might have to say. It's best to walk up to the real object being interviewed and ask questions out loud.

**Question for a Fallen Silver Maple**

Q: "Do you believe that trees
– just like people
and certain beloved house pets –
go to heaven when they die?"

A: "Sure."
(Sounding strangely optimistic
as a Roman Catholic priest
performs last rites,
crossing the tree's heart
and sprinkling it with holy water
scooped from the stream
that leads to Long Lake.) "What
do you think smoke is?"

– Jim Walker

## Looking Out: Found Poetry

For people looking with a poet's eye – that's you – raw material appears everywhere. Williams Carlos Williams said that anything from real life could be a poem, as long as it was unique and true to the experience. He lifted this poem nearly verbatim from a note to his wife:

### This Is Just to Say

I have eaten
the plums
that were in
the icebox

and which
you were probably
saving
for breakfast

Forgive me
they were delicious
so sweet
and so cold

-- William Carlos Williams

Keep your eyes and ears open. While many different kinds of poems originate in the world, "found poetry" tends to be the most complete.

This kind of poem operates under the same theories of the "ready-mades" of the art world. It may be a urinal when located in a bus station bathroom, but moved into a gallery it becomes something else. With poetry, the same can be true of graffiti written on the bathroom wall, the lines written on the back of an old post card, or a simple note – like the Williams poem above – written to a loved one.

After you remove the text from its original context, revise it. You will need to add linebreaks. You might cut some parts and expand others. As the poem moves through the revision process, it begins to belong to you. After all, you were the one who placed it into a next context and that changes it completely. It wasn't a poem, but it is now.

You may also find poems by merging words and phrases from signs you read as you walk down a city street. Try jotting down all of the written language you see in your local bowling alley. The lanes also serve as a great place to write a poem using overheard conversation and noise. This results in a found sound poem.

Cafes, bars, and break rooms are terrific places for writers to sit back and listen to people talk. Often, their conversations make great poems – or at least lines for poems. **Either way, the practice of actively listening to the human voice as a writer is beneficial to your work.** Ultimately, a blending of found text and found sound connected with your own thoughts and feelings can create a wonderful and cinematic collage poem.

Guillaume Apollinaire's poem "Monday on Christine Street" offers an example of this kind of poem. Considered a forerunner of the surrealist movement, Apollinaire simply – but deftly – merges his sensory experiences in a Paris café into this seamless collage of images and action. A portion of the poem reads:

**From Monday on Christine Street**

Those pancakes were divine
The tap's running
Dress black as her nails
That's utterly impossible
Here you are sir
The malachite ring

The floor's sprinkled with sawdust
It's true then
The redheaded waitress has run off with the bookseller

## Twenty-Four-Hour Poem

This prompt is an excellent way to train your self to pay attention to the poems that exist around you and within you. It requires that you carry your notebook with you at all times so you can write at least one poem for every hour you are awake.

This is challenging because you must create a poem even when no inspiration strikes and the muse is taking a nap. If you recall dreams from sleeping hours, these can be included in the sequence.

Instead of a diary narrative of your day, these poems are stopped-time moments that, together, can communicate an overall idea of what your day was like. From this, the reader can experience a microcosm of your life.

Poems in this exercise stem from observations of the outside world or interior thoughts and emotions. They key is to offer the reader a clear feeling of what it is like to be you and live in your world. This includes the world of your thoughts and emotions.

You might consider extending this exercise for an entire month. The project will result in several notebooks full of raw poems waiting for revision. But be careful to avoid poetic burnout.

## Place Poem

Similar to a short story, the setting of a poem can be crucial. Sometimes the poem can simply be about a place; or the place can become an important character or even a voice in the poem.

You can approach writing about place through direct observation – using the sensory lists to generate raw material. Or you can use the power of your memory to draw the sensory details out of your mind and re-create a place that means something to you on the page.

Whatever your approach, make the place you choose magical. Fill your poem with very specific details. Use the cinematic tools of patterned focus to make the place come alive. Start with a wide shot that establishes where we are. Move to a medium shot bringing us closer to what the poem's focus will be. Then, zoom in on the specific details, the tiny building blocks of the place you are exploring. Let us see and hear and smell and taste and feel these moving close-up pictures.

The magic of any place is found in its small details, in the things you find under the magnifying glass. If you are spending the time to write a poem about this place, reveal its big and small beauties (even if these come from pure ugliness). Make a myth of your place; make it bigger than life – mysterious, ghostly, glorious, one-of-a-kind. Some of the best places to visit to write this kind of poetry include junkyards, cemeteries, forests, strange small towns, farms, big city streets, your own home and neighborhood. Places to explore from memory might include old schools and neighborhoods, the baseball field where you learned to play; about anyplace memorable you visited that moved you and stuck in your memory.

Here's an example poem about a small Midwestern town that seemed to have an air of death about it:


**Brooklyn, Ind.**

This boy his blue
10-speed bicycle dumped on the ground
buries the dog right there yellow (you
can smell it as you drive by twice)
where it died
along Centenary Road.

Riverside Auto Parts trailer sky turned
over shatter 1972 tornado new Ford and Chevy
truck parts tiny purple flowers broken Plexiglas.

They send him out to clear off flowers and flags,
every month he piles them pink and yellow
silk with beer cans,
medicine jars and grass clippings
green behind the cinder block shed.
A wood chair inside there tiny and sharp
in shadows (to torture the living?)
The dead here talk in junkyards

listen to shapes of faces
in windshields.
Sideways school buses on fire
the plastic seats melting red.

You step on their black toy guns
break them up in dried mud.

– Jim Walker

## The Persona Poem

The persona poem, or dramatic monologue, is an age-old category for poetry. With this style, poets adopt a voice and speak to readers as if they were telling a story to another person in the room.

Such poems are always written in first person. Part of the reader's enjoyment of a poem arrives in getting to know the speaker as one might a real person. **The reader learns about the speaker from *how* he or she says things and *what* he or she says.**

In a persona poem, you can become anyone you like. You choose a voice for them – like you would for a character in a play or movie. Then you tell the character's story through that voice.

For this exercise, make a list of the people you'd enjoy pretending to be. They could be historical or mythological figures. They could be pop icons or current stars. They could be more general characters like a scientist working on human cloning or a jockey in the 1930s or a forty-five-year-old recently divorced factory worker who makes novelty toys just outside Memphis and lives with his mother. You can make up the character you want to be and make him or her come alive in your poem.

This exercise works well in a group setting. Begin by asking everyone to write a few details about a character on a piece of paper before placing the paper in a hat. Make the character as specific and outlandish as possible. Each person in the group then draws a character and writes an impromptu persona poem.

An interesting variation for an individual or group involves the *Weekly World News* found at the checkout line at the grocery store. This is a sensational newspaper full of stories about UFOs, Elvis sightings, outlandish predictions and otherwise normal people doing abnormal (and mostly fictional) things.

On your own, take characters in the stories and write persona poems about them. In a group, cut the headlines out of the newspaper and place them in a hat. Each person then writes a poem about the character and story they draw.

Another drastically different variation of the personal poem is the "portrait poem." Instead of writing the poem in first person and offering the character through his or her own voice, move to the third person and write a poem about the character.

Provide the reader a detailed picture of this person in the same way that you approached the place poem. Move from the wide establishing shot to the tiny details that make this person who they are. When we begin to know new friends, they will be blurry in our minds for a while, but soon becoming clearer as we know them better. The portrait poem can follow this same pattern.

Another variation of the persona poem is created by working with a partner and conducting an interview with that partner about a particular topic – like his or her first kiss. Once you've asked your partner questions, share your own story in detail, making some notes for later reference. Then you write two poems, one about your own experience and one about your partner's. The poems are written in first person and develop a character through the voice of the poem.

During the interview, be sure to capture your partner's speech patterns (*how* he or she says things) and try to replicate those in your poem. The better the questions you ask (who, what, when, where, why and how), the more detailed raw material you'll have for your poem. Avoid questions that lead to "yes" or "no" answers. It's always better to have too much than not enough once you begin the drafting and revision process.

Here's a persona poem written in the voice of a woman telling the story of her first kiss as a youngster. An interview drew out the details for this narrative poem:

## Gaylie Cotton's First Kiss

me: tall bone thin twin
absolutely nothing
my sister Gayle: bodacious

that's why she gets Henry
I get leftovers I get

Eddie

we heard a lot about their cars
but we never saw any cars
instead they pile out, 5 of them, from a yellow cab
15 minutes Gary over to East Chicago projects
Tracy's duplex where her mom isn't ever home

we all walk off our separate ways
Eddie and I back to Tracy's
she's upstairs with Eric doing
what our imaginations thought

Eddie turns the light down to set the mood
"Roxanne, Roxanne why you treat me so bad?"
raps out rattle speakers then Whitney Houston
"How will I know if he really loves me?"

Eddie

pair of black casual polyester slacks cuffed under
he dresses up white shirt all the time
his family real religious
wouldn't allow my Lee jeans white ruffle shirt
penny loafers with a nickel shining in them

glimpse of light I see he's hemmed his pants cuff
with safety pins shivering silver in soft light

hear Tracy and Eric upstairs on the bed
heart beating so fast my head rings in my ears
can only think those safety pins holding up his pants

Eddie

asks if he can kiss me and I say no I have homework
he begs and begs and all I can see is those safety pins

*Jim Walker & Mark Shaw*          85

I can't believe I'm going to let him kiss me
he gets closer I see the pins go all the way up
the hem of his leg all the way up and he kisses me
nothing like I imagined tries to stick his tongue
in my mouth and that's when I hit him
slobbering all over my chin

Eddie

tries again like the movies turning our heads
side to side to just right
and I land one much better
later he lies and says we did more
which wasn't true at all

– Jim Walker

## Exploring Multiple Points of View

This is a variation of both the persona poem and place poem as it blends several voices and perspectives into one poem as a way of telling a story or setting a scene.

Consider a little league baseball game and the different points of view that could tell the story of a particularly poetic moment in the game: The players (the star pitcher and the bored right fielder), the coach, the parents, the umpire, the concession-stand worker. You could even push things beyond the literal and write from the perspective of the ball, of a bird flying overhead, of the grass in the outfield.

In a poem with shifting perspectives, the reader needs to be signaled of this shift. Each stanza could be written from a different perspective and the lines are broken differently to indicate this. Or each new perspective could have a tiny subhead above it indicating the new character speaking.

This exercise can also work in a group setting. After the group identifies the story of the poem together, each member of the group can select a point of view and write that part. The parts can then be merged together into an interesting collaborative poem.

# The Object

The ultimate in outward poetry is the "object poem." The object itself isn't as important as the state of mind of the observer. You must look at whatever object you choose closely and imaginatively.

Begin with something you can hold in your hand. Describe the object in as many ways as possible. What does it look like, does it make a sound on its own or when you tap on it? What does it feel like when you touch it? What does it smell like? What would it taste like if you put it in your mouth?

Once you've answered all of the concrete sensory questions about the object, move to the abstract, using your imagination instead of your senses to answer. Where was the object born or created? What is inside the object? What could it be in an alternative universe? What kind of personality would it have? What would it say if it could talk? Why is it beautiful? Why is it important? Add your own questions as they come to you. Use interesting and unusual similes to help compare the object to other things.

Ultimately, the list of concrete and abstract answers and comparisons will become a poem. The object poem is about focus and zooming in to the important close-up pictures. Pay attention to the smallest aspects of the object as well as the big, conceptual one.

This prompt will generate a wealth of material, probably more than you need. But that's fine. Save the extra scraps – what poet Tom Lux calls "orphans" – for other poems.

Once you've practiced with an object you can hold in your hand, like a seashell or your grandfather's pocket watch, move to something bigger like a statue in the park, an animal in the zoo, or a body of water. This poem can become a persona or portrait poem of sorts too, an autobiography or biography of the object.

A variation of this exercise plays with the senses and involves collaboration. Consider wearing a blindfold while describing an object you can hold in your hand. Your partner, who supplied the object without you seeing it, writes down your descriptions.

Do the same for your partner and then work on your poems on your own without ever seeing the objects. Once you are both pleased with a typed and fairly realized draft, share your poems and reveal the objects.

Here is an example of an object poem:

## Object

The red garter strap
soaks harsh light
as my wife cries for me.

I am far away,
sitting at this cheap desk
turning its silk in my hand.

I brought it with me here
in a glass box,
a rose
etched dead on the front.

I dream of a time when I own time,
a time when I choose exactly when
to snap the strap against her thigh,
exactly when
to run my finger under it
tight as an emergency.

She could break.

And the stocking
– black fishnet –
would come rolling down.

– Jim Walker


## Art's Inspiration

Poets have a long history of writing about works of art. Paintings, sculptures, collages and photographs make perfect substitutes for the objects discussed in the preceding prompt. Music, plays and films can similarly inspire poems. Even folk art, like a quilt or a chain-saw carved black bear will work.

Once you choose your work of art, offer the same kind of sensory descriptions and ask the same questions you asked the object. The key is to make the work of art your own. In order to do this, walk inside the painting or photograph, live and breathe the music or movie.

As a poet, you filter and interpret your work, you add to it and compliment it. You are not photocopying it. You do not replace it. There should be no competition between the piece of artwork and your poem. You are not improving it. The work of art is a starting point. Eventually, it may not even appear in the poem at all and only you will know it is there.

When you compose from paintings or pictures, you may write narratives, explaining what is happening in the painting. You may write about who a certain character is in the painting and come up with a dramatic monologue or persona poem for that character. But you should also attempt to write lyrical poems about the emotions captured in a painting or sculpture. It is easiest for traditional artwork, with its built-in narrative elements, to lead to narrative poems. More abstract modern paintings, reflecting feelings and sensations, more readily lead to lyrical poems.

Try to go against that grain. Write wild poems about a Rembrandt painting and a narrative about one of Jackson Pollack's. Try to write from artworks you aren't immediately sure how to write about, things that puzzle you. See Robert Bly's poem "Rembrandt's Portrait of Titus with a Red Hat" in Chapter Three for an example of an art-inspired poem.

You may enjoy writing from found photographs and photographs you took yourself, old and new pictures and postcards purchased at antique stores, Max Ernst's surrealist collages, Ernst's, Magritte's and Francis Bacon's paintings, folk art, and work created by friends.

If you know any artists, suggest collaborating with them. You write a poem about one of their works of art as they create a work of art about one of your poems.

One excellent variation on this exercise requires at least one other person. Instead of ever seeing the work of art, you know of it only through a partner's description and through questions you ask to get the details for that description. You could even try to draw the picture from the description and then write your poem based on your own translated picture.

Either way, the exercise is exciting when you finish your poem and are allowed, for the first time, to see the original picture. For the sake of comparison, you and your partner should also write poems about the pictures you saw and described, creating a somewhat matched pair –

one seen and one unseen – that you can compare once you've revised them. The following poem was inspired by a series of Ernst's collages:

### The Girl as Weather

She is bending trees to the angle of her back.
She is the crest of a tidal wave
breathing everything a mile out from the shore,
growing a mile high.

Fish flopping over in silt.

She floats, a salted cloud, head first into stone.
She sees me, a bird who does not understand
compassion or the idea of falling down.

It is nothingness she falls through.
I am the nothingness she falls through.
The point of impact. The end
always darker than the beginning.

– Jim Walker


## Poems Prompted by Other Poems

Writing teachers and writing guidebooks often push beginning poets to write "imitations" of other poems, adopting the poems' voice, tone, style and content as launching points for new poems. This technique, while valuable in some ways, can be problematic for newer writers still growing into their own voices and styles. Duplication only creates more of the same. This is not what poetry is all about.

You should be inspired and influenced by things you read – the same way musicians are by listening to others' music. But don't try to imitate any poem at this point in your learning process. Focusing too much on imitation early on could restrict you as a new writer rather than expand your options. You do not need to try to sound like anyone else.

Be pleased if you don't. Finding a unique personal voice is a key to becoming a good writer. Once a writer is accomplished and can always fall back on his or her personal voice, then imitation is a good way to learn more about poetry, to study it from the inside. This is a much better technique for analysis of poetry, taking a poet's work apart in your head and putting it back together.

Yet, there are several good ways to use other poems as starting points for your own work. You can simply choose a poem you enjoy and respond to it. Answer questions the poem might ask. Write questions about it. Borrow the first line of a poem and make it your first line, writing the rest of the poem underneath. Borrow a last line of a poem and write your way to it. Once you are finished drafting, delete the borrowed line.

In a more involved technique, copy another person's poem longhand on a piece of paper, leaving extra space between each line. Compose your own lines in the spaces between the other poet's lines. Type it all in, revising along the way. Then delete the lines you didn't write and revise again.

## Working in Traditional Forms

Historically, creative writing teachers have introduced young writers to poetry by presenting them formal, structured verse and asking them to start by writing the same sort of rhyming, metered poetry.

This is like a music teacher presenting a beginning student with a Mozart concerto and saying "do one of these." To understand playing music, the student starts with the basics and moves up to the more complex. This should be the same for learning to become a poet. **The most important place to start in poetry is with content, not with the rules of formal structure.**

A poem is about what truth is communicated, as a message or a feeling, not about the structure in which it is communicated. It is difficult enough for new poets to learn to communicate their truths effectively without trying to shoehorn those truths into the limitations of a traditional form requiring them to pay attention to the line's meter and rhyme scheme.

Poetry is rooted in the traditions of rhyme, meter and formal rules. Once you have become comfortable with relaying your truths in free verse – akin to a musician learning to play rock and roll songs – you will be ready to consider moving to poetry's more complex equivalent of classical music. Rhymed, metered and otherwise formal verse is much harder for the beginner to write well. When these formal rhyming poems have content problems, they often unintentionally smack of sappy greeting cards and children's books.

**The haiku is a good place to begin writing structured verse.** Here, the form serves as a challenge to keep poems concise. There is no room for extra words in a three-line poem with five, seven and five syllables in those lines.

Here is an example written by one of the early masters of this ancient form:

Evening darkens. Hunched
On a withered bough, a crow.
Autumn in the air.

– Basho

This traditional Japanese poem is most often image-based, working like a photograph in words. Most often, the subject of these picture poems is something beautiful from the natural world. But this isn't a required purpose of the haiku. So try taking haiku pictures of something impressively ugly.

The haiku shouldn't rhyme. And each line needn't be end-stopped. By enjambing the lines, you can keep the reader moving forward in the poem. As short as they are, the haiku's lines can contain varied rhythms. But meter, or the conscious placement of certain stressed syllables in the line, isn't crucial to the haiku.

Pay special attention to the first and last words of each line, as these will receive extra attention. Titles are optional with haiku.

Haiku is great for writing in a series. Here are three from a series on nine by Ethridge Knight. These were written while he was in prison:

Easter guard tower
Glints in sunset; convicts rest
Like lizards on rocks.

Under moon shadows
A tall boy flashes knife and
Slices star bright ice.

In the August grass
Struck by the last rays of sun
The cracked teacup screams.

**The tanka is an ancient Japanese ancestor of the haiku form.**
Poets are allowed an extra couplet that follows the 5-7-5 haiku. These
two lines, with seven syllables each, allow the poet to reflect after
observing in the first three lines. Note how the first three lines present
the image and the last two show the poet's consideration of the scene:

The shore of a bay –
blowing through silent branches
of gray old pine trees
the wind acquires the voice
of crashing waves' agony

– Saigyo

**Another interesting Far-Eastern traditional variation is the
haibun.** This poem is built by alternating between haikus and short
blocks of prose. This style of poem is perfect for a poet visiting a new
place or going on a walk. The haiku work as pictures illustrating the
story. The prose sections between these pictures can be connected by a
narrative thread, keeping the reader attached to the poem.

In this example, prose written on postcards discovered at an
antique store is balanced with haiku written about the pictures on the
front of the postcards:

## From 14 Picture Postcards For Miss Ethel Hass

Columbia carved
Wallula Gap's pink clouds,
sweeps the sandstone floor.

Got a bit of volcano ash yesterday but it blew in off the roads
in Washington. If wind blows right, we could get ash from this
new eruption. Just watched a rerun of the parade.

Shining stuffed black bass
spliced huge on hunters orange canoe.
Could swallow Jack Engs.

Big fish for dinner. Now you can invite in all your friends. Still
hot and dry. Surely was good talking to you yesterday. Hope you
had a good, good day. We had such a nice trip (55 miles' drive
each way into the mountains) to the field station where our son is.

Imnaha River
cut ocean from mountain with
steel lunchbox blue ice.

Donna and I canned peaches Saturday. Made jam and pies too.
Baked cookies yesterday and made and froze two apple and one
peach pie today. Our friend is arriving on Friday. Tomorrow it's
clean house for me. Kitty is OK. She's busy exploring the big
outdoors.

Freedom of conscience
red leaf flames melt Mt. Hood ice.
Drip pan's asphalt curve.

A bright beautiful morning with the sun shining through the
gold leaves of the trees. Leaves falling now so I shall have to do
some raking today before the girl comes to mow my lawn. It needs
one last cropping. Scamp is OK and outside. I'm feeling much
better than I did last week. Will wash storm windows.

Constant lap of lake
smokes shoreline rocks like Piedmonts.
Blue mountains lean back.

Leaves are coming down fast these days. Will have to rake a
few more that blew across the street. Charles has another sore
tooth. He has to have it pulled next week. Now he's taking
medicine to reduce the infection. Kitty is snoozing in the chair
behind me. She's a lazy girl.

Brook trout jump syrup
blueberry stack Brown Lee Dam.
Crawdads here don't die.

– Jim Walker

Marianne Moore adapted the idea of the haiku's syllable-counted line to her free-verse poetry. She assigned a syllable count for each line in each stanza, keeping that count the same from stanza to stanza. Note in this excerpt from her poem, "The Mind is an Enchanting Thing," Moore's stanzas follow the same pattern of line number and syllables per line:

**From The Mind is an Enchanting Thing**

is an enchanted thing
like the glaze on a
katydid-wing
subdivided by sun
till the nettings are legion.
Like Giesking playing Scarlatti;

like the apteryx-awl
as a beak, or the
kiwi's rain-shawl
of haired feathers, the mind
feeling its way as though blind,
walks along with its eyes on the ground.

It has memory's ear
that can hear without
having to hear.
Like the gyroscope's fall,
truly equivocal
because trued by regnant certainty,

it is a power of strong enchantment. It
is like the dove-
neck animated by
sun; it is memory's eye;
it's conscientious inconsistency.

In this poem, the stanzas all contain five lines. The first line has six syllables, the second five, the third six, the fourth seven and the fifth nine.

Each of Moore's poems had a different syllable and line structure. She decided the syllabic rules of each poem and then followed the form throughout it. She occasionally broke from her syllable count within the poem, usually for one line, at fitting moments like the last line of the fifth stanza in "The Mind is an Enchanting Thing," above.

Some poets, like Robert Bly, feel that counting is crucial to keeping poems connected to the rhythms of the earth. He wrote: "If you are not counting anything in your poems, there is no form, no matter how much people talk about 'open form.' Marianne Moore counted syllables; she didn't care a bit about accents; she counted syllables. That brought her poems closer to nature, which always counts."

**To create syllabic poetry, write a stanza with six lines or so, count the syllables in each of the lines and then write the rest of the poem following that same count.** Another approach is to take an existing poem with no attention to syllable count and establish a pattern and follow it as a revision technique. This will probably require cutting words. Try to avoid adding any to make the form fit.

**Robert Bly is a proponent of another form that involves counting, the ancient Middle Eastern ghazal.** Increasingly popular, this form is comprised of five to 15 independent couplets (two-line stanzas) that leap associatively from couplet to couplet. In the ancient pattern, the last word or last short phrase of the first couplet rhymed. Then, the second line of the remaining couplets rhymed with that same last word. In the last couplet, the poet would then include a third-person self-reference.

Most modern ghazals focus less on rhyme and more on the power of the associative leaps between couplets. The ghazal opens poets to the possibility of placing far-reaching ideas and images next to each other without the need for transitions that muddy the water. Today, poets like Bly will count syllables and work from a set number per line – often twelve to 14 syllables.

Bly's "Rembrandt's Portrait of Titus with a Red Hat" and "The Difficult Word" found in Chapter Three are examples of his variation on the ghazal form.

**Other important traditional forms, like the sestina, sonnet, pantoum, and villanelle can be difficult to master.** These forms rely on intricate structural patterns – sometimes including rhyme and meter (the stresses of certain words in the lines). With so many structural layers operating at once, these forms should be tackled once you've become a more experienced poet. Only then will you be able to say what you want to say while working within the confines and possibilities of the form.

**The sonnet is characterized by fourteen lines of iambic pentameter and a rhyme scheme.** Sonnets usually end with a change in direction, thought, or emotion called a "volta" or "turn." This form has several variations including the Italian, Petrachan, and Shakespearean. Here is an example of the latter:

**Sonnet 18**

Shall I compare thee to a summer's day?
Thou art more lovely and more temperate:
Rough winds do shake the darling buds of May,
And summer's lease hath all too short a date:
Sometime too hot the eye of heaven shines,
And often is his gold complexion dimmed;
And every fair from fair sometime declines,
By chance, or nature's changing course, untrimmed;
But thy eternal summer shall not fade,
Nor lose possession of that fair thou ow'st;
Nor shall Death brag thou wander'st in his shade,
When in eternal lines to time thou grow'st;
So long as men can breathe, or eyes can see,
So long lives this, and this gives life to thee.

– William Shakespeare

Bly's "The Face in the Toyota" in Chapter Three is an example of a modern, free verse sonnet.

Other traditional forms to pursue:

- A **limerick** is a light verse form of poetry containing five lines. The first, second, and last lines scan like this: weak STRONG weak weak STRONG weak weak STRONG, and the third and fourth scan like this: weak STRONG weak weak STRONG.

- The **triolet** is a French form of poetry with eight lines. The first, fourth, and seventh lines are identical. So are the second and eighth lines. It usually is written in a combination of iambic tetrameter and trimeter.

- The **villanelle** is 19 lines and six stanzas long. There are two rhyming sounds with a rhyme scheme like this: aba aba aba aba aba abaa. Here's the confusing part: the first and third lines of the first stanza are repeated in alternation—the first line is the last line of the second stanza, the third line is the last line of the third stanza, etc. And the first and third lines are the third and fourth lines, respectively, in the last stanza.

- The **pantoum** is a form of Asian poetry and is unique in its repetition. The second and fourth lines of every stanza are the first and third of the next, and the second and fourth lines of the final stanza happen to be the first and third lines of the first stanza, giving a 'circle' effect. See Kovacik's "Herman Kafka's Dinnertime Pantoum" in Chapter 3 for an example.

- The **sestina** has seven stanzas, six with six lines and one with three lines. The six words that end the first stanza's lines are repeated at the end of the lines in the first six stanzas. The final stanza uses two of these "key words" per line.

- The **ballade** is a form of poetry containing three eight-line stanzas and an envoy that may be either four or five lines long. The last line of the first stanza is the last line of all others, including the envoy. There are only three rhyming sounds, and no word can be repeated as a rhyme.

- The **paradelle** resembles a word puzzle. There are six lines per stanza. In all stanzas but the last, the first four lines are two different lines repeated twice, and the last two lines use all the words of the previous line. The last stanza uses all the words of the previous stanzas.

- This **rondeau** is French in origin and contains 13 lines. It is built on two rhymes. What is unique about this form is that the first few words of the first line are repeated as the last lines of the next stanzas.


## The Language, the Language

Many of the prompts covered thus far are designed to help you find content for poems and match that content with the correct form. While it is important to write consciously about certain subjects, poets often enjoy writing that comes accidentally, like the found poems discussed earlier. Playing writing games and placing specific rules on writing can help produce poems you never imaged you'd write. Here are a few possibilities.

**Try writing primitive poems using a limited, earthy language**. This could mean limiting yourself to guttural one-syllable words or creating a language built from a brief word list that you or a group select. The list can be created randomly – by pointing into a dictionary or other books – or by your design.

Another way to limit your vocabulary options and involve the alchemy of accident is to write a set number of words on scraps of paper, place those words in an envelope and draw them at random, creating the skeleton for a poem.

Magnetic Poetry, words printed on thin magnet strips and sold in stores, works the same way. Be sure to draw your words blindly, as having too many words at your disposal and choosing them consciously is the same as writing on your own. You might as well just write in your notebook and use your own words.

**Another creative technique uses math.** Create a formula or code, assigning a word to each number when it appears as the answer in a math problem. Poet Maureen Seaton writes poems based on the infinite answer in the calculation for pi, assigning a single word to the decimal point and to numbers one through ten. When each number comes up in the answer, a form of the word assigned to it appears in the poem. Use a calculator or visit one of several pi-calculation sites on the Internet for the numbers.

Here is an example of a poem created using pi:

**Me**

I am shrinking man. I all human the broken
pieces. The I way. I human man gone way gone. Man
I human I way. Broken all the pieces. Way human man
shrinking. The broken shrinking. Gone. The I. The I broken.
All shrinking pieces. All human pieces. The broken man.
The man all the way pieces broken. Human shrinking. Gone.
Man pieces. Gone way. Human. Gone way. Pieces human.
Gone way. Man human all I man shrinking. Broken pieces
shrinking all the way to gone.

– Jim Walker

An easier type of math is involved in an exercise using any text
and a dictionary. Choose a block of writing, possibly a poem of your
own, and look up each of the words – except articles and other
indefinable words – and replace each of those words with the word
nine entries down from it in the dictionary. You'll be amazed at the
results.

Poet Charles Bernstein discovers poems by taking one written in a
foreign language and translating it by reading the words as units of
sound. He assigns each the closest English equivalent.

Beat Generation writer William Burroughs, author of *Naked
Lunch*, perfected the system of the cut-up. He would cut a page he
wrote into four pieces and then shuffle them so they didn't line up as
they did originally. He would sometimes replace one corner of the cut-
up with found texts from newspapers or other books.

**The cut-up creates a collision of sentences and phrases that
didn't originally go together, making something new and
interesting out of the collision.** Another option is to cut pages into
several vertical strips, allowing only phrases and short parts of
sentences to remain together before being taped down next to short
bursts that came from other texts.

Cut-up text can originate anywhere – plumbing catalogues, music
magazines, recipe books, old philosophy books – but the text shouldn't
come from poetry or other kinds of creative writing texts.

The key to the cut-up is to understand that what you discover when placing these disparate chunks of language together is just the beginning. The raw material, as with all of these language exercises, must be manipulated and revised and made your own.

Here is an example of a poem that started as a cut-up. Raw material included stories from science and home décor magazines, as well as a book about Old-West desperadoes:

### The True Story of My Failed First Marriage

We were married in copper wire.
I triggered a spark gap like a physician's teardrop.
You created a huge magnetic field.
I thought you were the daughter of a pipe bursting.
You took my delicate parts.
Your horse rode away toward a metal light pole.
I wanted it to leave but could not handle its current.
So I released the charge and did not come back
to find you in the space between sparks.
Then it happened. You cracked through the glass block
cellar window. You dropped the rose hard
and left me at the coil to belly-crawl the tunnel alone.

– Jim Walker

## Surreal Games

Before William Burroughs, the surrealists in France and Germany in the 1920s and '30s were already creating with the magic of accidental language, the universe of the dream.

**Surrealism is based, according to its French founder, Andre Breton, on the "disinterested play of thought."** This means the poet must release the chains of real-world logic. It is important to understand that the poem must create its own logic, must make its own sense independent of what we expect from the rules of life.

In this way, surrealist poems often create new worlds with rules we've never experienced. But we know when something isn't right in this new world. Consider those moments in dreams when we begin to realize "this isn't real" because, even in the twisted logic of the dream, something happens that tells us the dream is false. The logic is broken, the magic lost.

When you play a surrealist game, you will relinquish control and like it. Surrealism is about expressing pure thought, about being free of controls imposed by the prejudices stemming from religious morality and social standards. It can be very refreshing to ignore those things, embracing instead the imaginative and the unconscious – the silly, dreamy and dark sides – as well as the erotic and the childish.

Our imaginations are at their strongest when we are children. Why do we lose this? "If man retains some lucidity," wrote Breton, "he cannot help turning back towards his childhood which, spoiled though it was by his trainers, seems to him to be full of charms. There the absence of all known severity leaves him the perspective of several lives at the same time. Every morning children leave without anxiety. All is ready; the worst material conditions are excellent. The woods are white or black; they will never go to sleep."

**Surrealist poetry relies on the image.** French poet Pierre Reverdy wrote: "The image is a pure creation of spirit. It cannot be born of a comparison but of the bringing together of two realities, which are more or less remote. The more distant and just the relationship of these conjoined realities, the stronger the image – the more emotive power and poetic reality it will have."

Here is an example of an image-driven surrealist poem:

### The Man with the India Rubber Head

*Five clocks ring out the hour in a silent room.*

I desire the bones of a toy store clerk
sleeping in a pine box
that will leak clouds of flesh
when everything breaks apart and is gone.

*Until the end of his life he preferred to take the train.*

Wicked is the man who shoots down the joy of birdwatchers
breaks down the love that starts in Sunday newspapers
and fries sunshine in a dusty room.

*Time floats down like a blackbird full of BBs.*

– Jim Walker

**Surrealist games are about bringing together these distant realities and seeing what new comes from the collision.** These child-like games look to unlock words and ideas – often from the subconscious – through chance and accident, instead of the usual premeditation and deliberation. They bring out what Breton called "spontaneous, extra-lucid, insolent rapport between one thing and another which common sense hesitates to confront." These games can feel like alchemy.

Surrealist games require collaboration and interaction between you and at least one more open-minded and creative person. Sit at a table across from your partner. Each of you needs a piece of paper and a pen.

At the same time, both of you write a question on a piece of paper. Don't think much about it, just jot down the first thing that comes to mind. Remember, surrealist poetry usually starts with automatic writing. This, Breton said, is "the dictation of thought without control of the mind." Cover the question and hand it to your partner. Without reading the question, write an answer below it.

When you are finished, look at the surprising way the unseen question was answered. You can do the same thing in a variety of ways with one person writing a word, covering it, and the other person writing a definition. Also try collaborating with surreal if-then statements.

With a partner or group, select several non-poetry or creative fiction books – the stranger the better. Place those books on a table in front of you. Each writer needs a notebook or piece of paper and a pen. For this exercise, you will open the book, pick a line at random and write it on your paper. Then you will write the first line that comes to your mind. You'll cover both and pass the paper to the next person. You will then do the same thing on a new piece of paper and a new book until you have used a line from each book once.

A mathematics wiz in the group can figure out how to go around the exact number of times to have each piece start and end with the same poet and/or the same book. This is the preferred method as it can help bring the poem around full circle.

The next step is to share the notes for the poems and allow each poet to revise as he sees fit. Sharing the different versions of the raw material drafted into something more realized can be a revealing experience. Each poet will focus on different things in the revision of the same raw material.

This exercise is similar to what is known as the "exquisite corpse" or "telephone game" where you start a poem or story on a piece of paper, each adding a line before covering all but the last line and passing it on around the circle. The surrealists liked to do the same thing with drawings, starting in a corner of the page, covering all but the edge of the drawing and passing it to the next person to continue adding to the work.

Another enjoyable surrealist group game called "Around the Word" produces poems that are both collaborative and individual. Sit in a circle and go around, in order, calling out a word while free writing in short bursts.

The exercise starts with one person in the circle choosing a word. All of the poets have to use that word in the first line of their poem. After enough time is permitted to complete the line (30 seconds to a minute), the next person in the circle calls out a word. This word must then be used in the next line, and so on.

You can use any form or homonym version of the words called out. These poems can be fun to share immediately but will be vastly improved by revision. During revision don't feel that you have to keep all of the called-out words in your poem. This game is designed, as are all of these exercises, to generate raw material for poems. From there we go to work to make it a polished poem. This will be another final product to share with the rest of the group.

Here's an example of a poem that started with the "Around the Word" game:

**Photo Album**

I like sunshine better, books about New Jersey
more than school.

Green lights in pictures bright and I'm burning him.
Made him close his eyes.

I squint back the restaurant restroom.

White and pink, Kevin is next to the mirror.
I could just sleep in his sink.

Sun sets on the lake cottage floor
down from where we made picture postcards so pretty.
Sold them as cut-rate wheat to Wesleyans for communion bread.

Gradual, the light begins to fade
into a tulip bulb in your eye after God switched to a star.

-- Jim Walker

Hopefully the various prompts suggested above will inspire you.
And keep you working steadily as you grow as a poet. When ideas
don't flow naturally, and you are unable to decide what to write about,
return to these prompts as necessary.

Remember that your progress as a poet will be gradual. Try a
different prompt at various stages of your development and remember
- poets gather their material from many different sources. The only
restriction: the extent of your imagination.

# Chapter Seven
## Punctuation and Poetic Consciousness

### The Importance of Punctuation

Punctuation is defined as being the use of standardized marks and signs in writing to separate words into sentences, clauses, and phrases in order to clarify meaning. This seems simple when you are dealing with paragraphs. But poetry is another matter altogether. It begs the question, is there a *right way* to use punctuation in poetry?

In a word, no. But, of course, there is a best way.

Punctuation is used to summarize thoughts and ideas, to aid in lucidity and the manifestation of meaning, and especially to signal when and where to pause. Poetry may very well be a different animal from prose, but punctuation, because of its formulaic nature, serves the same function in both forms. With this in mind, it is easier to understand why punctuation is so important.

As with every word, every punctuation mark is an essential element in helping the reader come to a conclusion about the meaning of the poem. By not taking punctuation seriously, by not knowing some of the basic rules of punctuation or by randomly choosing places at which to break lines, the poet may be unwittingly leading the reader astray and leaving a plethora of room for an incorrect interpretation of the sentiment.

Robert Frost once said, "Poetry is a way to take life by the throat." This idea, that poetry is a powerful medium for grasping the essentials of living, is a clear sign that poetry is not an art form to be taken lightly. We must be conscious of every move, we must be diligent, awake, and aware of the logics we implore in every line of every poem we write.

### Standard Punctuation Marks

Let's consider a few standard punctuation marks, their usages and an example or two of how each of these points are applied in poetry:

The **comma** — A punctuation mark ( , ) used to indicate a separation of ideas or of elements within the structure of a sentence. A pause or separation; a caesura.

- Use a comma before the words "and" and "or" in a series of three or more, e.g., Walt Whitman's poem "Song of Myself."

  It may be you are from old people, or from offspring taken,
  It may be if I had known them I would have loved them,
  soon out of their mother's laps,
  And here you are the mothers' laps.

- Follow a statement that introduces a direct quotation of one or more paragraphs with a comma. But use a colon after "as follows." Examples: Dorothy Parker's epitaph reads, "Pardon my dust." Dorothy Parker's epitaph reads as follows: "Pardon my dust."

The **semicolon** — A mark of punctuation ( ; ) used to connect independent clauses and indicating a closer relationship between the clauses than a comma or period does.

- Look at the use of the semicolon in the first stanza of Elizabeth Bishop's poem "One Art"

  The art of losing isn't hard to master;
  so many things seem filled with the intent
  to be lost that their loss is no disaster.

The **colon** — A punctuation mark ( : ) used after a word introducing a quotation, an explanation, an example, or a series and often after the salutation of a business letter.

- Look at this section from Margaret Atwood's poem, **"Spelling"**. Notice the use of the colon in the second stanza show here:

  I return to the story
  of the woman caught in the war
  & in labour, her thighs tied
  together by the enemy
  so she could not give birth.

  Ancestress: the burning witch,
  her mouth covered by leather
  to strangle words.

The **dash** — A line, approximately the width of two hyphens ( — ), in writing or printing, denoting a sudden break, stop, or transition in a sentence, or an abrupt change in its construction, a long or significant pause, or an unexpected or epigrammatic turn of sentiment. Dashes are also sometimes used instead of commas or parentheses.

- In Emily Dickinson's poem "Ah, Moon— and Star!" notice her use of the dash in the first stanza of the poem:

    Ah, Moon—and Star!
    You are very far—
    But were no one
    Farther than you—
    Do you think I'd stop
    For a Firmament—
    Or a Cubit—or so?

The **hyphen** — A punctuation mark (-) used between the parts of a compound word or name or between the syllables of a word, especially when divided at the end of a line of text

**Parenthesis** — Either or both of the upright curved lines, ( ), used to mark off explanatory or qualifying remarks in writing or printing.

A qualifying or amplifying word, phrase, or sentence inserted within written matter in such a way as to be independent of the surrounding grammatical structure.

A comment departing from the theme of discourse; a digression.

- Look at the interesting and ingenious use of the parentheses in this poem:

**1(a...(a leaf falls on loneliness)**
e.e. cummings

1(a

le
af

fa
ll

s)
one
l

ness

The **apostrophe** — The superscript sign ( ' ) used to indicate abbreviations to show where a letter or letters are omitted, the omission of a letter or letters from a word, the possessive case, or the plurals of letters.

The **quotation mark** — Either of a pair of punctuation marks used primarily to mark the beginning and end of a passage attributed to another and repeated word for word, but also to indicate meanings and to indicate the unusual or dubious status of a word. They appear in the form of double quotation marks (" ") and single quotation marks (' '). Single quotation marks are usually reserved for setting off a quotation within another quotation in double quotation marks.

The **exclamation point** — A punctuation mark (!) used to indicate an emotional exclamation.

- Take a look at the last stanza of the poem "Ah, Moon— and Star!" by Emily Dickinson:

But, Moon, and Star,
Though you're very far—
There is one—farther than you—
He—is more than a firmament—from Me—
So I can never go!

The **question mark**— A punctuation symbol (?) written at the end of a sentence or phrase to indicate a direct question.
The **period**— A punctuation mark ( . ) indicating a full stop, placed at the end of declarative sentences and other statements thought to be complete, and after many abbreviations.

## Punctuation and Poetic Conciousness

Good poetry is not emotional in its mechanics. This is not to say that good poetry is not emotional, but rather conscious control over punctuation and logical choices in linebreaks hightlight the emotional content of your poem. It cannot be emphasized enough the importance of punctuation in a poem. The idea Frost articulated so well that, "Poetry is a way to take life by the throat," harbors the hope that every word, mark, and line break will be essential to the integrity, effectiveness and artistry of the craft. Use punctuation as a tool to show your reader the meaning in your poem. Becoming conscious of every point, mark and linebreak you use in every line of every poem is just part of the process of becoming a stronger poet.

# Chapter Eight
## Feedback

You may generate poetry sitting alone somewhere. You may shape and revise it at your computer while everyone else is away. But, once you are satisfied with your work, you will want to share it. You will *need* to share it.

You are the first point in the equilateral poetry triangle. For whatever reason, you have a desire to write. The words inside you are dying to get out. They hammer away at your mind, possessing it for a little while like noisy demons.

These demons – your interests, your obsessions – make up the second point in the triangle. This is the muse, the reason you write, the fuel behind the fire. You can write without the muse, you can write without being possessed by your demons, but that writing will be humdrum. It will not reflect any kind of truth about you or the universe and your place in it.

The third part of the poetry triangle, every bit as important as the other two in the equation, is the audience. Without an audience, the poem still exists, but it only exists in one way—in your way. Once others see this reflection, they blend it with their own experiences and ideas and make it their own.

**When a poem works, the audience owns the poem just as much as the writer; it is universal enough to open up a door to the reader while still remaining the poet's house. Remember, a great poem is about you but makes the audience believe it is about them.**

A poem is working best when the audience, as Li-Young Lee says, feels they are overhearing a dialogue between you and your demons or muse.

Poets are often discouraged when they complete a poem and show it to a friend or loved one who doesn't really understand the purpose of poetry. They will call your poem "interesting" or "nice" or maybe be honest and say they don't understand it or they don't really like it. Don't be discouraged by this. You can't expect everyone to like poetry. But you can expect to find an appreciative audience out there for your creations if you are working hard to put your artistic vision on the page.

You may be fortunate enough to have a close friend or family member who will give your poetry a chance and take the time to see what you are trying to accomplish with your writing. If you don't have this built-in audience in place, you'll need to find one so you can begin to receive feedback for your work. You need to know what poems are accomplishing your goals with the audience and what poems aren't.

You can discover information on open-microphone nights, poetry workshops and book groups led by local writing organizations, universities and colleges, and libraries in small towns and large cities alike. If you have a college in your city, call the English department or writing program office to see if someone there can lead you to any workshops or reading groups.

If you can afford it and never had a chance before, an introductory poetry class as a continuing student can provide a structured program that will launch your writing. If the college scene isn't possible, check with the librarian at your local branch for alternative courses or seminars.

Local newspapers and related organizations' newsletters list regular open-microphone poetry readings. To participate, you will need to bring along a poem you're comfortable sharing and a couple of bucks for coffee. A few tips for first-time readers: some poems are definitely better on the page than they are performed.

Read your work into a tape recorder and see what sounds best. Always start with shorter poems. The worst poet at any reading will invariably be the poet who reads the longest. Don't be that poet.

Another tip: take your time as you read. Use your line and stanza breaks as the sheet music for your voice. Speed up and slow down as the lines and stanzas dictate. Just relax and share.

While the Internet presents a viable option for those isolated geographically, poetry websites where you can post your work and receive feedback do not begin to compare to real face-to-face interaction. Don't be shy. Don't be afraid of other people's egos and insecurities. All artists have them. Many artists, poets included, can be self-centered and self-obsessed at times. But interaction is mutually beneficial and necessary. And remember that constructive criticism isn't personal.

After reading your work in public to receive specific, constructive feedback, join a poet's group or consider taking a leadership role in starting one. If you decide to do the latter, here are some tips:

1.  Meet on a set day. It could be every Saturday morning or the first Tuesday of the month. This will permit members of the group to organize their schedules around that day.

2.   Choose a facilitator. This person keeps things moving, watches when discussions go on too long or can help interpret comments that seem harsh or confusing. This person is the mediator, the referee and the timekeeper. Without a facilitator, any group will break down. This is often the role of the teacher in the college workshop setting. The person in this role can also point out ways that everyone in the group can learn from feedback given to one person. The facilitator can also compare and contrast work by different poets in the group.

3.   Meet somewhere comfortable, somewhere neutral if possible. If the group meets at your house every time, the group may soon feel that this is your group, not theirs. Rotate meeting places or do it at a relaxed spot like a friendly diner or coffeehouse.

4.   Work together on assignments. Workshops are best when the group is on the same page with their poetry. Look at the prompts in this book – many specifically designed for groups – and work through them together, comparing how each member of the group approaches the assignments differently. People in the middle of other projects can choose to opt out of the assignments.

5.   Be honest and constructive when offering feedback. This doesn't mean you must "be positive" all of the time. When poets share their work in the group, they need to know first if the purpose or goal for the poem was clear to the audience. Did they get what the poet was trying to do? Once this question is answered, the group can move to talking about what worked and what didn't work – and why or why not. Be as specific as possible.

Workshop groups sometimes struggle with the issue of members "rewriting" a poet's work by offering many suggestions for changing single words, linebreaks or other small details. While these suggestions can be helpful, some feedback can go too far into minutiae. Beware of tension that workshop nitpicking can create.
**After receiving feedback during the revision process, the poet can choose to accept or ignore the advice. The poem will only be rewritten the way the poet decides to rewrite it.**
Along with helping provide receivers for the signal that is your poetry, these sharing activities will help introduce you to an all-important network of fellow artists and poets. If you don't have close

friends or family members who share your understanding and passion for poetry, you will begin to relish new friends who do.

When you attend a reading and someone performs a poem that you especially enjoy or that seems to be in line with what you are trying for in your own work, meet that person. Exchange phone numbers or email addresses.

## Never Stop Reading

A terrific side benefit of this kind of networking is the discovery of great poets to read. Reviews of poetry books are hard to find. Publicity for new books is virtually nonexistent, with poets usually receiving only word-of-mouth advertising for their books. Listen to what other people are reading. You can also note suggested readings in the Appendix.

Write down names and titles that interest you and visit the library or an online bookstore such as Amazon.com. From this list, begin to outline your own reading plan. Poetry books, while available at larger chain stores, aren't as easy to find as the typical paperback best- seller. Trust friends to help you connect with poets you'd like to read.

Anthologies make a good starting point for people new to poetry. Certain poets will become instant favorites and you'll be able to find more of their work later.

Read literary magazines to discover work by current poets. Some of the most popular, such as *American Poetry Review* or the *Paris Review* can be found at most larger bookstores. Many of the best literary or "little" magazines are not as easy to find. Track down a few you are interested in and consider subscribing.

As a developing poet, you'll learn the most by reading a mixture of work by the great poets through history, established modern poets and poets newer on the scene who may be writing more experimental work. Ultimately, your best plan is to read the things you enjoy, and that can help improve what you are trying to create.

It is reassuring to find like-minded writers in print who help you see that you aren't alone in your poetic pursuits. **Reading is of the utmost importance for any writer. You should never leave home without your notebook and an unread poetry book. When you are waiting in line or taking a break at work, read.**

That way, these words and ideas will be constantly bouncing around in your brain and good things will come out. Reading will help your writing by raising your expectations and giving you an idea of your place in the world of poetry.

Poets should also read more than poetry. Think of it as research for poetry. If you are reading the *King James Bible*, the style of its poetry may work its way into yours. You may find yourself referring to the Bible's stories or making allusions to its characters. If you are reading a book about the Old West, you may also find stories and people from that reading popping up in your poems.

Consider your list of obsessions. If you can't stop thinking or writing about the Civil War, then read about it, learn more. If you are hooked on food and cooking – maybe even a specific dish – then study the history of that dish, the chef who invented it, and let this knowledge work its way into your poem.

Maybe you have always been fascinated with honeybees. Read all the books you can about the life of bees and write poems about them, maybe as metaphors for humans. Immerse yourself in topics you enjoy – science, math, history, mythology, folklore, art, music – and emerge with tons of inspiring information for poems that you can blend with your own thoughts and emotions.

Poetry's road is one that veers off into countless wonderful detours and side paths. Find friends – both in person and in print – to take with you along your journey.

One of the great joys of poetry comes from its abundance. It is an art form with thousands of years of history to explore. But the road goes two ways. Contemporary poets – published or sharing their work at local readings – can teach and inspire you.

In his poem "To Elsie," William Carlos Williams worries there may be "No one/ to witness/ and adjust, no one to drive the car" of poetry.

That is your job.

# Getting the Word Out

# Chapter Nine
## Becoming Published

Once you have taken the time to read and write a good deal of poetry, your goal is to begin sharing it in print form.

For any poet, the publishing process can prove to be a rewarding challenge. Once you branch out into a network of poets in your community, you will likely meet somebody publishing a local literary magazine or newsletter. These publications are a great way to get started. Their editors will be more likely to take the time to offer feedback and suggestions for your poems. They will tell you exactly what they want and don't want. And you will have access to back issues that you can review.

Best of all, if you know the work of the person who edits the magazine, you have a better idea of his or her poetic sensibilities. This can help you target the work that fits best with a particular outlet. With local publications, your work will not be competing with an influx of poems from all over the world. These little magazines will also be less likely to request work from established writers, leaving more room for newer ones.

Be aware that every editor who publishes a magazine knows other poets. Many have a tendency to publish their friends' work first. The hope is that these friends aren't being favored because of their status in the editor's life. The hope is that the editor is a friend of these poets, in part, because they share a similar taste in poetry.

If you have an inside track with local magazine editors, don't worry about the ethical dilemma of submitting poems to a friend. Just be prepared for your friend to say: "Sorry, not this time." And make sure you don't hold that against the editor who is just doing his or her job. **Bridges are very important in the small world of poetry. Don't burn any over petty publishing squabbles or an inflated ego.**

Local publications can range from photocopied and stapled pamphlets to very professional-looking glossy books. The packaging depends on the amount of money the editor has to invest in the magazine. Quite often, the most low-tech literary magazines are filled with the best poetry.

Regardless, the joy of seeing your work in print for the first time, the joy of holding that little book in your hand and knowing your poem was accepted as part of a product now sought by an audience of readers supercedes any concerns about printing quality. With this kind of publication, you will receive no pay for your work. You may only get a free copy or two of the magazine. But there's no disputing that you are a published poet.

Be sure to ask your editor friend for submission guidelines before handing over any poems. Unless you are told otherwise, follow these guidelines to the letter. Don't give any indication that you are expecting special treatment. The editor will appreciate this show of respect.

When you are told that your poem has been accepted, record this to help you avoid sending it out again to another magazine. Most editors will be insulted if they see a poem they published appearing at the same time in another magazine – especially one distributed in the same area as theirs.

Once you've worked through the process of seeking publication in local magazines, it is logical to consider moving to larger regional and national literary magazines. For many new poets, the first step toward that goal is purchasing a publishing guide like the *Poet's Market* and searching its listings for appealing literary magazines. The listings offer a general idea of what magazine editors are seeking and provide poets with guidelines for submitting their work.

You'll also discover the magazine's circulation is tiny or huge and what percentage of submissions is accepted for publication. Don't bother sending poems to magazines with a circulation of fifty readers. You might as well make photocopies of your poem and hand it out to your friends. The listings may also include sample poems chosen by the editor to demonstrate what kind of work the magazine has published.

These samples are helpful since you can see how your work compares. You may also check the listings for the names of other poets published in the magazine. From there, research these poets – the Internet is the best place for this – read their work, and see if it fits with yours.

If the magazine has a website, the *Poet's Market* listing will likely include that address. If the site includes more than just basic information, you can get a very good feel for the magazine and what kind of poetry it publishes.

Here's a brief explanation/analysis of a literary magazine listing in the *Poet's Market:*

**$ THE SUN** (*Tip: dollar sign indicates monetary pay for poems*)
107 N. Roberson St. Chapel Hill, NC 27516 (*Tip: no telephone number listed, don't call them*)
Website: www.thesunmagazine.org. (*Tip: your next stop in researching*)
Established 1974. Editor Sy Safransky. (*Tip: well-established publication*)

**Magazine Needs**: The sun is "noted for honest, personal work that's not too obscure or academic. We avoid traditional, rhyming poetry, as well as limericks, haiku, and religious poetry. We're open to almost everything else: free verse, prose poems, short and longer poems." (*Tip: pay close attention to these specific requests; no formal poems here*)

Has published poetry by William Snyder Jr., Allison Luterman, Donna Steiner, David Budbill, Susan Terris, and Michael Chitwood. (*Tip: if you aren't familiar with these poets, search for them on the Internet or at your local library or bookstore – see if their writing is anything like yours.*)

As a sample, the editor selected these lines from "Dog on the Floor in the Pet-Food Aisle" by Ruth L. Schwartz:
We watch our lives through airplane windows,/small and dim and scarred,/ and even so, life noses up,/ rolling before us/ like a black dog,/ its brown
eyes steady as the sun/ its belly in the air, asking for touch.
(*Tip: in the sample, slash marks indicated linebreaks*)

The Sun is 48 pages, magazine-sized, printed on 50 lb. offset, saddle-stapled, with b&w photos and graphics. (*Tip: this is a heavier paper stock and attractive binding method*)

Circulation is 50,000 for 48,000 subscriptions of which 500 are libraries.
(*Tip: a very large circulation for a literary magazine*)

Receives 3,000 submissions of poetry/year accepts about 30; has a 1-3 month backlog. (*Tip: Only a slim percentage of poems are accepted*)

Subscription: $34. Sample: $5. (*Tip: Don't expect subscribing to increase your chances at publication, but a sample can help you determine if this is the publication for you*)

**How to Submit:** Submit up to 6 poems at a time. Poems should be typed and accompanied by a cover letter. (*Tip: Send in as many poems as permitted. This will increase your odds of being published. Keep your cover letter brief.*)

Accepts previously published poems, but simultaneous submissions are discouraged. Guidelines available for SASE. (*Tip: many magazines refuse to print anything previously published – SASE is Self Addressed Stamped Envelope*)

Responds within 3 months. Pays $50-$200 on publication plus copes and subscription. Acquires serial or one-time rights. (Tip: this is *big money for poetry. Latter sentence means rights to poems revert back to the author after publication.*)

Finding and reading literary magazines is the best way for you to determine where to send work. These have their own shelf in the periodical section at many larger chain bookstores. Some newsstands also stock a variety of literary magazines.

If you find a store that sells literary magazines, spend time browsing the selections. Buy a few that you would like to read anyway. In the backs of these magazines, read the contributors' biographies. They often list other publishing credits. If you feel you have something in common with a contributor or two, make note of the other magazines in their biographies and research those, too.

Once you've identified current published poets you feel write in a style similar to yours, research these poets to discover where they submitted their work. Most new poetry books include an Acknowledgements page listing the literary magazines that published the individual poems comprising much of the book.

Make a list of these magazines, look them up in *Poet's Market* or on the Internet and, if they still seem like a fit, send your work. Anthologies, especially the Best of American Poetry series, also make great places to research poets and the literary magazines that published their work. Anthologies will list the names of the magazines in the acknowledgements section.

Taking time to research before submitting can save you time and money and save magazine editors trouble.

For example, consider a poet who writes experimental poetry. He finds a magazine listed in the *Poet's Market* with an experimental sounding name. He then sends the recommended three or four poems with the recommended self-addressed-stamped envelope (SASE). Little does he know, because he didn't research, that this isn't an experimental magazine, but one that publishes inspirational poetry.

Unfortunately, this poet wasted his time since he sent something that, no matter how good it was, did not fit with the editor's interests. He waited eight weeks only to get a rejection slip and not know why.

Another option open to poets is submitting to Internet journals. This can help save money in postage and the responses may arrive quicker. Do the same sort of research of these web-only magazines. And be sure to follow the technical submissions guidelines closely. Most online magazines are very particular about sending attached files because of computer virus issues.

To optimize your chances concerning magazine submissions, consider the following tips"

## Make a Submissions Worksheet

Some magazines accept simultaneous submissions, others do not. The poetry-publishing world is a small one. Note when you receive word if your work was rejected or accepted. Refer to this sheet in your next wave of submitting poems. This will help make sure you don't send poems to a magazine that already rejected them once.

**Don't let rejection bother you.** Some poets have wallpapered entire rooms with rejection slips – tiny form responses that usually say "your submission does not meet our needs right now" or something similar.

**A hand-written rejection note is a good sign, especially if the editor writes something like "close, send more."** Don't expect commentary on most rejections. Eventually, an editor will accept one of your poems and you'll feel the joy of beating the odds. This, and a free copy or two that will arrive months later in the mail, makes it all worthwhile.

# Read Submission Guidelines Closely

Some magazine editors are particular about the number of poems you send or even the kind of envelope you use for your submission. **Many editors only read submissions during certain times of the year.** Don't make the mistake of sending poems during the off-times. Fall and early spring are the best times to send work to journals associated with universities. These publications don't read during the summer because professors and students who serve as editorial staff are away from campus.

With too many poems to handle in the first place, editors wisely use violations of these requirements as a way to reduce the load submissions.

Additional tips: be sure to include your name on every page of poetry you submit. Your name, address and email should be listed on each poem. Don't staple pages together.

Always include a SASE with your submission. Most editors will pitch your poems in the trash if they don't see a return envelope in the packet. Be prepared to wait up to six months to hear back. While calling to check after a month or two is acceptable, don't expect to catch editors at their phones very often.

# Write a Cover Letter for Each Submission

Address letters to the editor by name, if possible. You should mention why you decided to send your work to the magazine. Mention the name of the magazine so it doesn't seem like a form letter. But don't be excessive with the compliments. Letting them know that you have read poetry they published by a poet you admire is acceptable.

If you've been published, mention this in the letter. Make the letter brief and be sure that it, like your poems, is closely edited for spelling and grammar. A typo-filled cover letter is another excuse for an editor to disregard your work.

Here is an example of good cover letter:

Dear Mr. Jones and staff:

Please find enclosed five poems and the two-sentence biographical sketch per your guidelines.

As an avid reader of *Lost Highway* and a poet with a growing number of publishing credits, I would like very much to be included in an upcoming issue. I especially enjoyed Charles Simic's poem in the winter issue.

I see your magazine as printing what must be the future of poetry. Thanks for your time. I hope something here will fit your needs.

Sincerely,
A. Poet


## Never Pay Reading Fees

Avoid sending poems to any publication that asks for payment before reading your work. This is most likely a scam. There are many high-quality literary magazines that don't charge poets anything more than return postage. Start there.

**As stated in Chapter Ten, do not commit to having your poetry published by a subsidy publisher who charges you for publication costs.** They are not interested in your publishing career; only in making money. If you can not secure a traditional publisher, self-publish your work. Information about doing so is readily available from several self-help books including Book Report, Publishing Strategies, Writing Tips, and 101 Literary Ideas For Aspiring Authors and Poets, a Books For Life Foundation publication.

Working to get your poems published is a difficult but rewarding pursuit. When your poems find their way into literary magazines or onto websites accessible across the globe, you know that hundreds and thousands of like-minded strangers are connecting with your creative thoughts – just as you have connected with poets you've read.

Your work is now part of the wonderful world of poetry.

# Chapter Ten
## Understanding The Publishing Industry

As you continue to learn and improve as a poet, take the time to understand the publishing world. By examining the current state of affairs in the poetry publishing industry, you can discover how your work fits into the world of published poetry.

"Being published" assumes many forms. They include binding several copies of a personal memoir or journal entries for family and friends, writing a magazine or newspaper article, penning a short story or essay for publication in magazines or writers' journals, writing a short article to be published on an Internet site or the company newsletter, crafting a poem to be included in a magazine or anthology collection, writing several poems for inclusion in a poetry book or chapbook, or completing a fiction or non-fiction manuscript that will be self-published or released by a traditional publisher.

This said, whether you have created a book idea, a few sentences, a paragraph or two scribbled on a torn sheet of paper, a chapter outlining characters, partial text ripe for a short story, essay, or magazine article, half of a non-fiction book revealing that Neil Armstrong did *not* walk on the moon, the first draft of the great American novel, or several pages of poetry—**STOP**. Before proceeding, enter the real world of publishing.

A common error committed by many aspiring poets is to complete a manuscript or collection of poetry while possessing little knowledge of the inner workings of the industry. Writing for publication without researching the literary marketplace is akin to listing a home before assessing its market value. Lack of information decreases the chances of selling the house just as lack of expertise about the publishing industry hinders the potential to be traditionally published by a company that will cover all costs of releasing a book.

Laborious reading or extensive research isn't required to begin a sojourn into the publishing world. Instead, visit a large bookstore or an independent outlet. This scouting mission is guaranteed to enlighten, since bookstores are packed with written works published in many forms and through many means, often involving writer ingenuity and alternative publishing strategies.

The key is to understand where you fit into the world of poetry, both as it was written in the past and as it is written today. Use the bookstore as a way to discover current trends regarding the types of poetry specific publishers are marketing to bookstores.

## Publishing Industry Overview

As you browse your way to the area where poetry is displayed, note the ambience of the bookstore—the whispering of customers discussing which book to purchase while reading snippets from jacket covers or the first pages of the text. At the store's café, people read, flip through magazines, write in notebooks, or type away at a laptop as the aroma of cappuccino drifts through the air.

Remember that those meandering around the store are potential customers for *your* book. They are the very people who may pay as much as $29.95 for a hardback edition. If enough of them can be convinced it is a must-read, strong sales result.

When you discover the poetry section, pick up the books, feel their texture, and note the colors, the graphics or photographs, and the style of print. Notice that the quality of cover stock, paper and binding varies from small presses to big publishing houses reissuing handsome collectable editions of classics like Walt Whitman's *Leaves of Grass*.

Read the inside jacket cover text, the author or poet biography, and the back cover text. On the second or third page, the name and location of the publishing company is provided.

While glancing at the books, become familiar with the major players in modern poetry. Don't forget that you are not a poet from a different time in history. As much as that poetry continues to sell, you'll notice that little contemporary poetry mirrors work written in centuries past. With this in mind, scribble a note or two listing publishers that have published work similar to yours. As the writing process continues, add to the list. When the time arrives to seek publication, the list will be helpful.

To learn more about the team who collaborated to publish a book similar to one under consideration, check the "Acknowledgments" page. Besides the publishing company and the author or poet, the team may include the writer's agent and an editor or editors who championed the book. Note these names for future reference.

Notice the titles and subtitles on the book covers. Jot a few down, since the title is as important to marketing the book as the words written within. Publishers develop ulcers worrying about titles guaranteed to *hook* the reader.

**While touring the bookstore, remember your mindset is one of an** *aspiring poet*, **not a** *customer.* This is a research mission involving investigation. Plan to spend an afternoon or a full day or two browsing the shelves. Consider what is being written, how the books look and feel, their length, and how they are presented. **Each book has its own self-contained marketing program designed with one thing in mind: sell the book.**

With this goal in mind, examine the packaging, the cover, and how the poet is showcased. Reading the poet's biography on the inside back jacket cover will provide insight as to his or her background and previous publications. You can also garner inspiration from finding work by first-time poets who have been published.

### Reference Magazines

To learn more about publishing, check the magazine section. To complete the first day's "training" regarding the book business, select publications such as ***Publisher's Weekly, The New York Times Sunday Edition, Writer's Digest, Poetry Magazine,*** and ***Poets and Writers*** **magazine.** Just as those immersed in the financial world consult *Forbes* to stay abreast of developments in that field, these publications are a guidepost to what's occurring in the book world.

Other sources of knowledge about the publishing industry are publications by chain bookstores and *Book Sense*, a directive of books recommended by independent outlets. Each provides insight regarding current trends in the publishing industry.

### Publisher's Weekly

*Publisher's Weekly* **is a must-read for aspiring poets.** The first half features advertisements for new releases, publishing news detailing sales records, the revolving door shifts of executives from company to company, and the names of authors or poets signed to write new books. These include celebrities who are advanced a million dollars to write about the color of their toothbrush and the epiphanies that surfaced during their rehab. One year, it seemed every issue carried news of yet another body part that actress/author/fitness guru Suzanne Somers could perfect.

Publishing excesses aside, becoming familiar with the names of those in positions of power in the literary industry is important because they are the ones who consider a book for publication. Even if a book concept is rejected, the person rejecting it may rotate to a new literary agency or publishing company and later consider another book written by the same author or poet. This is why it is wise to never write a nasty letter after being rejected. Accept the decision and move on.

The middle pages of *Publisher's Weekly* feature interviews with publishing heavyweights. Valuable tips emerge based on their experiences.

Several pages near the back of *Publisher's Weekly* are dedicated to reviews of books being published in the coming months. They are catalogued under the banners of fiction, non-fiction, audio, poetry, and paperback. This section keeps the writer current on the latest news about books being published, while providing insight into reviewers' comments regarding their content and potential.

Included with the review section is a column titled, "Poetry Notes." In one issue, the magazine featured information about publications such as *Poetry In Motion From Coast to Coast, Good Poems*, and *Poems For America: 125 Poems That Celebrate the American Experience*.

Spring and fall editions of *Publisher's Weekly* are important issues for poets. They feature multiple pages listing book titles being released during those seasons. These pages provide insight into publishers and the types of books each company favors. It also presents a glimpse of the varied subject matter that becomes fodder for publication. Keep in mind that one season's hot topics may be cold by the time a new book on the subject is written.

## Poets and Writers Magazine/Poetry Magazine

*Poets and Writers* magazine is a prestigious publication packed with useful information for aspiring writers and poets. Founded in 1970 to "foster the development of poets and fiction writers and to promote communication throughout the literary community," the magazine presents vital facts about every aspect of the writing process. Published bi-monthly, one issue featured *8 Editor's Tips On Getting In*

*The Glossies*, as well as sections detailing *News and Trends, The Literary Life*, and *The Practical Writer*. Special notices and advertisements for awards, grants, conferences, and residencies are also included.

Another excellent source of information for poets is *Poetry Magazine*. Checking their Web site at www.poetrymagazine.com provides current information about the poetry-publishing world. The magazine sponsors the Ruth Lilly Poetry Prize, an annual competition awarding a deserving poet, $100,000.

Another poetry competition to consider is the $2500 Jack R. Leer International Poetry Awards. More information is available at www.booksforlifefoundation.com

---

Exploring the poetry publishing world provides confidence and confidence is power. By understanding how your book idea relates to the workings in the industry, you won't feel as if you are in the dark regarding the sojourn your poetry must take toward publication. By reading industry publications and visiting bookstores on a regular basis, you are preparing yourself for the day when you decide to submit your poetry collection.

# Chapter Eleven
## Publishing Alternatives

Those with aspirations to become a published poet must define the word "published," since **there are publishers** *and then there are publishers.*

Publishing alternatives include: Traditional Self-Publishing, Print-On-Demand Publishing, Vanity Publishing, Subsidy Publishing (traditional and Internet), E-book Publishing, and Traditional Publishing through national/international companies, regional/small presses, or university presses. For the first-time writer, each possesses advantages and disadvantages.

**Poets intent on building a publishing career should consider each publishing alternative in light of their goals and the industry perception of each publishing venue.** A strategy that has proven most successful is to exhaust the potential to be traditionally published before self-publishing. This excludes other alternatives including, above all else, subsidized publication.


## Traditional Publishing

Many poets choose subsidy presses because they do not thoroughly research the options. Some give up, believing no traditional publisher will be interested in their material.

**Before committing to any alternative publishing options, seek a traditional publisher.** These include large, medium, and small publishers, as well as university presses. These companies pay all costs involved in publishing the book.

**There are a number of traditional publishers with a love of poetry that are seeking the next bestseller. Think positively.** If you believe your book is worthy and should be accepted for publication by a traditional house, give it a try. If this fails, traditional self-publishing is always possible.

Regardless of your attitude toward the craft, having one book published by traditional means is paramount to launching a career. It can be done.

Successful small presses continue to publish terrific books. More about small presses can be discovered at the *Poets and Writers* web site or through www.cbsd.com/pubs.cfm, the site for Consortium Book Sales and Distribution.

**Traditional publishing has several advantages, but one is most significant: The publisher pays for all costs involved with releasing the book. On occasion, a publisher will provide the poet an "advance" so it can publish the book.** The amount (usually half up front—half upon acceptance of the manuscript) is based on the number of books the publisher anticipates selling.

Using sophisticated data, the company determines the number, calculates the sum the author or poet would earn under the proposed royalty agreement, and then offers a percentage of the total. Advances range from a small amount to a million-plus. Regardless of the advance, remember that the publisher believes in the potential of the book to the extent they are willing to fund printing and editing costs, disperse up-front money, and permit sharing of royalties instead of asking for money. This is significant since industry statistics confirm publishers earn a profit on fewer than 10 percent of the books they release. Publishers don't expect poetry books to be among their most profitable.

**Poets earn revenue from the sale of each copy of the book.** The royalty may be based on the retail price or the publisher's net income (wholesale price). In today's marketplace, garnering a percentage of the retail price is rare, since publishers provide the retailer with at least a 40 percent discount. More likely, the royalty will be based on the "invoice price," a term referring to the price indicated on the publisher's invoice to wholesalers (distributors) and retailers (sales outlets).

This figure subtracts the discount from the retail price. Any royalty paid will be based on the "net copies" of the book sold. This refers to the total copies invoiced less those returned to the publisher. Since retailers have the right to return books they cannot sell, the publisher will keep a reserve account (revenues withheld from the poet) to cover the anticipated returns.

**Typical royalty schedules call for the poet to be provided revenue percentages based on increments of books sold.** Each agreement will differ, but a standard split could call for the author or poet to garner a 10 percent royalty on the first 5,000 books sold, 12½ percent on the next 5,000 sold, and 15 percent thereafter on the sale of hardcover books.

Royalties for the trade paperback edition of a book will vary, but the percentage is less, based on a lower retail price. Seven-and-one-half percent is reasonable.

Poets wonder whether it is advantageous to consider a traditional publisher since the royalty amount is low as compared with traditional self-publishing where the writer keeps all of the revenue. This is a matter of choice, but self-publishing requires the poet to have a financial outlay of funds to finance the publication of the book. With a traditional publisher, you do not since they cover all of the costs.

**To the budding poet, securing a publishing deal with a traditional publisher—big, medium, or small—is cause for a celebration. Drink, eat, and be merry for a week.**

Securing a publishing commitment, regardless of the advance amount (the advance for the first *Chicken Soup* book was $1,000), or lack thereof, is important to building a career. It provides credibility. **The first publication can lead to a second, since you are "publishable."**

Poet interaction with publishing house editors varies according to the size of the publisher. At a smaller "house," the editor may be responsible for one book or as many as three. This scenario permits them to spend considerable time with the poet on everything from final editing to promotion.

Editors at medium-sized or large publishers may not have this luxury, since their job responsibility dictates interaction with several poets. Many times the first- time poet is relegated to dealing with an assistant to the editor. Sustaining a good relationship with the editor and his or her assistant is vital to the success of the book.

**Never forget that while some editors may not be great writers, they possess terrific instincts. Listen to them, learn from them, and respect them, for they are the foot soldiers regulating the flow of material into the publishing industry.**

**Traditional Self-Publishing**

Traditional Self-Publishing dictates that poets write the book, design and lay out the pages, design and prepare the book cover or jacket, contact a printer and bookbinder, and pay to have the book printed and bound. Using a commercial layout program such as Pagemaker or Quark ensures a professional appearance for your book.

Since keeping the "cost per book" to a minimum is important, obtain several printing and binding quotes. Printing a book of approximately two hundred pages for less than five dollars a copy is possible if sufficient copies are ordered.

**On the day your book is delivered, celebrate since you have accomplished a goal others covet.** You can give or sell the book to family, friends, and colleagues—whomever you want. You retain any revenue, since no agent or publisher receives a percentage.

When you self-publish, print as many as you wish, whenever you wish. You can sell them at flea markets, on a table on your front lawn, or at book signings organized at bookstores and other outlets.

**If you choose Traditional Self-Publishing, you are the writer, editor, promoter, marketer, warehouser, and bookkeeper for your book.** If it succeeds, it is because of your efforts. To gain a better understanding of a game plan for self-promotion, consult *The Self-Publishing Manual, How To Write, Print & Sell Your Own Book* by Dan Poynter, *How To Publish, Promote, and Sell Your Own Book* by Robert L. Holt, or *The Complete Guide to Self-Publishing* by Tom and Marilyn Ross. Author Poynter's website at www.parapublishing.com provides extensive information about the self-publishing process. Additional information is available at www.booksforlifefoundation.com.

Self-help books may focus on self-publishing fiction or non-fiction, but many of the suggestions are relevant to poetry. If you know someone who has traditionally self-published their works, discuss their game plan and learn from their experiences. Many times it is advantageous to select a release date for the book and work backwards. Set deadlines for completion of the poetry, editing, cover layout, selection of a printer, through promotion and marketing. This will provide organization for the release of the book. Remember to make certain that your book will be printed and available for release before your promotion campaign is undertaken. After all the hard work, no poet wants to have the book publicized when books aren't ready for sale.

Since you will not benefit from advice and counsel offered by a publishing company while finalizing your manuscript for self-publication, hire an accomplished line editor to review the manuscript. Doing so will strengthen the writing style and prevent careless grammatical and spelling errors from infiltrating the text. Every word written is a reflection of your writing ability, and you want the book to be first rate and professional.

Many self-published poets who do not hire a line editor are embarrassed when their book is released. Careless mistakes ruin good writing.

**Remember there are line editors and** *then there are line editors.* Request samples of edited works of fiction, non-fiction, or poetry to ensure credibility. Choose an editor with experience in the particular genre that you have chosen.

To help locate reputable printers, visit Dan Poynter's website at www. parapublishing.com or www.booksforlifefoundation.com. Before submitting orders, writers should request sample copies of printed material to ascertain quality. Keep in mind that the printer and the bookbinder are often the same company. If this is the case with the printer you are contemplating, request a sample of a bound book that is similar to yours (hardcover or paperback). Be sure to get in writing their policy of replacing substandard or damaged copies.

To aid your self-publishing efforts, read the *Writer's Digest* publication, *Publishing Success, The Writer's Survival Guide to Self-Publishing and E-Publishing.* Articles include "8 Steps To A Good Book" (Learn about the eight most common reasons self-published books fail), "Get Your Book On The Shelf" (find out who the middlemen are, how books get into stores and how you can get your book in stores), "Get Booked On Oprah," "Tips From The Pros" (eight successful self-published authors share their stories), and "Words From The Wise" (nine successful e-authors discuss the advantages and disadvantages of e-publishing). Included is a complete listing of publishing companies with specifics about each.

Key to any poet's efforts is securing a distribution pipeline so the book can be exposed in bookstores and libraries. Beware of any distribution companies demanding payment in advance for their expenses. If they agree to represent the book, they should assume the risk based on a percentage of the revenue garnered from the sale of the book.

One poet discovered a chain store in his area willing to stock a few copies of his book on consignment. To his delight, the store agreed to charge a 30 percent fee, well below standard. Independent bookstores will stock self-published books on a similar basis.

Besides bookstores, you may consider non-traditional outlets. Depending on the genre of your book and its anticipated target audience, you can locate outlets where potential customers will congregate

Don't forget the Internet as a distribution outlet. Amazon.com is an excellent way to reach both broad and specialized audiences. Their "Advantage" program encourages self-published poets to expose their books on the website. Other Internet sites, including Barnes and Noble, are also available.

Most poets who self-publish establish a personal website to promote themselves and their book. If you do so, make certain it looks professional. Sloppy websites with cheap graphics will inhibit your reputation as a budding writer instead of enhancing it.

If you decide to sell your book on your website, consider PayPal, the "poor man's VISA" account. Information is available at their website and start-up costs can be kept to a minimum.

Entering your book in reputable competitions, such as those sponsored by *Writer's Digest* or prestigious poetry magazines, is advisable. You never know who will read your works and decide, "Hey, this is a poet I want to know." A list of selected competitions is available in *Poets and Writers* magazine, including the $2500 Jack R. Leer International Poetry Competition, sponsored by Books For Life Foundation.

While marketing and promoting your book, consider spending funds to hire a public relations company to represent it. This adds a professional edge to your efforts and provides access to media you may be unable to reach otherwise.

Editor Amy Pierpont believes self-publishing can be a definite asset. In *The Writer*, a recommended publication for aspiring authors or poets, she states, **"Publishers are always looking for talented writers, and when we find they're already self-published, it is often an added plus because the author comes with a built-in audience."**

## Print-On-Demand

Print-On-Demand publishing is an alternative for the first-time poet to consider. Trade paperback-sized books are stored electronically and printed one at a time based on the demand. Turn-around time can be less than forty-eight hours. If a greater quantity is requested, shipment is possible within a week.

Fee-based Print-On-Demand companies are not publishers in the traditional sense. They charge "set-up" fees ranging from ninety-nine dollars to a thousand dollars or more. Some also offer marketing packages and other services. You normally submit your book in electronic form on a computer disk.

Writers receive royalties from the sales of the book. Royalties can range from 20 percent for hardcover books purchased directly from the publishers to 10 percent on those purchased by bookstores, libraries, and the author or poet. This may seem advantageous, but investigate what the fee-based Print-On-Demand publisher can do that you cannot do simply by traditional self-publishing.

The main differences between fee-based Print-On-Demand publishers and traditional self-publishing concerns **control** (when you self-publish, you control all aspects of the book as compared with Print-On-Demand where you choose from the publishing services offered), **book revenue** (traditional self-publishing permits you to keep all book proceeds while Print-On-Demand outlets only provide a royalty), and **book rights** (by traditionally self-publishing, you keep all the rights while some Print-On-Demand outlets require you to contract with them for an extended period of time).

**If you are determined to print only a few copies of your book for family and friends with no potential for commercial success, fee-based Print-On-Demand has merit.** If you are a public speaker interested in "BOR" (Back of Room) sales, or a businessperson seeking publicity for a specific economic issue, POD can also make sense.

If you do choose a fee-based Print-On-Demand outlet, be certain to hire a line editor with experience in your genre to edit the book. Many POD books are released that include typos and grammatical and punctuation mistakes. Make certain that you have the right to check the final version of the book before it is printed to verify printing quality. When you receive your books, check immediately the printing quality and whether the text includes your revisions. If it does not, return the book to correct the mistakes. Your book is a reflection of you and many are released that prove embarrassing to the writer.

**Writers attempting to build a traditional writing career should avoid fee-based Print-On Demand outlets.** In the true sense of the words, they are simply subsidy publishers and viewed as such by the traditional publishing industry, bookstores, and libraries. Certain stigmas that attach are described in the next section and reviewers will most likely pass when requested to review the book.


**Vanity Presses/Subsidy Presses**

Vanity Press is a misunderstood term. Some define it as a company that charges a poets for all of the production and marketing costs of their books, but to many, it indicates writers who decide to publish their book for family and friends.

There may be many reasons for doing the latter. A Philadelphia trial lawyer wrote a book chronicling his courtroom adventures. He wanted his children and grandchildren to learn about the justice system during his lifetime. This was worthy and had nothing to do with ego. The accurate term for his effort was self-published.

**The term often interchanged with Vanity Press is Subsidy Press.** These companies are easy to locate. Vantage Press is the most well known. They accept manuscripts, guide efforts with regard to finalizing proper form and substance for the material and the cover, and then print the book. Editing services and promotion ideas are offered at extra cost.

Similar companies exist on the Internet. **All promise your book will get a look-see from the national chain stores, but the promise doesn't guarantee the book *will be stocked* in those stores.** Most times it will not unless the book stirs enough interest to entice the stores to stock it.

Subsidy Presses have published millions of books. Writers who choose this option have achieved the goal of being published. They are free to sell their books any way they choose, albeit with the press or the publishing company taking its share of the profits. This can range from 25 percent to 50 percent.

**As mentioned, a hybrid of subsidy publishers has appeared in recent years. These fee-based Print-On-Demand companies claim to be the author's and poet's best friend and some do not demand a share of any book revenues.** Nevertheless, organizations that bill themselves as fee-based PODs are in fact subsidy publishers by the very definition of the word "subsidy" since the poets are subsidizing publication. One company, for instance, advertises through mailings "monthly specials" akin to a used car dealer. They also hoodwink the author or poet by making the claim that they will "make [your] book available through more than 25,000 bookstores worldwide." This may be true, but the reality is that few will actually stock the book.

Other Subsidy Press outlets promise that authors and poets will keep the rights to their book. This is acceptable, but the Subsidy Press will receive a hefty portion for each book sold at a price they determine. Website advertisements alert the poet that they have a "variety of options regarding payment percentages." Read the fine print before committing and ask, "What can this subsidy publisher or fee-based POD do that I can't do by traditionally self-publishing where I keep all the revenues?"

If you decide to publish through any outlet that is, in effect, a Subsidy Press, you must have realistic expectations based on the understanding of the advantages and disadvantages of the subsidy press you choose. Some are better than others, but the basic agreement unfolds as follows: The author or poet pays a fee to have a certain number of copies printed. At Vantage Press, 450 copies is the minimum. The company guarantees the book will appear at least once in their *New York Times Book Review* advertisement, and that the book will be distributed through Baker and Taylor, a reputable company. The book will be listed in *Books In Print, Publisher's Trade List Annual*, and the *Vantage Press* catalogue. Book publicity is circulated to local media in the author or poet's area or selected national media through a list the author or poet provides. For this service, the press is titled to a certain percentage of book revenues.

Vantage Press and other such outlets promise to forward review copies to bookstores and local libraries in the author or poet's area. Major bookstore chains and online book outlets are advised of the publication. If the author or poet schedules book signings, the company will assist with providing books.

**Since Subsidy Presses offer such services, many poets wonder why their books do not sell in large quantities.** Ninety-nine percent won't because a first-time poet has no name recognition, no backing from a nationally known publisher, and no solid marketing and promotional campaign behind them. The national chains and independent stores are reluctant to stock a book by an unknown. They are too busy promoting books by well-known authors or poets.

**Libraries frown on all Subsidy Press books.** They have limited budgets and are influenced by the bestseller lists. Poets may contact them, but the chances of libraries purchasing the book are slim.

**Above all, remember that any Subsidy Press earns most of their money by *charging authors or poets to print the books and for other services, not by selling the books.*** Before committing, request a list of best selling books published by the Subsidy Press under consideration. Understanding their operation can prevent a naive poet from being suckered by promises the Subsidy Press can't deliver.

**A distinct disadvantage to Subsidy Presses is the stigma attached to it.** Many fine books have been published, but there is the perception among traditional publishers, libraries, and the public that a subsidy book is an ego trip not to be taken seriously. Those who publish with Subsidy Presses are marked as rank amateurs who could not be otherwise published. Right or wrong, this is the perception. **As self-publishing guru Dan Poynter says, "The name of the subsidy publisher on the spine of the book is a kiss of death."**

When you copyright material, whether it is the book manuscript or a Book Proposal, you may receive a solicitation letter. The opening line may read, "One of our researchers has come across the manuscript you registered with the Library of Congress and has forwarded your name to us as a possible candidate for publication with our company." The second paragraph mentions "problems" authors have in finding a "commercial publisher." It then reads, "Just having your manuscript read by most commercial publishers is difficult and involves long delays."

This type of language can adversely influence those not familiar with the publishing industry. Beware of such information, or any that discourages traditional publishing or traditional self-publishing. It may not be directly misleading, but there are multiple traditional publishing companies that will consider material and contact the author quickly with an opinion.

**Poets should be wary of contests promising that the winners will be included in a published book.** Oftentimes, everyone submitting poetry is a "winner," since the contests are intended to lure poets into purchasing the books. Such "pre-purchase" agreements are part of a "publishing trap." It also includes subsidy publishers and literary agents who charge in advance for their services.

Other organizations promise to include poetry in an anthology if the poet will pay a certain fee or purchase books. It is important to distinguish those publishers from the legitimate ones. Those preying on a poet's excitement that her or she will be a "published poet" don't care about how many books are sold, only how many fees they can collect. Avoid such publications for there is a stigma attached to them.

**Subsidy publishers rely on the desperation of aspiring poets who believe there is no other way to be published.** As stated, **beware of the "publishing trap" and consider alternatives before being sucked in by a subsidy publisher, an unprofessional literary agent, or "pre-purchase" poetry book publishers. Investigate before committing.**

### Internet Publishing

Internet publishing provides a vast array of publishing opportunities similar to standard Subsidy Presses. For a cost, the Internet provider will publish a book as professional as those released by the major publishing companies.

Costs differ for hardcover and paperback editions. Additional fees are charged for editing, cover layout, and other services. Some of the publishers provide free books to the poet; some do not. Most retain a hefty percentage of sales revenue. Be wary of promises made that a book will be forwarded to bookstores or other outlets. Many of these companies, like standard Subsidy Presses, earn their revenue from providing author or poet services and not by selling books.

**Regardless of the publishing method, poets should not agree to a contract clause binding them for more than a year.** Flexibility to accept an offer from a traditional publisher is important.

### Publisher Information

**Locating publishers is simple—gaining their attention is more difficult.** While various publications list publishers and contact names, an author or poet submitting material faces long odds. Estimates vary, but publishers confirm they receive thousands upon thousands of manuscripts, Book Proposals, and Query Letters, each *week.*

For information regarding the submission of poetry, consult *Poet's Market.* It reveals submission guidelines, contact names, and other important information. A list of chapbook publishers (release of small volumes of poetry) is included as are the names of reference books helpful.

***Poet's Market* is an important reference source for an aspiring poet. Read it from cover to cover.** Included with each publisher listing (see Appendix for sample Publishers) are addresses, telephone numbers, fax numbers, e-mail addresses, and contact names. Most listings tell how long the publisher has been in business and what types of books it features.

**Important to note is the "How To Contact" section.** Here the publisher provides an explanation of the rules and regulations for presentation of material. For one company, it reads, "Query [letter] with outline plus three sample poems. Reports in one week on queries. One month on manuscripts."

---

### Publisher Research

A most common question among aspiring authors and poets is: "How can I find a publisher who will be interested in my book?"

**Organizing a list of publishers who should be interested in your book narrows the field for submission.** A separate Rolodex listing of those names is warranted. When you are ready to submit your Query Letter and Book Proposal, the list will serve as a guide. Contacting those individuals will cut the odds, since you will know that these publishers have shown interest in the type of book you are considering. Otherwise, you waste time and effort submitting material to publishers who will have no interest.

**Don't be afraid to use non-traditional means of contacting publishers.** Anyone can scan the "help-books" and discover names, but if you are dedicated to being published, you will not only hone in on the "usual suspects" interested in the contemplated book, but use friendships, acquaintances, or the bartender down the street to your advantage. **Remember that any publisher will consider Book Proposals and/or manuscripts in the following order: those submitted by poets they have published, those referred by poets they have published, and those arriving unsolicited.**

If you know someone who has been published, ask for a referral. Don't be afraid to approach published poets since the worst that can occur is for them to say "no."

Meeting editors at poets' conferences or conventions is a terrific way to begin a relationship. Resist the temptation to overwhelm them with ideas for several books. Simply make the acquaintance and then follow up with a letter or telephone call at a later date.

Remember that most publishers are not receptive to receiving a completed manuscript. Instead they welcome a Query Letter and a Book Proposal. Some make it clear that if a manuscript is submitted, it will be deposited in the nearest receptacle.

Since your goal as an aspiring poet is to be considered on your talent and not be rejected because of the form of your submission, be alert as to the publishing guidelines provided by various companies. Remember that these companies cannot exist without poets and welcome your submissions, albeit in the correct form.

**Book Proposals**

**To maximize the potential to become traditionally published, prepare a professionally written Book Proposal.** Poets ask whether they should write the Query Letter or the Book Proposal first. Methods will vary, but it is logical to start with a Book Proposal first since you will use portions of the information formulated in the proposal in the Query Letter. Remember that the Query Letter is simply a mini-proposal setting up readers for the extended information about the book contained in the Book Proposal.

The journey toward completing a draft of the proposal begins with understanding what a Book Proposal *is* and what it *is not*. **Above all, the Book Proposal *is* a sales tool.** Within the scope of twenty to thirty pages, less in many cases, the "written pitch" outlines the poet's game plan so an agent or editor at a publishing company can consider its merits.

**What the Book Proposal should not be is promotional, boastful or pompous. A well-conceived Book Proposal doesn't *tell* the reader the book is the greatest one ever written. Instead, the text *shows* them through good writing and interesting facts that the book has merit.**

A sample Book Proposal for poetry is presented in the Appendix. Use this proposal as a guidepost, noting the proper form. Self-help books vary about the components of the Book Proposal, but the Appendix samples follow a form that has proven successful.

Many writers abhor the idea of writing Query Letters or Book Proposals. The process appears difficult and time-consuming. But with a well-planned strategy, writing the letter and proposal can be completed without actual loss of life. And doing so will pay off.

Even when poets receive a rejection letter, most include a compliment regarding the Book Proposal and the offer to consider future book ideas. Plain and simple—forwarding a professionally written Query Letter and Book Proposal gains the attention of publishing company editors. Believe it.


## Taglines

**Any book can be described in ten to fifteen words or less, preferably less. This can be more complicated for poetry than a how-to book, but it is still possible and important. The Tagline, a.k.a. "hook for the book," or "handle," is akin to "pitches" made to motion picture studios by producers and screenwriters attempting to convince executives to produce a film.**

Taglines for poetry are as varied as the material submitted. **Since most collections of poetry have a common theme, the poet must provide a snappy hook providing the reader with a clear indication as to the message being conveyed.** One poet decided he intended to write a chapbook designed to enlighten divorced fathers regarding their responsibilities toward their children. When asked by an editor what the theme of the collection was, he simply answered, "Dads, Don't Be A Dope." Another whose collection featured the "dark side" of religion used the Tagline, "Christ's Underbelly."


## Book Titles

**Book titles must be snappy, concise, and descriptive. Above all, they must pique the reader's curiosity.**

With non-fiction, the subject matter is a star and the title will depict a certain person, event, or issue. Titles such as *Ghandi,*

*MacArthur, Truman, Dolly (Dolly Parton), In Cold Blood, DiMaggio,* and *Hoffa,* are examples. *One Hundred and One Ways To Invest, Race and Responsibility, A History of National League Ballparks,* Suzanne Somers' *Eat, Cheat, and Melt Away The Fat,* and *Gay Men In The White House* provide instant recognition regarding subject matter.

For works of fiction, clever word usage provides clues to the book's content. Hemingway's *The Old Man and the Sea,* John Dunning's *The Bookman's Wake,* and Scott Turow's *Presumed Innocent* reflect recognition of the themes presented.

**A check of the *USA Today* bestseller listing provides a plethora of creative titles.** *Who Moved My Cheese?* and *Venus Envy,* the book about Venus Williams and female tennis professionals, are examples of creative titles. Others are *Sacred Sins, The Last Precinct, Wild Justice, Body-For-Life, Earthquake in the Morning, The Red Tent, Four Blondes,* and two personal favorites, *Drowning Ruth* and *The Man Who Mistook His Wife For A Hat.* James Patterson's book, *The Lake House,* sounds intriguing, especially when readers learn that the main character's name is Ethan Cane.

Titles for collections of poetry must reflect the theme of the poet's intentions. *Sailing Around The Room* by Billy Collins, *Elegy For A Southern Drawl* by Rodney Jones, and *Misery Prefigured* by J. Allen Rosser achieve that goal.

**Aspiring poets must create a title so strong it will catch the attention of a publisher. If this is accomplished, it kick-starts a mindset that says, "I must read this material."**


**Book Proposal Components**


**If you have decided traditional book publishing is your first choice, written a collection of poetry, conceived a book title, and described your intended publication in fifteen words or less, you are ready to attempt a first draft of the Book Proposal.**

For collections of poetry, it should include:

Cover page information

Contents page, (optional)

Book Tagline (Hook)

Synopsis

Poet's Biography

Book Audience

Similar Successful Books

Book Promotion Ideas

Sample Text (5-10 poems)

Some poets decide to submit only the Query Letter and sample poems, but including the additional information mentioned above guarantees that the writer has provided all of the essentials about his or her book idea. Take the extra time to prepare material for each section listed. It will pay off.

Remember: the first page of the Book Proposal will provide the title, a subtitle if there is one, and your name. The second will present the snappy excerpt from one or more poems. The third page provides a Proposal Table of Contents. This is optional.

Beginning on the fourth page, with the title of the book at the top, are the components of the Book Proposal. They are: the Tagline followed by the Synopsis, Poet's Biography, Book Audience, Similar Successful Books, and Promotion Ideas. The Sample Poetry follows these compartments. There is no need to separate the compartments on individual pages—they should flow from page to page.

Sample length is less important than presentation of material showcasing your talent. When mentioning photographs, you should indicate "photographs available on request." Some publishers shy away from books requiring an extensive number of them due to cost factors.

**Regardless of the genre of the book, the Book Proposal must be adapted to the material being presented for consideration.** Emphasis should be placed on the merits of the book that you believe are most important. Providing the literary agent or editor with concise, well-organized information is a key.

## Poetry Book Proposals

Poetry book publishers expect the following from an aspiring poet: **a professionally written Query Letter accompanied by a Book Proposal including a Tagline describing the book in fifteen words or less, a Synopsis of the book of poetry contemplated, information about the poet, details regarding the potential book audience and marketing potential, a list of similar successful books, promotion concepts, an outline, and several sample poems.** Attaching a self-addressed, stamped envelope is required. *Poet's Market* and other publications such as *How To Publish Your Poetry* by Helene Ciaravino list specific requirements for submission.

Poetry submitted should be typed, not handwritten, on fine quality, 8.5 x 11, bond paper. A paper "weight" of more than 24 is suggested. The accompanying materials will be double-spaced, but the poetry is single-spaced with double spaces between the stanzas. If you are writing non-traditional types of poetry such as free form, the layout will differ.

Proper form includes a cover page listing the title of the work, a subtitle, if any, and the name of the poet. A second page can include a few lines from the poetry to catch the eye of the literary agent or publisher. The third page begins with a Tagline specifying the theme of the poetry followed by the Synopsis, Poet Biography, Book Audience, Similar Successful Books, Promotion Concepts, an Outline if there is one, and the Poetry Excerpts. The various compartments follow one another on the pages to provide a flow to the material. An example of a Poetry Book Proposal is featured in the Appendix. It is general in nature and can be modified for alternative forms of poetry.

Most poetry publications are impressed by poems that are not too lengthy. Do not be afraid to be experimental, since uniqueness is a cherished quality. Each poem should be titled for clarity. The pages of the proposal should not be stapled or bound so copies may be made for multiple readers.

Miriam Sagan, a published poet and UCLA instructor, suggested seven tips for aspiring poets she believes are worthy in *Writer's Digest*. They include: "Line breaks should feel natural, not forced, repetition of lines with a similar number of syllables can add to free verse, the opening word of each line should be compelling: use nouns and verbs whenever possible, and ending lines should strive for maximum reader impact."

To enhance publishing opportunities, photographs or illustrations can be helpful. Many poets forward a self-published book along with the suggested new material. This can be helpful to show agents and editors the worthiness of previous work.

E-mailing of poetry Book Proposals is possible, but discouraged since a hard copy of the proposal is much more impressive. See *Poet's Market* for details regarding submissions.

Book Proposals for poetry chapbooks (25-50 pages) compare with those for full-length books of poetry. Potential chapbook publishers and guidelines for submission can be found in *Poet's Market*. Additional publishing alternatives are available in *The Directory of Poetry Publishers*, a Dustbooks publication. They also publish *The Directory of Small Press/Magazine Editors and Publishers.*

**Regardless of whether you are submitting a Book Proposal for a full-length book or a chapbook, check publisher guidelines.** Failure to do so is a death wish. Be aware of suggested "reading periods" when publications indicate they will consider submissions. For a university publication, this may be during the school year or the summer months.

## Book Proposal Magic

Whenever possible, the aspiring poet should submit a Query Letter and Book Proposal. Length of the proposal will vary, but it will seldom be more than 20-30 pages in length. As stated, a concise proposal of twenty to thirty pages can work to your advantage even when the agency or publisher under consideration requests that only Query Letters be submitted. If the Query Letter is sensational, the concise Book Proposal will gain attention and provide needed information about the book that cannot be specified in a one-page Query Letter.

**When your Book Proposal and Query Letter are the best they can be, forward them to a publishing company using priority mail, Federal Express, or UPS.** This indicates that you are dedicated and serious about the work and separates you from the thousands of others submitting material. Equally important, it provides you with a tracking number to make certain your package arrived.

**A final note regarding Book Proposals—it is imperative that each section stands alone.** The writer cannot predict if an editor will read from cover to cover or leaf through sections that are of particular interest. He or she may skip ahead to the Sample Text section first to decide if the writing has merit, or glance at the Poet's Biography or the Similar Successful Books material. With this in mind, write each section as if it were being submitted individually for consideration.

**The Query Letter and Book Proposal submitted to a publisher enter a hierarchy differing from company to company.** At the top sits the publisher who operates as a quarterback dealing with editorial issues, as well as sales and marketing. Reporting to the publisher is the editor-in-chief to whom all of the editors report. Most publishers require that the editor-in-chief and/or the publisher sign off before a deal is finalized.

Reporting to the editor-in-chief, or the production director among larger publishing companies, is the managing editor. He or she deals with deadlines and coordinates information about the book. Reporting to the editors, or senior editors, are editorial assistants, normally young people new to the business. Any one of these people, or all of them, may read the Book Proposal before a final decision is made.

When a traditional publisher agrees to publish a book based on the Query Letter and Book Proposal, the cycle from idea to publication is complete. The accompanying chart at the end of this chapter provides a simplistic view of this process.

**The Book Proposal, and its partner, the Query Letter, reflects the heart and soul of the book contemplated.** By preparing ones that are professionally written, you boost your chances toward the ultimate goal—becoming published.


## Query Letters

To gain a publisher's interest, you must implement a well-founded strategy. **Since yearly submission numbers approach seven figures, you need to be creative so your book idea gains the attention of the publisher under consideration.** This way it won't be thrown in the dreaded "slush" pile to die a slow death.

**As stated, checking publisher guidelines is the key.** Remember: the material you submit is unsolicited; therefore readers will pay little or no attention unless you follow the guidelines.

Despite publisher guidelines requesting only a Query Letter, few will dismiss a Query Letter accompanied by a Book Proposal. You will decide the best strategy for you, but it is extremely difficult to capture a publisher's attention with only a one-page Query Letter. Providing them with additional information about the book in a proposal provides your best chance of gaining interest in your book.

Mastering the art of creating Query Letters is challenging since most writers are not used to this form of writing. Guidance on the proper form and substance is available through many publications such as *Writer's Market*.

**Brevity is a key—one page is sufficient.** Literary agents or editors have no interest in leafing through an eight-page letter beginning with announcement of the author or poet's birth and ending with a sentence touting the book as the best ever written.

Journalists Don Prues and Cindy Laufenberg provide excellent advice regarding the substance of Query Letters. In *Writer's Market*, they state, **"The tone of the writing is important. Create a catchy Query with confidence but devoid of cockiness."**

Mention of the book tagline, a "what if" scenario, or a compelling problem requiring a solution work well in the Query Letter's opening paragraph to hook readers. Regarding a poet's credentials, **it is important to explain why you are the one person in the world to write this book.** Include information about the target audience, a built-in audience due to your expertise, and reference the enclosed Book Proposal. Conclude the letter by writing, "A completed manuscript is available upon request."

Remember to include a self-addressed, stamped envelope for return correspondence. Literary agents and publishers appreciate saving the cost of the postage necessary to return the Query Letter and/or Book Proposal.

Never mention past rejections of material in a Query Letter. You may or may not inform an editor of multiple submissions. Most realize that you are doing so to speed up the process.

**Treat the Query Letter as a prologue to the Book Proposal when they are submitted together.** Edit it thoroughly, checking spelling, grammar, and punctuation. Most agents and editors will not consider the Book Proposal if the Query Letter contains multiple mistakes. An editor once said, **"The Query Letter is your three minutes to sell the book. Don't screw up."**

Marie Butler-Knight, publisher of Alpha Books, an imprint of Penguin Group, USA, offers this warning. "If you submit the same Query Letter to multiple publishers and you customize the contents to each recipient, read each letter carefully before you send it out. Make certain the letter isn't addressed to one agent or publisher but references another agent or publisher in the body of the letter. You'd be amazed at how often this occurs."

## The Poetry Query Letter

Poets attempting to reach publishing companies regarding their work must write a better-than-best Query Letter. Since there are thousands upon thousands of poetry submissions, poets must write outstanding prose to describe the poetry they have written. Again, the letter should be no more than one page written on 8.5 x 11 inch paper.

**Begin the letter with a sentence that will captivate the reader.** Use a Tagline (the hook for your book) to pinpoint the theme of the poetry and then provide titillating information designed to make readers say, "I must read the manuscript."

Paragraphs two and three of the Query Letter expand upon the theme of the material. Once there is a clear description, offer biographical material that illustrates why, just as with any aspiring author, you are the one best person in the world to write poetry on this theme. Inclusion of publishing credentials is critical as is information on built-in audience for the book. Comparisons to famous poets regarding style and content can be helpful. If you believe your book is similar to one represented by the agency or publisher you are contacting, note the name of the book. This will show the agent or publishing company you have researched their recent books.

**As with all writing, clarity, brevity, good word choice, and excellent sentence structure is essential.** Any agent or editor questioning the writing ability of a prospective poet will wonder if he or she is a competent wordsmith when writing poetry.

**Arrogance must be absent from any competent Query Letter.** Lines such as "People say that I am the next Billy Collins or Maya Angelou" will deaden any chances to be published. Be humble while showing the editor that you believe in yourself and possess a fresh voice that must be heard.

Within the letter, provide readers with exact information as to why your poetry is perfect for representation or publication. Once again the goal should be obvious: **you want the editor to say, "I must publish this material or someone else will and I will be sorry."**

In the final paragraph of the Query Letter, explain that besides the poetry submitted, there is additional material to be read upon request. Then thank the editor for his or her consideration and close with something akin to "Yours truly."

**Above all, be certain the person you are writing to is still employed at the agency or publishing company.** There is nothing more embarrassing than writing a letter to a former employee.

The Query Letter for a collection of poetry titled, *Columbus Was Wrong,* reads as follows:

Dear Publisher,

Is the world still round, or were the ancient naysayers correct? Answers to that question and more are explored in a new collection of poetry I have written titled, *Columbus Was Wrong.* Ten poems are included with this letter. Among them are: Flat or Round, Who's To Say, Christopher Was A Baboon, Not An Explorer, The New World or The Old One, and Gold Blinds Us.

The audience for *Columbus Was Wrong* includes those fascinated with Christopher Columbus, as well as the historical significance of the discovery of America. Similar works regarding whether men walked on the moon, why Charles Lindbergh did not cross the Atlantic, and how mankind has been hoodwinked into believing global warming threatens our very existence have been published in *Poets Of The Far East, Art Bell's Collection of Serious Poetry, and Dubsdread's Odd Poets of the Twentieth Century.*

The poet's perspective on these issues has been formed from extensive travel throughout the world. During a recent trip to southern Italy, the current collectionwas created after intensive investigation of Columbus' true mission when he assaulted the new world. The poet believes she is the first to offer through her poetry significant evidence that Columbus' name was actually O'Reilly and that he never set foot on Italian soil.

Thank you for considering the enclosed book proposal. Further samples of the poetry are available upon request.

Thank you.
Best,

Olathobal Moffit


Query letters are the key to unlocking the door of the publishing industry. Cleverly written with an eye toward exciting the reader, they operate as your invitation to those you hope will share your passion for the subject matter of the book. Strong words and visual images optimize your chances that an editor will say, "I must read the book proposal," a second step toward gaining a publishing commitment.

# Chapter Twelve
## Once You Have a Book

You've learned about poetry. You've learned about the publishing industry. Some time has passed and you've grown comfortable with your work. Now you are ready to test your mettle and discover if your poetry is worthy of publication.

**To begin the process toward becoming published, it is suggested that aspiring poets forward their individual poems to the country's small press magazines.** Many are available such as *American Poetry Review, Open City, The Kenyon Review, Hanging Loose*, or *Glimmer Train*. When any well-recognized magazine like one of these agrees to publish one of your poems, you begin to build credibility and can say with pride, "I am a published poet."

Building a reputation and being able to list your publishing credits is critical to your next step, submitting poetry to book publishers. After you've seen your share of rejection from literary magazines and you've weathered the disappointment and reveled in the joy of occasional acceptance, you are ready to begin the process of approaching book publishers.

**Competition is fierce as most poetry is currently published by small private or university presses.** Few major publishing houses print contemporary poetry, especially by unknown authors, since poetry doesn't possess the market appeal of fiction and non-fiction prose.

While traditional publishing routes, such as seeking a literary agent, may yield some success, the lack of monetary motivation permits few unrecognized poets to be represented by agents. Without their assistance, it is up to you to sell yourself and your work so that you gain exposure.

A full-length poetry manuscript features fifty or more pages and may contain as many poems. These books are usually thematically or stylistically connected. This means the poet may have hundreds of other poems that simply don't fit into the puzzle of a particular book. The books are often divided into sections representing shifts in theme, like chapters in a novel.

Established poets often release "greatest hits" collections of work written over several years. These are called "selected" or "collected" poems and are culled from previously published books and chapbooks.

**A chapbook is a short collection of poems - twenty to fifty pages printed inexpensively and distributed in small numbers.** Chapbooks can be traditionally self-published or published by local presses. Newer poets will discover that assembling thirty or so well-honed poems a more feasible goal during the first stages of becoming a published poet

For many poets, selecting enough quality poems for a full-length book takes serious dedication to the craft. This is why there are few overnight sensations in the poetry world.


## Creating a Chapbook

Once you have enjoyed success with literary magazines, collecting poems for a chapbook makes good sense.

Chapbooks, like full-length collections, can be groups of poem arranged by theme or style. These books are organized in different sections or can be one long collection.

Like any book, chapbooks will contain a Publication Page, noting where poems, if any, have been published. The book should have a Dedication and possibly a fitting quote from another text introducing your work. A Table of Contents at the beginning and a biographical sketch at the end are suggested.

**Many of the literary magazines that published your poems may print chapbooks.** Send a query letter to these presses and inquire if the editors are interested in assisting you. If so, ask for specifics including printing quotes.


## Book Contests

While researching printing alternatives, scout *Poet's Market* or other poetry publications for chapbook contests. For a small fee – usually $10 to $25 – there is the potential to be selected for publication by a reputable publisher.

Be sure you research the publisher just as you did magazines before sending your work. Learn the judge or judges' names for the contest and attempt to discover their credentials. If you think you match well with one or all, send in your manuscript. Make certain that you follow the contest guidelines to the letter. And keep track of each contest you enter.

**Publishers also offer contests for full-length manuscripts.** Follow the above-mentioned guidelines for entering these contests once you are confident that you have enough quality poems for submission. Many poetry publishers discover new poets through these contests and select non-winners for publication.


# Contacting a publisher

While poets often use contests as a way to have a first book published, many poetry book publishers accept unsolicited queries, proposals and manuscripts from new poets. *Poet's Market* is, again, the best place to turn to research these publishers.

**Most often, the smaller, independent publishers are more open to providing new poets a chance.** As with researching and targeting literary magazines, take the time to investigate a publisher before sending anything.

Start by looking at the books of poetry you find similar to your manuscript and make note of who published these books. Visit Amazon.com or your local bookstore to become more familiar with poetry publishers.

Once you've targeted a few possibilities, check *Poet's Market* for details. Here's a brief analysis/explanation of a poetry book publisher's listing:

**COFFEE HOUSE PRESS** (*Tip: not affiliated with a university)*
27 N. Fourth St. Suite 400, Minneapolis, MN 55401. (612) 338-0125. Established 1984. Managing Editor: Christopher Fischbach. (*Tip: website not listed, search for it yourself since nearly every publisher – including this one – has a website with an online catalogue.*)

Coffee House Press books have won numerous honors and awards. As an example, *The Book of Medicines* by Linda Hogan won the Colorado Book Award for Poetry and the Lannan Foundation Literary Fellowship. (*Tip: This shows a strong reputation and connection with the best of contemporary poetry*)

**Book Needs**: Publishes 12 books/year, 4-5 of which are poetry (*Tip: even smaller presses also publish prose selections*)

Wants poetry that is "challenging and lively; influenced by the Beats, the NY School, LANGUAGE and post-LANGUAGE, or Black Mountain." (*Tip: These are major movements in modern poetry – all of which were experimental at the time – should be researched before sending in work*)

Has published poetry collections by Victor Hernandez Cruz, Anne Waldman, Eleni Siskelianos, and Paul Metcalf. (*Tip: look them up and compare*)

**How to Submit**: Submit 8-12 poems at a time. Cover letter and vita required. (*Tip: don't send more poems than requested – they will request more if they want to see them; "vita" is your publishing history and brief related biography*)

"Please include SASE for reply and/or the return of your ms." Seldom comments on rejected poems. Responds to queries in 1 month; to manuscripts in up to 8 months. Always sends prepublication galleys. (*Tip: you get to proof the book before it is printed*)

Send SASE for catalog. No phone, fax, or email queries. (*Tip: don't test this*)

## Traditional Self-Publishing

If you decide publishers aren't for you, or you have little luck securing one, chapbooks can be self-published inexpensively using a home computer and the services of a local quick-print shop. If you have access to a digital camera and can import photographs to your computer, add the professional touch of a nice cover image and a photograph of the poet for the back of the book.

Don't use fancy fonts or other artwork inside the book. Poetry should be about the words, not the design. Keep it simple and clean and easy to read. Make sure to read every poem and find others to help proof your poems before you take the final version to the printer.

If you don't feel comfortable assembling the chapbook on your computer, or don't have an artistic flair for basic design, find a friend to help at no cost. Paying someone to design and print a chapbook will be expensive and prove a waste of resources. With the technology available, self-published chapbooks look just as good as ones printed by low-budget small presses and subsidy presses.

**Beware of small presses asking to publish your chapbook if you'll "split" the cost.** Make sure you're getting what you pay for. These presses publish chapbooks in the same way you could at home, but don't allow you full creative control and charge you more than you would have to pay to do it yourself.

Once you've delivered your completed book to the printer for self publishing, wait for a proof to review. Examine it closely, or have someone with an objective eye do so. Look at the formatting. With the importance of the linebreaks in your poem, nothing can be more disappointing than to have a computer or printer break a line in a new place. Take your time as you review these proofs. Don't be in a hurry.

A regular-length, staple-bound chapbook using card stock for the cover and regular paper inside will not cost much more than $2 or $3 per copy. Start with fewer than fifty copies and the entire expense will be under $100. You should sell your chapbooks for no more than $8. You will not become wealthy, but you will be able to showcase your work to an attentive audience.

Any beginning poet with aspirations to become published will realize benefits from a well-grounded strategy. Deciding what form of poetry is right for you, honing that poetry into its best form and content, investigating publishing alternatives, submitting to and attaining success with publication in poetry magazines to build publishing credentials, publishing chapbooks to expose your works, and then deciding to begin submitting your poetry collections to publishers will optimize your chances to become a published poet.

# Chapter Thirteen
## The Poet's Life

People don't decide to write poetry for fame and fortune, but because they love what the art form does to enrich their lives, how it allows them to communicate with themselves and others, how it makes them feel good and bad and more fulfilled. Once you are truly a poet, it isn't something you do as a hobby and pick up and drop like fly fishing or needlepoint.

**Poetry is always with you.** It is a crucial part of your life. It is not recommend that you quit your day job and move to an isolated mountain overlook to write poetry twenty-four hours a day. Poetry is not as important as your family, your friends, or your religious beliefs. But poetry is ingrained in all of those things. It is part of who you are. And, at least some of the time, it becomes a job with specific duties and responsibilities.

As a poet, you can never stop being a student. You can never stop striving to discover something new about your art form. It is impossible to ever know enough about poetry. Once you feel you've mastered certain techniques, try others that have eluded you. Try something you never found interesting. You'll be surprised at what happens.

**Continue reading others poets' works for inspiration.** With all of the poetry written through the centuries and all of the new poems released every day in print and on the Internet, sources are endless. Read poets you love and branch out to find related poets. Or, read against the grain. The key is to never decide you know enough and to stop reading.

Discover poems you love and gather them into a personal anthology of your favorites. Memorize them, including some of your own that please you most. You will bring them inside of you so they will be bouncing around in your head as you write more poetry.

**Help keep poetry alive with your pocketbook.** Join societies for poets and subscribe to as many magazines as you can afford. Buy as much poetry as you can, as often as you can. Poetry books make great gifts for everyone.

Think of this benevolence as helping support your craft and the other poets out there – all while introducing poetry to new people. You are a missionary spreading the good news of poetry to people who don't understand how wonderful it is. Select books carefully for people, especially for those not yet introduced to poetry. Much contemporary poetry is accessible and enjoyable for everyday readers. And people will appreciate your selecting something to match their tastes.

If you can't afford to purchase poetry collections, give your own poems as birthday and holiday gifts. Slipping a poem into a card adds a nice touch, even for someone who doesn't like poetry. Consider composing a poem with a loved one in mind, or a friend. They will be touched by your efforts.

Composing poetry with your children or other young people is rewarding. This is true even if the poems seem silly with rhymes that don't make sense. The creativity is terrific for kids, and writing poems is easy and fun for them.

**Don't be afraid to let people know you are a poet. Few painters or sculptors or short-story writers would ever shy away from telling a new acquaintance of their artistic passions.** Yet poets rarely want to tell non-poets who they are. Don't be afraid. Take the time to explain to them what it means to be a poet. Tell them what poetry is, that it's alive and full of passion and remains an important part of our culture. Then recite a poem—maybe one of your own.

Above all, be proud of your poetry whether it is published or waits in a desk drawer where you retrieve it on occasion. **Your poetry is a reflection of who you are and what you think, a friend always there for you.**

# Epilogue

The authors trust that *Poetry Report* will assist your efforts as an aspiring poet with intentions to let the world know of your thoughts and feelings about whatever subject it may be.

Our hope is that the book provides practical information that will guide you from the first moment you create a poem to the day when you can say with pride, "I am a published poet." This is so very important since writing poetry is like having a conversation with the reader but you are not there. Despite your absence, and inability to answer any questions, your words speak your message whether it is for amusement, inspiration, or a poem that provides your viewpoint about an important aspect of life.

Poetry is, in effect, your communication with the world. In restricted space, and with few word choices, you are pouring out your emotions and thoughts. When they are sent into the world through publication in magazines, chapbooks, or books, they filter into the minds of readers, and make an impression. No one can ever know what effect his or her poetry will have on an individual but the Good Lord somehow seems to touch those in need of an inspirational lift, a belly laugh, or a unique perspective on an issue with just the right poem.

Remember that your published poetry may live forever - passed down from family member to family member, by friend to friend, and kept alive by publishers that continue to release new editions of works written years ago. Hundreds of years from now someone may pick up your works and discover a message that will be meaningful to them.

This said, get busy and begin your sojourn with one of the most rewarding creative crafts available. Poetry can be your window to the world, and we look forward to hearing from you as to the progress made with your poetry efforts. Each of us is available to assist your efforts through the contact information at the end of the book—and don't hesitate to ask for help. *Poetry Report* is our gift to you, and we look forward to the day when you inform us that your book is available in the bookstores, on the Internet, or through the self-publishing route.

Meanwhile, God speed to you with the mystical adventure from idea to poetry publication. May you change the world through the magic of your words.


Jim Walker
Mark Shaw

Authors

# Appendix

This reference material, much of it excerpted from *Book Report*, the companion publication to *Poetry Report*, is designed to assist your efforts at different stages of the poetry writing process – idea to publication.

## Poetry: Key terms and ideas

<u>Verse</u> – This is writing that pays attention to not only each word, but also each line as a singularly important unit. The opposite of this is **prose**, writing unconcerned with the way the lines break as individual units. There is a movement in poetry called **prose poetry**. Here, the writers are unconcerned with linebreaks and lines as individual units while staying concerned with the importance of single words in terms of meaning, symbol and sound.

<u>Open form and free verse</u> – No strict pattern in repetition, rhyme, or meter. But, certainly, still verse.

<u>Purpose</u> – What is poem/poet trying to do? Poems can have many purposes – from telling a story, to expressing an emotion to presenting an image, to creating a sound, to delivering a message. Poems can have multiple purposes.

<u>Dramatic situation</u> – This is all about message. Who is sending the message? Who are they sending it to? Why do they need to send a message? Figuring this out is one of the first steps of interpretation.

<u>Pattern</u> – This is the arch of the poem – the way it moves, content and structure wise, from beginning to end. It is the way the whole poem comes together. Key elements include using repetition and using certain techniques to build to an ending. Pattern works quite differently in prose.

<u>Words</u> – Remember, each word can function on multiple levels in poetry. 1. How the word contributes directly to meaning by connotation, denotation or symbol (see previous handout). 2. The

second come with sound. Certain words, especially in conjunction with other words, give poems a certain sound and that can create a feeling, or lead to an interpretation, by the reader. 3. The third comes in rhythm. Words structured in a pattern or form, repeated or rhymed, can create a sound for the poem that also leads to a certain set of ideas or feelings from the reader. If a poem is to work well, the direct meaning of the words, and the sound and rhythm should compliment each other.

**Language** – Poetic language includes **idioms** (personal words that mark one's poetry), **diction** (the type of words chosen and why); archaisms (old words found in old poems, hopefully); **denotation** (literal meaning of words); **connotation** (the feel a word creates); **syntax** (the selected order of words); **inversion** (altering usual syntax to make poems rhyme or follow meter or beat); **pun** (using a similar sounding word to connect readers to another meaning).

**Image** – These are considered the building blocks of many poems. Images allow you to experience the poem on a sensory level. Sight is often the most important imagist sense. Images create pictures that stand for feelings and ideas when received by the reader. Images help create setting.

**Concrete and abstract diction** – Concrete words and phrases connect readers with things they can directly sense. These vivid words create **imagery** for the reader to see or hear or experience ("fresh cut grass on the baseball field"). Abstract words and phrases present meaning and ideas and feelings ("I love baseball"). These work in conjunction with the concrete to build a poem that can been seen and felt by the audience.

**Figurative language** – **Metaphor** makes a single comparison between two unlike things, usually linking concrete things with abstract ideas ("the ball field is my heaven"). If you use a *like* or *as* in there, then it is a **simile** ("Ty Cobb played like a demon"). **Central metaphor** comes when a poem contains a running metaphor that may not appear directly in a poem (see "Stone", "The Tunnel", or others). **Allusions** make metaphorical connections to historical or cultural events or characters ("Ty Cobb" was Napoleon in spikes"). **Personification** gives human characteristics to non-human things or abstract ideas ("the tree branch waved hello in the window").

**Symbol** – **Symbols** are concrete things or actions in a poem that provide meaning beyond the literal, surface, sense. **Traditional symbols** carry the same ideas with them for most people (colors, flowers, things in nature, religious emblems). Private symbols are often created by poets and can be interpreted different ways. The placement of certain words and the context of the poems can turn many common things into symbolic ones.

**Allusion** – This is making reference to something outside of the poem that pulls in feelings, ideas or connections for the reader. Alluding to icons from popular culture is a frequent technique of modern poets. But writers have long alluded to mythical, biblical and historical figures. Allusion works well when the reader can see the reference as a kind of shorthand. But it fails when the reader can't grasp the allusion. This, though, places more responsibility on the reader – keeping him or her involved in the process.

**Tone, theme and voice** – **Tone** is the speaker's implied attitude presented in the poem. It could reflect an emotion, be sarcastic, ironic, or satirical. **Theme** is the central idea of the poem, what it's all about and what holds it together. **Voice** combines tone with style and contributes to the overall feel of the poem and the creation of a persona or character for the speaker.

**Speaker** – This is the voice in the poem. It's who is sending the message. And the speaker is not always the writer of the poem. Even autobiographical or **confessional** poetry can be written through the voice of a **persona** created by the poet.

**Auditor** – This is the intended receiver of the message. It's the "you" of the poem. Sometimes, although infrequently, that "you" is the reader in general. Sometimes the "you" is a specific person addressed by the speaker of the poem. When the poem is released from **personal** poetry to **public**, then the writer must consider the idea of **audience**. Who will be receiving this message? What will they need to receive it as hoped? Remember, the auditor is not necessarily a member of the audience of the poem — just as the audience is not necessarily an auditor of the poem.

**Genres** – These are the recognized categories of poetry made clear by **style, form** and **content**. These genres include: **lyric poetry** (usually **abstract**, emotional and always non-**narrative** poems); **narrative poetry** (tells a story in the archaic forms of **epic, ballad, heroic metrical romance**); **dramatic poetry** (a spoken monologue or dialogue establishing character, slice of life).

## For a deep reading of a Poem:

*Take your time when reading. Give extra attention to the first and last lines of poems and the first and last lines of each stanza. Don't dismiss a poem until you've determined its purpose.*

1. Consider the purpose of the poem. Identify its speaker, auditor and dramatic situation. Note how you concluded all of these things and if you remain unsure about any.

2. Pick out key words and images and note why they are so important. Look at the emotions in the poem. Discuss this. Examine the overall pattern of the poem, in terms of both content and structure. How effective is it?

3. Next, look at it in terms of metaphor, simile, symbol the connotations of words, allusions. Examine the tone, theme and voice of the poem.

4. Last, consider how the poem connected for you. Why do you feel the way you do about it? What have you experienced or learned by reading it? Was this especially rewarding? Why or why not? This evaluative response should come last – after you've completed all of the above interpretive steps.

# Copyright

**To ensure no one steals your book concept, copyright the material.** This is essential even if you believe it will never be seen by anyone but Aunt Myrtle.

First consider copyrighting your material when you have a satisfactory draft of your book. Book Proposals and Query Letters may also be copyrighted.

**A copyright protects literary work under United States law for the life of the author or poet plus seventy years.** Copyrighting material is easy. **For details, consult the Library of Congress web site.** The necessary documents can be downloaded.

Proper authentication of the literary material is required. After a few questions are answered, the completed document and a copy of the literary material, accompanied by a filing fee, are mailed to the address provided. Within weeks, a letter is forwarded designating a copyright number. File this document in a safe deposit box.

A terrific reference source regarding copyright is *Kirsch's Guide To The Book Contract*, by attorney Jonathan Kirsch. In simple language, he explains why you should protect your writings.

When a book is traditionally published, the copyright continues in the name of the author or poet even though the publishing company obtained specified rights to publish it. **The book will be assigned an ISBN (International Standard Book Number) to distinguish it.** Internationally recognized, this ten-digit number (1st digit—country of origin, 2nd digit—publisher designation, 3rd set of digits—title of book, last digit—self-check) identifies the book for purposes of commerce and supply chains. **If you self-publish, you can obtain, for a fee, an ISBN number at www.bowker.com.** Once it is issued, you should register the number with *Books In Print* to insure the book information is available to major retailers, librarians, and independent booksellers across the country. Book titles can be registered at www.bowkerlink.com.

**A barcode used by bookstores and other retailers to record sales and price will be printed on the book.** Most popular is the 10-digit ISBN. Other barcodes may be printed on the cover or jacket, including UPC and EAN numbers. A traditional publisher will handle this for you.

There is one barcode per book. More information can be obtained at the Bowker web site.

# The Writing Process

There is nothing more personal than writing. Thoughts originating in the deep recesses of the intellect are unique. When these ideas are reduced to writing, they become a direct reflection of one's spiritual and intellectual being.

Those who choose to write professionally must do so with passion and a sense of responsibility since their words will affect the reader's mindset. Thoughts and ideas expressed verbally flutter through the air like multi-colored butterflies and seldom are accurately recalled. A famous psychologist once stated that people don't comprehend the substance of spoken words unless they are repeated six or seven times. Written words expressing thoughts and ideas are more likely to be recalled since readers choose quiet time to enjoy the very essence of published works. **Poets have the opportunity, in a day and age when people don't listen, to inspire, inform, challenge, and entertain whether they write fiction, non-fiction, or a collection of poetry.**

For those choosing to pursue a writing career at an early age, the battle plan is clear: keep an open mind and absorb everything life has to offer. For suggestions on how to be more creative, read *Pencil Dancing, New Ways To Free Your Creative Spirit* by Mari Messer.

Formal education is available through writing classes, books on writing, seminars, and college courses. Search for competent instructors with traditional publishing credits or outstanding academic skills.

To bolster the ability to write with sufficient knowledge, the aspiring writer must garner a sense of history, of what occurred to alter the course of mankind and why. Course study in psychology, philosophy, history, and classical literature provides a solid foundation.

**Extensive travel is the comrade of good writers.** Spanning the globe opens the door to a rich heritage. Sojourns to Greece, Egypt, Italy, England, France, and many other countries are valuable. Asked his advice for young writers, William Faulkner stated, "Travel and read."

While visiting foreign countries, learn about the people, the history of the country, and the customs. Working in a foreign country provides a wealth of knowledge. Don't shy away from what might be considered taboo employment. Faulkner wrote, "The best job ever offered to me was to become a landlord in a brothel."

Writing workshops, seminars, and writers' conferences are meat and potatoes if writing professionally is your goal. This is the perfect environment in which to gather valuable tips and nuances from those who have achieved the goal of being published. Many such events are publicized in independent, creative-arts oriented newspapers such as *The Village Voice.*

---

If you decide later in life that writing is a profession of choice, the alternatives differ. Workshops, seminars, and conferences are valuable tools for learning, but a crash course on writing professionally is a prerequisite if you have not exercised this skill in many years.

Education is essential to learning the craft of writing, but those who proclaim that someone with no formal literary training cannot succeed should recall the background of no less a "scholar" than William Shakespeare. While he was schooled in Greek and Latin literature, rhetoric, and Christian ethics, there is no evidence that the Bard was ever taught the art of writing. History indicates he left school at age fifteen, never pursued further formal education, and was not considered a learned man. This did not prohibit him from writing what many experts consider to be the most extraordinary body of works in the history of literature.

Poet Walt Whitman further proves that formal training is not linked to literary success. His formal education ended at age eleven. Unlike other writers of his time who enjoyed structured, classical educations at private schools, Whitman learned about writing in the local library. He then joined a newspaper, *The New York Mirror,* where he wrote his first article in 1834. Less than two decades later, after dabbling in short-story fiction, Whitman wrote the classic, *Leaves of Grass.*

In his book *On Writing,* famed author Stephen King stated, **"If you want to be a writer, you must do two things above all others—read a lot and write a lot."** Best selling romance writer Nora Roberts echoes King's sentiments. She began her career as a stay-at-home mother who wrote ideas in a notebook during a snowstorm in 1979.

Pleased with her efforts, she continued to write. The result was her first published work, *Irish Thoroughbred*. Since then she has written several bestsellers, all because, as she says, "I don't believe in waiting for inspiration. It's my job to sit down . . . and write."

Whether you are interested in writing fiction, non-fiction, or poetry, read, read, and read some more. Read the classics— Hemingway, Joyce, Dickens, and Steinbeck. Poets can learn from Whitman, Frost, Edgar Allen Poe, and Edna St. Vincent Millay. Each of these great writers admits their education about writing was influenced by the books they read. Asked what authors he enjoyed, Hemingway listed more than thirty-four before confessing that to list them all "would take a day to remember." Among them were Mark Twain, Bach, Tolstoy, Dostoevsky, Chekhov, Kipling, Shakespeare, and Dante. Hemingway admitted he also gained education from artists and composers. "I learned as much from painters about how to write," he stated, "as from writers . . . I should think that what one learns from composers and from the study of harmony and counterpoint would be obvious."

**Competent poets are superb storytellers.** While reading the classics, note how the canonized poets weave a story or present a message. Poetry must be clear, have a good beginning, middle, and end, and never be boring. Reading well-written poetry books helps you realize how others have accomplished the feat. In *On Writing*, Stephen King states:

> Good writing . . . teaches the learning writer about style, graceful narration, plot development, the creation of believable characters, and truth-telling. A novel like *Grapes of Wrath* may fill a new writer with feelings of despair and good, old-fashioned jealousy— I'll never be able to write anything that good, not if I live to be a thousand—but such feelings can also serve as a spur, goading the writer to work harder and aim higher. **Being swept away by a combination of great story and great writing . . . is a part of every writer's necessary formation.** You cannot hope to sweep someone else away by the force of your writing until it has been done to you.

Poets must sweep readers away just like fiction writers. Strong, visual word usage is the key as evidenced by an excerpt from *Presumed Innocent* by Scott Turow. It reads:

The atomized life of the restaurant spins on about us. At separate tables, couples talk; the late-shift workers dine alone; the waitresses pour coffee. And here sits Rusty Sabich, thirty-nine years old, full of lifelong burdens and workaday fatigue.

I tell my son to drink his milk. I nibble at my burger. Three feet away is the woman whom I have said I've loved for nearly twenty years, making her best efforts to ignore me.

Besides being a terrific storyteller, character description, a must for any poet, was Jack Kerouac's specialty. An excerpt of *On The Road* reads:

> He was a gray, nondescript-looking fellow you wouldn't notice on the street, unless you looked closer and saw his mad, bony skull with its strange youthfulness – a Kansas minister with exotic, phenomenal fires and mysteries.
>
> He had studied medicine in Vienna; had studied anthropology, read everything; and now he was settling to his life's work, which was the study of things themselves in the streets of life and the night.

In *Balzac and the Little Chinese Seamstress*, author Dai Sijie sweeps the reader into his novel portraying life during China's Cultural Revolution. An excerpt reads:

> The room served as shop, workplace, and dining room all at once. The floorboards were grimy and streaked with yellow-and-black gobs of dried spittle left by clients. You could tell they were not washed down daily. There were hangers with finished garments suspended on a string across the middle of the room. The corners were piled high with bolts of material and folded clothes, which were under siege from an army of ants.

As stated, poets must create poetry that visualizes their thoughts by providing the same dramatics utilized by the best fiction writers. To gain a better understanding of this point, re-read the poetry written by Karen Kovacik, Robert Bly, and Li-Young Lee featured in Chapter Three.

# Journals and Idea Books

Learning the craft of writing poetry is a continuing process. One of the best means to hone the craft is by writing in a journal or diary. It promotes discipline while providing a chronology of your life. This can be done through prose or poetry.

Author John Fowles (*The French Lieutenant's Woman*) stated, "I am a great believer in diaries, if only in the sense that bar exercises are good for ballet dancers; it's often through personal diaries that the novelist discovers his true bent." This comment is applicable for non-fiction writers as well.

**One exercise to consider requires writing in a journal each day for a week.** Content and length are optional, but the goal is to complete the task. Then cast aside the journal for a few days before reading it. If you're satisfied with the text, and the process involved, then you have the potential to write professionally. If you hate what you wrote, and the discipline of having to write each day, then consider basketry, modern art, or some other means of expending creative energy.

Another useful exercise to composing poetry is to organize a folder containing observations about others. Good writers are people watchers. Whether you do so in a park, at sports events, or at a bus stop, chronicle your thoughts and observations. Vivid description and words evoking emotion are the earmarks of the good writer. To enhance this skill, study speech patterns, how people move, what habits they possess, and face and body features. Make lists of these characteristics; then add other elements. A fat notebook may include pages listing names (Avon Privette, Paris Wolfe, Tootie Witmer, Audrey Wink, Holly Furfer, Bobby April, David Duck), smells (bug spray, moth balls, fresh strawberry pie, chemical fertilizer), descriptions (salty, speckled, overripe, furry), hair style (butch, raggedy, ponytail, mousy), and body parts (webbed feet, spindly toes, stubby arms, firm butt, limp face, spidery fingers, slumping posture, drooping eyes, artificial eyes, whiskey nose, parched lips, dead legs). Another list includes weather descriptions (gray drizzle, sideways rain, Oklahoma wind) and sky descriptions (primrose, veined with dry lightning, streaky blue).

Listing "useful phrases" is also helpful. Examples include soft laughter, hushed giggle, black scuff marks, pocket change, replied indifferently, fork patrol, pigeon toed, steady gaze, shimmered in the moonlight, and crumpled pompadour.

Before beginning the writing process, consult your lists and permit words and ideas to fill your brain with creativity. Clever words and phrases spice up the text, providing the reader with the all-important asset that E. B. White emphasizes: **visualization.** Learned author John Cheever endorsed White's viewpoint when he stated, "The books you really love give the sense, when you first open them, of having been there. It is a creation, almost like a chamber in the memory. Places that one has never been to, things that one has never seen or heard, but their fitness is so sound that you've been there somehow." This observation is applicable to poetry as well.

---

## Word Usage

While reading, note the author or poet's word choice. There are those who love the vocabulary and appreciate hundred dollar words that claim, "I'm a literate son-of-a-gun with a graduate degree in Webster's." But language must never be vague, elusive, or downright inaccessible. A story loses much of its flow and meaning if the reader spends too much time opening a dictionary. Phrases like "revelatory episodes," "epigrammatic prose," and "diorama of American plenty" will confuse and dismay 95 percent of the population.

**Remember, writing is personal, not only for the *writer*, but for the *reader*.** As the writer, you are conveying information regarding a story intended to captivate the reader. You want your words to leap off the page and infiltrate the reader's brain to entice, excite, entertain, or make them stop and think. When readers purchase a book, it will be successful if they ask, "Who is this author or poet and what is he or she trying to show [not tell] me?"

---

# Professional Advice

Modern day study guides for the aspiring writer abound. If you are a beginning writer, consult a basic book on style, grammar, and punctuation to guide your efforts. There are few hard and fast rules regarding these areas, but standards and guidelines exist to assist your understanding regarding how to write according to publishing industry standards.

Once you have learned the basics, consider two books to aid you as you become more proficient at writing.

The *Chicago Manual of Style* is a dense book not vacation reading. Set aside ample time so you can focus on its contents. A better idea is to consult the book in spurts, taking notes, and then referring to it again and again like a close friend who tells the truth.

Publisher's prefer that authors and poets adhere to the rules presented in this publication, but *Elements of Style*, by William Strunk Jr. and E. B. White, is ninety-five pages long, the perfect length for obtaining good, solid information about writing. Spending less than ten dollars for the book is one of the best investments an aspiring author or poet can make.

Professor Strunk published the classic for his students in 1919. It soon became known as the "little book that could." Over the years, White, most famous for writing *Charlotte's Web*, has revised it for modernization purposes, but the gem features Strunk's brilliant mind probing the depths of writing and what is proper and correct. Under titles such as "Elementary Rules of Usage," "Elementary Rules of Composition," "A Few Matters of Form," and "Words and Expressions Commonly Misused," the Cornell professor provides simple, clear, and brilliant guidelines. Among the jewels are warnings against overuse of adverbs and adjectives, advocacy of active voice and positive words, and rules for positioning pronouns. *Elements of Style* explains the whys and wherefores so even a dunderhead can understand. I recommend putting the book under your pillow while you sleep with the hope that the knowledge will seep into your brain.

While the first four sections of the book are a must-read, E. B. White added Book V titled, "An Approach To Style." He writes, "Up to this point, the book has been concerned with what is correct, or acceptable, in the use of English. In this final chapter, we approach style in its broader meaning: style in the sense of what is distinguished and distinguishing. Here we leave solid ground. Who can confidently say what ignites a certain combination of words, causing them to explode in the mind?"

Regardless of the caveat, White's suggestions *are* on solid ground. Sections include: "Placing yourself in the background," "Write in a way that comes naturally," "Work from a suitable design," and "Write with nouns and verbs, not with adverbs and adjectives." White discusses the need to revise and rewrite, not to overwrite, and not to overstate.

A quick reference book to complement *Elements of Style* and *The Chicago Manuel of Style* is *Grammar Report, Basic Writing Tools For Aspiring Authors and Poets.* Published by Books For Life Foundation, it contains useful hints regarding common grammatical and punctuation mistakes.

Absorbing the lessons outlined in any of these publications provides a basis for developing writing skills. Each author or poet chooses a storytelling method, but proper usage of language guarantees that errors won't signal lack of talent. Editors at publishing companies dismiss a manuscript or collection of poetry if there are misspellings and grammatical errors, but they also pay close attention to word usage.

Learning good writing skills at an early age will benefit aspiring poets. Parents interested in supplemental materials to improve children's writing skills may consider the Shurley English method. More information is available at www.shurley.com.

---

## Clarity

In *On Writing Well*, author William Zinsser states, "Good writing has an aliveness that keeps the reader reading from one paragraph to the next, and it's not a question of gimmicks to 'personalize' the author. It's a question of using the English language in a way that will achieve the greatest clarity and strength."

Fiction writers and poets must ask themselves several questions regarding clarity. Is the story time-oriented so the reader understands the time frame being presented? Are the characters well defined and do they act in a manner consistent with the background provided? Is there a believable backdrop for the story, one that is vivid? Have I written a clever dramatic story with a ticking clock to add suspense?

Non-fiction writers face a comparable question—will a story that is quite clear to the writer be as clear to the reader? Will the reader understand the message being conveyed by the text? This applies to poets as well.

Author John Updike provided a guidepost regarding clarity. He wrote, "When I write, I aim in my mind not toward New York, but toward a vague spot a little to the east of Kansas. I think of the books on library shelves, without their jackets, years old, and a countryish teenaged boy finding them speak to him." Author Zinsser suggests, "Clutter is the disease of American writing. We are a society strangling in unnecessary words, circular constructions, pompous frills, and meaningless jargon."

As the writing process continues, writers must be certain they have told the story they intend to tell, and with accuracy. Many times we read what our brain *wants* to read instead of what *is* on the page

**One method of determining clarity while proofreading for errors is to read the material aloud. By inspecting and hearing each word, meaning becomes clearer and mistakes are revealed that would otherwise have been overlooked.**

---

## Writing Skills

Information about how to write and writing style are referenced in many books. Professor White was correct when he wrote that no one understands why a certain group of words carefully joined produce magic on the sheet of paper for one author or poet while resulting in gobbledygook for another. Each writer's composition of words will differ according to his or her skill and experience.

In his book, *On Writing*, Stephen King offered a simple explanation for what he believes is important when considering writing style. He wrote, "Book buyers want a good story to take with them on the airplane, something that will first fascinate them, then pull them in and keep them turning the pages." Mystery writer Tony

Hillerman (*Hunting Badger*) told *Writer's Digest*, "I feel my first priority as a writer is to entertain the audience."

Never forget every book, including poetry collections, is an adventure—Write it like one. This is true whether you are creating a tortoise and hare story, a book about the inner workings of the latest computer, a chronicle of the evolution of Red Lobster stores as an American success story, a biography of the gifted poet Etheridge Knight, or a collection of poetry about why birds fly south for the winter.

Author James Patterson espouses a unique perspective of writing. In *The Writer's Handbook*, he states, "In the beginning, I really worried a lot about sentences in my books. But at some point . . . I stopped writing sentences and started writing stories. And that's the advice I give to new writers. Sentences are really hard to write. Stories flow. If you've got an idea, the story will flow. Once you have the story down you can go back and polish it for the next ten years."

No one doubts that clear, concise storytelling, including poetry collections, featuring language that *shows,* but does not *tell,* is paramount to success. Some writers sprinkle flowery language throughout their manuscripts. Others write like Hemingway and produce some sentences that are never-ending. Regardless, the finest writers, whether they are writing fiction, non-fiction, or poetry, are brief and visual, two great talents gained through experience. Being visual means to flavor your writing with the five senses—sight, smell, touch, taste, and hearing—so the reader consumes and is consumed with the text.

Professor Strunk wrote in *The Elements of Style*, "If those who have studied the art of writing are in accord on any one point, it is this: the surest way to arouse and hold the reader's attention is by being specific, definite, and concrete. The greatest writers—Homer, Dante, Shakespeare—are effective because they deal in particulars and report the details that matter. Their words call up pictures." Strunk added, "Vigorous writing is concise. A sentence should contain no unnecessary words, a paragraph no unnecessary sentences, for the same reason that a drawing should have no unnecessary lines and a machine no unnecessary parts."

Author Nora Roberts believes visualization means proper selection and description of characters whether the book is fiction or non-fiction. She told *Writer's Digest,* "Your characters have to jump off the page. They have to appeal to the reader in some way . . . They need to be appealing, humorous and human."

Literary agent Julia Castiglia echoes Roberts' words in *Writer's Digest*, "What we really look for are books that are well written, with a certain zing to them that climbs off the page and wraps itself around our brains, that so entrance and seduce us that we just can't say no." This applies to poetry as well.

---

## Word Choice

The requirement that the writer *show* the reader and not *tell* cannot be over-emphasized. Word choice is key. Mark Twain wrote, "The difference between the right word and the nearly right word is the same as that between lightning and lightning bug."

To improve a story, use active words portraying concrete images instead of abstractions: avoid crutch-words ending in "ly;" avoid "not" and "no;" use active verbs like "clawed," "swatted," and "pawed," instead of linking verbs like "is" and "was;" avoid overuse of gerunds (verbs used as nouns by adding "ing"); and use stronger nouns instead of adjectives. Regarding the need for active verbs, author William Zinsser wrote, "Verbs are the most important of all your tools. They push the sentence forward and give it momentum. Active verbs push hard; passive verbs tug fitfully."

Avoid words such as "a little," "very," "kind of," "pretty much" or "really," qualifying other words. They are often unnecessary and make your writing sound trite.

Concise word usage translates to paragraph length. Reader attention span is short, so use of a few sentences separates the text and keeps the flow of the story at a steady pace. Long paragraphs are bulky and can bog down the reader. Avoid them.

Strong word usage is essential at the beginning of a verse. Words completing a verse must tantalize and urge the reader onward.

---

## Keys To The Writing Process

**If you decide to write an entire manuscript or collection of poetry before completing a Query Letter and/or Book Proposal, remember one important rule: Once you start, don't stop.** The main reason most people intending to write a book never do is because they encounter a stumbling block regarding word choice, punctuation, or grammar usage. Before they know it, the creative juices turn sour.

Author and literary writing guru Natalie Goldberg speaks to this in her book *Writing Down The Bones*. She believes initial thoughts "capture the oddities of your mind." She writes, "First thoughts have tremendous energy. It is the way the mind flashes on something." Author Goldberg provides a list of exercises in her book to inspire writers toward creative thinking.

Author John Steinbeck (*The Grapes of Wrath*) spoke to the importance of completing what you begin. He stated, "Write freely and as rapidly as possible and throw the whole thing on paper. Never correct or rewrite until the whole thing is down. Rewrite in process is usually found to be an excuse for not going on. It also interferes with flow and rhythm which can only come from a kind of unconscious association with the material."

In a 1947 letter to Jack Kerouac, writer Neal Cassady, upon whom Kerouac based the character Dean Moriarty in *On The Road*, wrote in a letter to Kerouac:

I have always held that when one writes, one should forget all rules, literary styles, and other such pretensions as large words, lordly clauses and other phrases as such . . . Rather, I think one should write, as nearly as possible, as if he where the first person on earth and was humbly and sincerely putting on paper that which he saw and experienced and loved and lost; what his passing thoughts were and his sorrows and desires. . .

Actor Sean Connery, playing the part of fictional author William Forester in *Finding Forrester*, addressed the subject in an interesting manner. He stated, "You write the first draft with your heart. You re-write with your head."

Instead of worrying about mistakes or lapses in the text, plow ahead with your poetry first drafts. There will be time later to fill in the blanks or correct errors.

---

## Writing Regimen

There is no definitive answer to how much text a writer should complete each day. Stephen King states in his book *On Writing*, "I like to get ten pages a day, which amounts to 2,000 words. That's 180,000 words over a three-month span, a goodish length for a book."

Esteemed author John Updike (*The Power and the Glory*) writes 1,000 words a day, six days a week. This process has resulted in more than fifty books, two of which have earned Pulitzer Prizes.

Ernest Hemingway, who never began writing unless twenty sharpened pencils were close at hand, described his daily routine by stating:

> I write every morning as soon after first light as possible. There is no one to disturb you and it is cool or cold and you come to your work and warm as you write. You read what you have written and, as you always stop when you know what is going to happen next, you go on from there. You write until you come to a place where you still have your juice and know what will happen next and you stop and try to live through until the next day when you hit it again. You have started at six in the morning, say, and may go on until noon or be through before that. When you stop you are as empty, and at the same time never empty but filling, as when you have made love to someone you love.

Poet Maya Angelou's regimen is classic. "I have a hotel room in every town I've ever lived in," she stated. " . . . I leave my home at six, and try to be at work by 6:30. To write, I lie across the bed, so that [my] elbow is absolutely encrusted at the end . . . I stay until 12:30 or 1:30 in the afternoon, and then I go home and try to breathe."

Tom Wolfe (*A Man In Full, The Right Stuff*) sets page goals. He stated, "I set myself a quota—ten pages a day, triple-spaced, which means about eighteen hundred words. If I can finish that up in three hours, I'm through for the day."

Many writers believe they deserve a magnum of champagne in celebration if they can write four to six pages a day. Others write less, some more. It all depends, but never let anything prohibit progress toward the appointed goal. This means the telephone, loved ones, pets, door-to-door salespeople, radio, television, grammar problems, spelling miscues, mosquitoes, or children. All are the writer's enemies since they obstruct completion of the task.

Block out these enemies, begin to write, then write and write, and write some more. Be sure to "save" the material paragraph by paragraph while working and then save it on a disk when you have completed the day's task so computer "crashes" won't eliminate your text. Mother Nature is another enemy of the writer and her electrical storms are computer killers.

When words are dashing out of the brain, there is exhilaration beyond comprehension. While the juices are flowing, the fingers can't work fast enough. The rush is better than any chemical "high."

A proposed regimen is as follows: The poet decides on Sunday to complete three poems in one week. He or she writes a first draft of one on Monday, another on Tuesday, and one on Wednesday. Thursday is set aside for review of each poem, with finalization of the poetry on Friday. This night is reserved for celebration, Saturday for recovering from the Friday night hangover, and Sunday for the Sabbath.

By not touching the manuscript on the weekend, the poet will have a fresh perspective on Monday. Best selling author Truman Capote (*In Cold Blood*) was a proponent of this method. After describing himself as a "horizontal author [who] can't think unless I'm lying down," he stated, "when the yellow draft is finished, I put the manuscript away for a while, a week, a month, sometimes longer. When I take it out again, I read it as coldly as possible, then read it to a friend or two, and decide what changes I want to make."

---

# Revisions

The process of rewriting is complex. Pulitzer Prize winning author Elie Wiesel stated, "Writing is not like painting, where you add. It is not what you put on the canvas that the reader sees. Writing is more like a sculpture where you remove; you eliminate in order to make the work visible. There is a difference between a book of two hundred pages from the very beginning, and a book of two hundred pages, which is the result of an original eight hundred pages. The six hundred pages are there. Only you don't see them."

When you are in the revision stage, as opposed to when you are rushing through a first draft to complete it start to finish, speed is the enemy of quality. To be sure the work is the finest it can be, take your time. Columnist James Kilpatrick wrote, **"Edit your copy, then edit it again; then edit it once more.** This is the hand-rubbing process. No rough sandpapering can replace it." William Zinsser stresses the importance of revisions. He concludes, **"Rewriting is the essence of writing well; it's where the game is won or lost."**

Every time text is revised, it improves. Many times writers return to words they've written and are amazed at the flow and clarity. Other times the material embarrasses them. How I wish I could re-write many of the first books I had published using the skills learned over the years. Nearly every published author or poet I know feels this way.

Revising material is a constant process. In *On Writing Well*, William Zinsser proclaims, "Writing improves in direct ratio to the number of things we can keep out of it that shouldn't be there. Examine every word you put on paper. You'll find a surprising number that don't serve any purpose." He adds, "Most first drafts can be cut by 50% without losing any information or the author's voice."

Laurie Rosen, editor of thirty-seven bestsellers, advises novelists to follow ten basic steps while considering revisions. Among the ones she listed in *Writer's Digest* are: Revise toward a marketable length (Average novel length is between 60,000 and 100,000 words. Manuscripts exceeding 100,000 words are a tough sell), torque the power of your scenes (emphasize the purpose of the action), tease the reader forward into the next chapter, give your antagonist some depth, and dramatize, dramatize, dramatize."

Some poets set deadlines for completion of revised drafts. Meeting them is an excellent form of discipline. **Setting reasonable**

**deadlines is suggested.** No writer should create or edit when the brain is weary.

---

## Critique

When an acceptable draft of your poetry is completed, let others review it. It doesn't matter if your reviewer is a spouse, a relative, or a friend down the street.

**Writers need a variety of people to provide objective opinions.** Being removed from the material, reviewers can spot flaws and misinformation, and correct mistakes. They may even suggest an alternative means of telling a story.

The key is locating people not afraid to say what they think. Then, when criticism is leveled, swallow your ego and be receptive.

Good writing requires dedication and perseverance since words are the writer's communication with the world. Only through hard work will the message be strong. For poets attempting to impress editors, good writing is their most important calling card.

# Manuscript Techniques

When submitting poetry for publication:

**Don't** type more than one poem to a page.

**Do** single-space the text (whenever possible).

**Do** leave two spaces between stanzas.

**Don't** include name, address, and so forth on each page.

**Do** include above information in Query or Cover letter.

**Do** begin title of poem four-five lines from top of each page.

**Do** leave three spaces between title of poem and first line of poem.

## Book Promotion Ideas

The book has been written. The publishing deal is completed. The champagne celebration has produced a hangover the size of Ted Turner's Montana ranch because the long-awaited book is being released.

So what now? **Should you sit back and watch your publisher do all the work to promote the book?** Is it time for a vacation to the French Riveria to frolic on the shores of the Mediterranean?

The answer, of course, is "no," since the real work to promote the book has just begun. **Regardless of whether the publisher is large, medium-sized or small, or the book is being traditionally self-published, you are responsible for promotion, promotion, and more promotion.**

If a traditional publisher has released the book, there may be obligations regarding publicity. **Book promotion clauses are common in most publishing contracts.** They focus on what is expected of the poet and what is expected of the publisher when the book is released.

Without sufficient promotion, chances for success are doomed. The extent of the publicity and marketing program will depend on the size of the publisher releasing the book and the perceived importance of the book in the publisher's overall list. Having a major publisher release your book is worthy, but this does not guarantee a big promotion campaign. While negotiation is occurring, be certain to learn of the publishing company's commitment to promotion. This factor may be as important as the dollar amount of any advance being provided to you.

If there is a strong commitment to a promotion campaign, the publishing company will assign an expert in this field to coordinate the effort. The campaign may include a nationwide tour featuring television, radio, and print opportunities.

Medium-sized and smaller publisher's commitment to promotion will vary. They may or may not employ in-house experts to deal with publicity. Yours will depend on what is expected of you in tandem with efforts by the publisher.

Medium-sized and smaller publishers without an in-house promotion or publicity department rely on free-lance book promoters. These experts are hired on a project by project basis to expose the book to the media. Campaigns vary in cost depending on whether they involve print, radio, television or a combination of all three.

The publishing contract should contain specific language regarding the extent and length of the campaign and who is responsible for the cost. You may be required to expend funds to promote the book. If so, a clause should be included in the contract providing for this likelihood.

If you are willing to fund publicity or a promotion campaign for your book, consider noting this in the Query Letter and Book Proposal. A clause in the contract will provide guidance.


## Book Signings

Book signings provide an opportunity for you to meet the public and sell your books. Major publishers will coordinate the appearances. Medium-sized and smaller publishers may assist, but the poet will assume an active role with scheduling.

**The publishing contract should clarify respective roles and provide guidelines for book signing promotion, since it is essential to success.** At least one month before the event, a coordinated campaign involving the author or poet, the bookstore, and the publisher should be planned. Storefront signs and signs in the store are critical as is the announcement of the book signing in print publications and on radio and television.

**Book signings must be strategically planned.** Competition from other local events can impede success. Research newspaper and magazine calendar sections to discover competing events that may draw potential customers away. Discussing the best day and time for your book signing with the bookstore owner is essential. Some stores are "dead" on the weeknights; others flourish. Weather may play a part regarding scheduling. During the winter, few customers flock to book stores when there is five feet of snow on the ground. Summer months can be terrific weather-wise, but when the weather is too good, customers will stay away from their favorite bookstores.

Book signings during seasonal holidays can be advantageous. Books are great gifts for Christmas, Mother's Day, Father's Day, and Valentine's Day.

Mall bookstore signings can be terrific since there is normally a steady stream of customers walking about. Coordinating a book signing during peak hours is advisable.

**Self-publishing guru Dan Poynter suggests poets consider holding mini-seminars instead of book signings.** In a *Writer's Digest* article, he quotes Teri Lonier, author of *Working Solo*. She stated, "An autograph party says, 'Come and appreciate me and buy a book;' a seminar says, 'Come on down, and I will give you something for free that will improve your life.'" Poynter and Lonier agree that it is important to think of, "the potential benefit to the customer. How can you lure them out of the house and down to the store?"

When you appear at the book signing or seminar, remember people love stories. They may be interested in the ones featured in the book, how you decided to write it, or the research tools employed. **The more entertaining you are, the greater the chances you sell your books.**


## Attracting Publicity

If the publishing company funds the promotion campaign, you will gain needed exposure. If the publishing company cannot fund the campaign, or if you are self-published, consider expending funds to cover promotion costs. **Outstanding public relations companies exist, but make certain they specialize in book promotion.** Ask for references and copies of public relations campaigns they have designed for other poets.

Regardless of who is funding the promotional campaign, you must be clever to promote the book through any means possible. The saying, "The Lord helps those who help themselves," is most appropriate.

To circulate interest about your book, keep an "address book" listing every friend and acquaintance since childhood. When book signings or other promotional appearances are scheduled, mail invitations to everyone in the area you know. You will form a group of loyal readers who will purchase future books.

**Free publicity is the poet's best friend.** Convince magazines or newspapers to print an excerpt from the book. To gain exposure, telephone radio shows, contact libraries to schedule readings, and work through local writer's centers. Public speaking also provides the opportunity to promote the book.

Internet websites for poets are a must in the twenty-first century. Designing them has become an art form, and there are multiple companies available to assist the writer. How fancy the site is depends on your pocketbook, but you can promote your book online to enhance sales opportunities.

To further publicize a book, consider creating a full-color flyer, brochure, or a "One-Sheet" (book cover on one side—descriptive material about the book on the other). Postcards displaying the book cover can be forwarded to media outlets, prospective purchasers of the book, and friends.

**Publicizing a book not yet in the bookstores is the kiss of death.** If buyers interested in the book based on media exposure visit the store and the book is unavailable, chances are they will not return to buy it. Make certain the publisher and the bookstores coordinate stocking the book at least a month before the promotion campaign begins. If you self-publish, handle the matter yourself.

Double checking everything about your book signing is essential until the day it occurs. Make sure media exposure is secure and check the store a week or two before your book signing to see if posters are on the front window and displayed throughout the store. Most bookstores employ "community relations" managers to handle book signings, but they have many other duties. Good communication is a key to assurance that your book signing will be a success.

Regardless of how many books you sell at the book signing, request the opportunity, if it is not offered, to sign multiple books to be stocked in the store. Most stores do this as a courtesy, but publishers relish this opportunity since a signed book cannot be returned to them. This also applies to self-published poets, guaranteeing that you will be paid for the books left at the store.

If you are self-published, negotiate your share of the cover price with the bookstore. Splitting the revenue is fair, but many stores will permit you to keep as much as 70 percent.

If you appear for a book signing at a library or not-for-profit organization, consider donating a portion of the cover price. This promotes goodwill.


## Book Promotion References

Several worthy publications will help you better understand book promotion. One is ***The Complete Guide To Book Publicity,*** written by Jodee Blanco, a seasoned professional who is also an expert on self-publishing. Using the tips she includes in her book can be very worthwhile. One discourages authors or poets from mentioning their book more than once or twice during an interview. Another discusses what to wear for television appearances.

Blanco suggests that authors or poets write a book with promotion in mind. She believes that to successfully expose the book to the reading public, there must be a "promotional" tone, one signaling to the media that the book is timely and important. **Integrating an issue or cause into the story permits a built-in promotional package.** This permits a hook for the poet, the publisher, and the public relations firm representing the book.

Blanco's advice is questioned by those who believe a writer must write true to their heart and not with commercialism in mind. This "one or the other" stance fails to recognize that one can do both. Many poets believing in an issue or cause convey their feelings while keeping an eye open toward promotion. As long as they don't sacrifice their beliefs, they are being true to themselves, as well as being practical.

Promotion ideas must be considered in light of expense and coverage. Make certain you are targeting the right audience for your book. Spend money wisely to reach the largest group of people who will be interested in the type of book you have written. Be creative and you will be amazed at the amount of publicity you can generate for your book.

## Building A Career

**Book promotion is an important component to building a professional writing career. The goal is to create interest in both the current book and the next one.** To this end, remember to act like a professional when dealing with those who take the time to visit a bookstore, chat about the book, and purchase one. Keep a mailing list so you can advise them of the next book being released.

Continued contact with the bookstores is important, as well. Many poets send "thank you" notes to the manager after an appearance. When the poet is ready for another appearance, the manager will recall the good manners with a smile.

**Publishers take note of how poets handle public appearances.** The writer may or may not be interested in securing the same publisher for the next book, but don't gain a reputation as someone who is difficult. The book publishing industry is small and a bad reputation with regard to promotion can impede chances regarding the next book and the next.

Above all, be proud of your book. From nothing but an idea, you have produced a bound book presenting your message to the world. Shout "hooray" and enjoy the experience.

# Sample Poetry Book Proposal
# With Comments

---

## Cover Page

*(Ten spaces)*

*(title)* **A Parade of Ladies**

*(36 Font, Bold)*

*(three spaces)*

*(poet)* **Diana Meadows** *(24 Font, Bold)*

*(No copyright information)*

(Tip—It is recommended that titles be six words or less. Titles should be symbolic of the story being told. They must be strong— unforgettable—titles sell the book.)

## Tagline (14 Font, Bold)

*A Parade of Ladies* is a collection of poems that depict a time gone by when respect for the fair sex was the call of the day.

*(Tip—clarity is a key. If someone asked you what your book is about, what would you say?)*

## Synopsis *(14 Font, Bold)*

Where have all the ladies gone, I ask in a tone familiar to that of a professor addressing his students? Have males forgotten that the fair sex is to be pampered with love and affection and not demeaned for standing up for their rights. Whose to say that those women that choose to stand up for what they believe in still aren't as feminine as the ones that stay at home, keep their mouths shut, and raise children?

Twenty-five years ago, women were respected for their opinions and not chastised as "feminists" on the prowl. But all that changed when men, threatened by the strength shown by their wives, girlfriends, and sisters decided enough was enough. Soon women were being looked down upon and laughed at for speaking their minds. Too often they were threatened with reprisal, sexual or otherwise, unless they promised to shut up.

In *A Parade of Ladies*, this poet tells stories of those women, unknown though they may be who stood their ground and said "take me as I am or leave." Woven through the collection is a theme of pride and believing in oneself despite the odds. In "John Waterford's Wife Carol," the woman of the house tells her husband that she is applying for college since their four children have left the nest. "Rex Walter's Girlfriend," Olivia decides to join the NAACP despite warnings from her spouse that she will be pigeonholed as a "communist sympathizer." In "Ralph Johnson's Sister," Sidney Anne Johnson is a mother of eight that intends to leave her abusive husband in spite of threats that he will kill her.

Twenty-four poems are presented featuring twenty-four women with stories to tell, each essential to *A Parade of Ladies.*

*(Tip—Outlining the theme of the poetry collection is imperative. Catch the interest of the agent or publisher with an exciting overview of the stories to be told by the poems.)*

## Poet Biography

Diana Meadows is a single parent to six children, ages four to eighteen. After being abandoned by her husband, she worked sixteen-hour days while studying for her bachelor's degree in education on the weekends.

Diana began writing poetry to suppress spousal abuse. After her husband left, she began to write in earnest. One poem from her self-published first collection, *A Family of Flowers*, was printed in *Poets and Writers* magazine. Other poems have appeared in the *Village Voice* and various newspapers. In September of 2002, she received first prize in the poetry and prose competition conducted by Books For Life Foundation.

Ms. Meadows, a first grade teacher at Northwest School in Louisville, Kentucky, resides with two of her children, four dogs, and five cats, in the woods near Lexington, Kentucky.

*(Tip—Presenting the poet's credentials, her platform for speaking through her poetry is essential. Any agent or publisher will realize this lady knows about the subject matter being featured.)*

## Book Audience

Women interested in overcoming any self-doubt will be readers of *A Parade of Ladies*. Inspirational in nature, the material is hard-boiled but right on point. Through the women featured, readers will understand that the poet is expressing her thoughts regarding the state of womanhood today. The *Louisville-Courier Journal* properly dubbed the poet's first collection of poetry, *A Family of Flowers*, "the hard knocks of family life." *A Parade of Ladies* promises a similar hard-edged style while making women stop and think about whom they really are.

*(Tip—Publishers seek the largest audience possible for a book. Attempt to show that there may be multiple readers that will be interested in the poetry.)*

## Similar Successful Books

*A Parade of Ladies* is written in the spirit of *Ollie's Fables*, a series of poetry books emphasizing the rights of women. This collection is unique because it examines the subject matter in an objective manner based on the poet's personal experiences.

Another similar collection is *Peace On Earth*, by Elouise Johnson. *A Parade of Ladies* compares favorably with this book, but extends the subject matter.

## Promotion Ideas

Through her exposure as a leading advocate of women's rights, and a monthly newsletter sent throughout the country to battered women, the poet has a built-in audience for her collections of poetry. *A Family of Flowers* was promoted through the poet's web site at www.standonyourown.com and more than three thousand copies were sold. *A Parade of Ladies* will be promoted through the newsletter and the website and at the poet's speaking appearances.

*(Tip—Attempt to validate that the poet has readers interested in the book either through previous works or media exposure. Agents and publishers know sales are dependent on promotion, promotion, and promotion.)*

## Collection Status

The poet has written sixteen of the poems for the collection. The remaining eight will be completed within two weeks of contract.

*(Tip—Provide the agent or publisher with the status of writing. This shows professionalism and good organizational skills.)*

## Outline
**(Partial List of Poems)**

**John Waterford's Wife Carol**
**Peggy First, A Woman Alone**
**Rex Walter's Girlfriend**
**Pink Dye's Older Sister**
**Wilma Pam's Dead Lover**
**Ralph Johnson's Sister**

**Olivias Creek's Missing Husband**
**Bart Black's Dead**
**Have You Seen Christina Applebaum?**
**Poor Little Red Chambers**

*(Tip—Provides agent or publisher with thumbnail sketch of poetry. Titles are catchy, easy to remember.)*

## Sample Poems

*(Tips—Sample poems will be typed one to a page. If a Cover page is not used, then type in upper left hand corner name, address, telephone number, and e-mail address. Space down six lines or so, center, and print the title of the poem in 18 Font, Bold. The poems will be single-spaced, double-spaced between stanzas. If the poem stretches beyond one page, continue to the next by indicating your name, a keyword from the title of the poem, and the page number at the upper top left hand corner of the page.)*

# John Waterford's Wife Carol *(18 Font, Bold)*


She was a lovely thing, you see,
When John Waterford spied her in the bar,
He was smitten like never before,
Carol was his dream come true.

The wedding was a day to recall,
Special feelings all around,
Four children soon filled the household,
John and Carol, the perfect couple.

But Carol wasn't certain who she was,
A high-school graduate but nothing more,
She wanted to find herself,
When the children left the nest.

An ad for a college caught her eye,
But John laughed at the idea,

Carol raised her voice,
John raised his fist.

Months went by,
Carol afraid to try,
John the roadblock,
To self-respect, a chance to change.

Then God paved the way,
When John was hit by a truck,
She was sad to see him go,
But not that sad.

And then the day arrived,
College student Carol,
How proud she was to be in class,
Her dream instead of his fulfilled.

Six years hence,
And Carol found her way,
She loves life,
Most of all herself.

*(Tip—Use strong words, words that improve pacing of the poem.
Remember that all good stories are love stories.)*

*(Note: Between five and ten poems would follow this one.)*


# Appendix

*(Includes photographs, illustrations, media coverage for the poet, etc.)*

*(Tips—If you are offered a publishing agreement, hire an
entertainment lawyer or utilize the services of a literary agent to
represent you, if you can afford these options. They can best protect
your interests. Regardless, familiarizing yourself with a publishing
agreement can be helpful.)*

# Publishing Agreement

This is an agreement between Poet (hereafter referred to as "Poet") and Afterlife Publishing Company (hereafter referred to as "publisher") regarding the publication of the book titled, *Guardians of the Heavens*.

*(Sets out parties to the agreement and subject matter.)*

**Poet and Publisher agree:**

The poet will write for publication a book tentatively titled *Guardians of the Heavens*. To the publisher, the poet grants all rights including but not limited to the exclusive right to publish, sell, create derivative works and distribute the book during the full term of the copyright and renewals thereof throughout the world and in all languages. The poet reserves the electronic rights and the motion picture and television rights.

*(Details the issuance of rights to book from author or poet to publisher. Tip—Delete the words, "including but not limited to" if possible. This will prevent confusion. Also—If all rights are not being transferred, specify exact countries where publisher can market book. Also—It is important to reserve motion picture and television rights for later sale.)*

**The publisher shall have the right to copyright the book in the name of the poet.**

*(Important that copyright remains in the name of the author or poet. Tip—Never give up that right.)*

The poet will complete and submit to the publisher a manuscript of not more than 100 pages by ____. After the manuscript is accepted by publisher, it shall be published at the publisher's own expense within eighteen months. The publisher reserves the right to prevent publication due to circumstances beyond its control. If they do not publish the book within eighteen months, all rights revert to the poet.

*(Details the conditions for publication including length of manuscript and due date. Also specifies period of time within which publisher can publish book. Tip—Attempt to shorten period of time for publication to one year or less. If possible, pin down publication date. Also—be certain that the reversion clause is included to protect your interests.)*

Publisher will pay to the poet an advance against royalties in the amount of $5,000. Half will be paid upon acceptance of the manuscript and half will be paid on the date the book is published.

*(Sets terms for the advance to be paid to author or poet. Tip—Attempt to obtain as much of advance as possible up front. Also—if possible, add clause specifying that no portion of the advance will be returned to the publisher if they do not publish book.)*

Publisher will pay to the poet royalties based on retail price of the book. The breakdown for such payments shall be: 10 percent of revenues produced by sale of 10,000 books, 12½ percent of revenues produced by the next 5,000 books, and 15 percent of revenues thereafter.

*(Details standard revenue-sharing terms for most books. Tip—Attempt to negotiate "retail price" or "invoice price" as standard for measuring royalties. "Net revenues" will provide less money due to discounts.)*

No royalties shall be paid to poet on copies given to or purchased by the poet, sample copies, damaged copies, returned copies, or copies given away for publicizing the work or to promote sales. Royalties on non-trade special sales may be independently negotiated with the mutual consent of the poet and the publisher.

*(Specifies books that will not be subject to royalties. Tip—Limit this category as much as possible.)*

The publisher shall have the right to reserve a percentage of royalty payments, not to exceed 20 percent, in anticipation of copies of the works being returned by its customers. If the poet has previously submitted to the publisher a work that was subsequently published by the publisher, then publisher has the right to combine royalty statements for multiple works written by the poet for the publisher. If the poet has purchased books from the publisher and has not paid the publisher's invoice, the publisher may deduct the amount due on the invoice from the amount of the royalty due the poet during any royalty payment period.

*(Protection language for the publisher. Tip—Restrict the reservation amount as much as possible. Attempt to bring all revenues owed current after two years.)*

Net proceeds derived from the disposition of "subsidiary rights" shall be divided equally between publisher and poet. They include: digest, abridgment, condensation or selection, book club first and second serialization, reprint edition through another publisher, syndication, translation and foreign language book publication, publication in the English language outside the United States, the right to public display, the right to grant reprints and other uses to third parties, and all other rights and uses now known or hereinafter to become known.

*(Sets out other potential sources for sale of book. Tip—Restrict this clause as much as possible. Delete general languages such as final phrase above concerning "all other rights.")*

The publisher will report on the sale of the work by providing royalty statements on a quarterly basis. All balances due poet shall be paid at that time.

*(Denotes publisher obligation regarding earnings statements. Tip— Even thought most publishers report twice a year, attempt to secure quarterly reporting.)*

The poet is responsible for submitting the manuscript (electronically/floppy disk, and hard copy) including a Table of Contents, Foreword, Epilogue, Appendix materials, and Bibliography. The poet shall also submit suggested photographs

**applicable to the book. Publisher shall be responsible for all costs of printing the book, including the inclusion of photographs.**

*(Details materials to be submitted by author or poet. Tip— Photographs can be expensive so make certain the cost is the responsibility of the publisher.)*

**The poet warrants that he or she is the owner of the work and has full power and authority to copyright it and make this arrangement. He or she asserts further that the work does not infringe any copyright, trademark, trade secret, or other intellectual property, violate any property rights, or right of privacy, or contain any scandalous, libelous, or unlawful matter. The poet agrees to defend, indemnify, and hold harmless the publisher against all claims, suits, costs, damages, and expenses that the publisher may sustain by reason of any scandalous, libelous, or unlawful matter contained or alleged to be contained in the work, or any infringement or violation by the work of any copyright or property right; and until such claim or lawsuit has been settled or withdrawn, the publisher may withhold any sums due to the poet under this agreement.**

*(Asserts publisher's rights if publication is challenged. Tip— publishers will insist on this clause. It will be a deal breaker.)*

**The publisher shall have the right to edit the work for publication, but the poet shall have final approval of the text prior to release of the book. The poet shall also have final right of approval over the cover art and text, back, front, inside front, and inside back, and the photographic insert, if any.**

*(Language re approvals. Tip—Many publisher agreements do not provide author or poet with final approvals. Seek to gain this right.)*

**The publisher shall provide twenty-five copies of the book free to the poet.**

*(Poet free copies. Tip—Attempt to induce publisher to provide as many free copies as possible for give-aways as well as personal use.)*

If the work is not in print for a period of six months or the publisher declares that the work is no longer worthy of print for continued sale, all rights revert to the poet. He or she may purchase all remaining copies of the book at publisher's cost. He or she may also obtain from publisher all plates, books, sheets, and photographs.

*(Out of print circumstances. Tip—Require publisher to relinquish rights to book if it does not sell a certain amount of copies per year.)*

The poet agrees that during the term of this agreement he or she will not agree to publish a work on the same subject that will conflict with the sale of this book.

*(Key terminology is "conflict with the sale of this book." Tip—Make certain language is definitive regarding this point.)*

The poet agrees to submit their next work first to publisher for their evaluation. Publisher shall have thirty days to either agree to negotiate in good faith a publishing agreement or decline to do so.

*("Next book" language. Tip—Avoid if possible.)*

The poet agrees to provide publisher with an eight by ten snapshot. He or she also agrees to promote the book as requested by the publisher. This includes interviews for newspaper, radio, television, book signings, and other promotional events. Publisher shall be responsible for all expenses incurred by poet to promote the book. Publisher agrees to expend $___ to promote and market the book.

*(Sets out poet obligation. Tip—Keep language as broad as possible. Attempt to bind publisher to expend x dollars to promote book.)*

The poet designates Sleepy Time Literary Agency as his or her representative. All revenues due poet and other correspondence with the agency shall be forwarded through its address at 345 Park Avenue, New York, New York 20002.

*(Designates poet's literary representative.)*

This agreement constitutes the entire agreement between the parties. It supercedes any oral or written proposals, negotiations and discussions. The agreement may not be altered in any form without the express, written consent of all parties to the agreement.

*(Standard language)*

This agreement is binding and shall inure to the benefit of the heirs, executors, administrators, or designees of the poet and to the assigns of the publisher. The poet may assign their rights under this agreement as they wish. The publisher cannot do so without the written consent of the poet.

*(Specifies future rights. Tip—If possible, do not permit the publisher to assign the rights to the book with your consent.)*

This agreement shall be binding under the laws of the state of Massachusetts. Any and all conflict shall be first submitted to the American Arbitration Association.

*(Provides guidelines re conflict resolution. Tip—Attempt to include languages providing your state as governing body for law.)*

Signed this _____ day of ___, ____.

_____
**Afterlife Publications**

_____
**Poet**

# Publisher Submission Record

**Document: Book Proposal—*A Parade of Ladies*** *(Tip—Prepare one sheet for each submission. Print and collect in loose-leave notebook marked "Submissions.")*

**Submission Date -**         June 12, __

**Agent/Publisher Information -**         Rosalie Thompkins Agency
56 West 57th Street
New York, NY 20002
212-789-7890
RThompkinsAgency@aol.com

**Contact at Agent/Publisher -**         Jeanette Furber, Agent

**Four – Six Week Reaction -**         No response, telephoned agency. Spoke with Furber's assistant. Proposal in stack to be read. Estimated time—two weeks.

**Follow-up -**         6/17-Furber's assistant telephoned. Requested full collection of poetry. Forwarded by Fed Ex.

**Revisions, if any -**         _____
_____
_____
_____
_____

**Decision -**         Hooray! Jeanette has agreed to represent book. Suggested revisions being forwarded.

**Outcome -** Revisions completed. Submitted to Jeanette. She submitted it to four publishers. Riverhead books' offer accepted. Hooray again!

*(Tip—First submit material to four or five literary agents. Follow-up, keep four to five in play at a time. If no positive response, then repeat process to selected editors at publishing companies. Continue process until successful, but keep good records for future use.)*

# Bibliography/Recommended Reading

How To Write a Book Proposal, Michael Larsen, Writer's Digest Books, Cincinnati, Ohio, 1997

Jack Kerouac, Selected Letters, Edited by Ann Charters, Penguin, New York, 1996

Novel Ideas, Barbara Shoup and Margaret Love Denman, Alpha Books, Indianapolis, Indiana, 2001

On Writing, Stephen King, Scribner's, New York City, 2001

On Writing Well, William Zinsser, HarperCollins, New York, 2001

1,818 Ways To Write Better and Get Published, Scott Edelstein, Writer's Digest Books, Cincinnati, 1991

The Complete Guide To Book Publicity, Jodee Blanco, Allworth Press, New York, 2000

The First Five Pages: A Writer's Guide to Staying Out of the Rejection Pile, Noah Lukeman, Simon and Schuster, 2003

The Writer's Chapbook, George Plimpton et al, The Modern Library, New York, 1999

Twentieth Century Dictionary of Quotations, Edited by The Princeton Language Institute, The Philip Lief Group, Bantam Doubleday Dell Publishing Group, New York City, 1993

Writer's Guide To Book Editors, Publishers, and Literary Agents, Jeff Herman, Prima Publishing, 2002

Writing Down The Bones, Natalie Goldberg, Shambhala, Boston and London, 1986

# Resources

Daniel Alderson, Talking Back To Poems: A Working Guide for the Aspiring Poet

Briggs, John, Fire in the Crucible: The Self-creation of Creativity and Genius

Brande, Dorothea, Becoming A Writer

Burroway, Janet, Writing Fiction: A Guide to Narrative Craft

Buzan, Tony, Use Both Sides of the Brain

Epel, Naomi, Writers Dreaming

Forster, E. M. Aspects of a Novel

Hartwell Fiske, Robert, The Dictionary of Concise Writing: 10,000 Alternatives to Wordy Phrases

Hemingway, Ernest, A Moveable Feast

Hirsch, Edward, How to Read a Poem and Fall in Love with Poetry

Keyes, Ralph, The Courage To Write; How Writers Transcend Fear

Maisell, Eric, Staying Sane In The Arts

May, Rollo, The Courage to Create

Nachmanovitch, Steven, Free Style Improvisation in Life and Art

Perry, Aaren Yeatts, Poetry Across the Curriculum

Rico, Gabrielle Lusser, Writing the Natural Way

Uleland, Brenda, If You Want To Write

Welty, Eudora, One Writers' Beginnings

# Recommended Poets and Poetry Books

Alberti, Rafael (*Looking for Poetry*);
Alexie, Sherman (*First Indian on the Moon*);
Apollinaire, Guillaume (*Selected*);
Ashberry, John (*Self Portrait in a Convex Mirror*);
Atwood, Margaret (*Good Bones and Simple Murder*);
Baus, Eric (*The to Sound*);
Bishop, Elizabeth (*Geography III*);
Blake, William (*The Marriage of Heaven and Hell*);
Bly, Robert (*Eating the Honey of Words; translations of Jimenez, Machado, Kabir*);
Borges, Jorge Luis (*Selected*);
Brautigan Richard (*Trout Fishing in America*);
Breton, Andre (*Earthlight*);
Brooks, Gwendolyn (*Selected Poems*);
Bukowski, Charles (*Run with the Hunted*);
Carver, Raymond (*All of Us*);
Collier, Michael (*The Folded Heart*);
Creeley, Robert (*Collected Poems*);
Cummings, E.E. (*Complete Poems*);
de Nerval, Gerard (*Aurelia*);
Dickinson, Emily (*Complete Poems*);
Di Prima, Diane (*Selected Poems*);
Dobyns, Stephen (*Velocities*);
Donne, John (*Collected*);
Duhamel, Denise (*Queen for a Day*);
Edson, Russell (*The Tunnel*);
Eluard, Paul (*Selected*);
Erdrich, Louise (*Baptism of Desire*);
Factor, Jenny (*Unraveling at the Name*);
Fanning, Roger (*Homesick*);
Fried, Daisy (*She Didn't Mean to Do It*);
Frost, Robert (*North of Boston*);
Gander, Forrest (*Science & Steepleflower*);
Gass, William H. (*In the Heart of the Heart of the Country*);
Ginsberg, Allen (*Collected Poems*);
Hass, Robert (*Human Wishes*);
Hoagland, Tony (*Donkey Gospel*);

Kalamaras, George (*Borders My Bent Toward*);
Keats, John (*Collected*);
Hayes, Terrance (*Muscular Music*);
Hughes, Langston (*Collected Poems*);
Jordan, A. Van (*Rise*);
Kasischke, Laura (*Fire & Flower*);
Kerouac, Jack (*Pomes All Sizes*);
Knight, Ethridge (*The Essential Ethridge Knight*);
Koertge, Ron (*Making Love to Roget's Wife*);
Kovacik, Karen (*Beyond the Velvet Curtain*);
Larkin, Phillip (*Collected*);
Laux, Dorianne (*What We Carry*);
Lee, Li-Young (*The City in Which I Love You*);
Lewis, Lisa (*The Unbeliever*);
Lux, Thomas (*New and Selected*);
Mallarmé, Stéphane (*Collected Poems*);
Moore, Marianne (*Complete Poems*);
Neruda, Pablo (*The Book of Questions*);
Notley, Alice (*The Decent of Alette*);
O'Hara, Frank (*Collected or Lunch Poems*);
Olds, Sharon (*The Father*);
Oppen, George (*New Collected Poems*);
Orlen, Steve (*This Particular Eternity*);
Parra, Nicanor (*Selected*);
Plath, Sylvia (*Ariel*)
Pound, Ezra (*Personae*);
Rice, Stan (*Fear Itself*);
Rilke, Rainer Maria (*Selected Poems*);
Rimbaud, Arthur (*A Season in Hell and Illuminations*);
Roethke, Theodore (*The Lost Son and Other Poems*);
Seaton, Maureen (*Little Ice Ages*);
Sexton, Anne (*The Complete Poems*),
Shakespeare, William (*Various collections*)
Shepard, Sam (*Hawk Moon*);
Simic, Charles (*The World Doesn't End, The Book of Gods and Devils*);
Snyder, Gary (*The Gary Snyder Reader*);
Spicer, Jack (*Collected Books*);
Stafford, William (*The Darkness Around Us is Deep*);
Stevens, Wallace (*Collected Poems*)

Szporluk, Larissa (*Dark Sky Questions*);
Takahashi, Shinkichi (*Triumph of the Sparrow*);
Tate, James (*Memoir of the Hawk*);
Trakl, Georg (*Autumn Sonata*);
Transtromer, Tomas (*Selected Poems*);
Valentine, Jean (*Growing Darkness, Growing Light*);
Vallejo, César (*Selected Poems*);
Voigt, Ellen Bryant (*Kyrie*);
Wenderoth, Joe (*Letters to Wendy's*);
Whitman, Walt (*Leaves of Grass*);
Williams, William Carlos (*Selected Poems*),
Wright, C.D. (*Steal Away*);
Wright, Franz (*The Beforelife*);
Wright, James (*Above the River: The Complete Poems*);
Young, Dean (*Skid*)

# Recommended
# Poetry Guides, Anthologies, Textbooks
# And Essay Collections

Addonizio, Kim and Laux, Dorianne. *The Poet's Companion*. Norton, 1997.

Behn, Robin and Twichell, Chase. *The Practice of Poetry*. HarperCollins, 1992.

Bly, Robert. *American Poetry, Wildness and Domesticity*. Harper & Row, 1990.

Bly, Robert. *Leaping Poetry*. Beacon, 1975.

Bly, Robert. *News of the Universe*. Sierra Club Books, 1995.

Brotchie, Alastair. *A Book of Surrealist Games*. Shambhala, 1995.

Collom, Jack and Sheryl Noethe. *Poetry Everywhere*. Teachers and Writers Collective, 1995.

Drury, John. *The Poetry Dictionary*. Story Press, 1995.

Dobyns, Stephen. *Best Words, Best Order*. St. Martins Press, 1996.

Guth, Hans, Rico, Gabriele. *Discovering Poetry*. Blair Press, 1993.

Gwynn, R.S. *Poetry, a Longman Pocket Anthology*. Longman, 1998.

Hall, Donald. *Claims for Poetry*. University of Michigan, 1982.

Hass Robert. *Twentieth Century Pleasures*. The Ecco Press, 1984.

Hugo, Richard. *The Triggering Town*. Norton, 1979.

Kennedy, X.J. *An Introduction to Poetry*, HarperCollins, 1994.

Kowit, Steve. *In the Palm of Your Hand*. Tilbury House, 1995.

Lehman, David. *Great American Prose Poems*. Scribner, 2003.

Levertov, Denise. *New and Selected Essays*. New Directions, 1992.

Lewis, Richard. *Still Waters of the Air: Poems by Three Modern Spanish Poets (Lorca, Jimenez, Machado)*. Dial Press, 1970.

Lorca, Frederico Garcia. *In Search of Duende*. New Directions, 1998.

Marshall, Tod. *Range of the Possible: Conversations with Contemporary Poets*.

Eastern Washington University, 2002.

Mayes, Francis. *The Discovery of Poetry*. Harcourt, 2001.

Olson, Charles. *Selected Writings*. New Directions, 1966.

Oliver, Mary. *A Poetry Handbook*. Harcourt Brace, 1994.

Nims, John Frederick. *Western Wind*. McGraw-Hill, 1992.

Oates, Joyce Carol. *Telling Stories: An Anthology for Writers*. Norton, 1998

Rexroth, Kenneth. *Love and the Turning Year: One Hundred More Poems from the     Chinese*. New Directions, 1970.

Timpane, John. *Poetry for Dummies*. Wiley, 2001.

Waldman, Anne. *The Beat Book*. Shambhala, 1999.

Wallace, Robert. *Writing Poems*. HarperCollins, 1991.

Williams, William Carlos. *Selected Essays*. New Directions, 1969.

# Credits

Bly, Robert, "Driving to Town Late to Mail a Letter," "The Russian," and "The Face in the Toyota" from *Eating the Honey of Words*. Copyright 1999 by Robert Bly. "Rembrandt's Portrait of Titus with a Red Hat" and "The Difficult Word" from The Night Abraham Called to the Stars. Copyright 2001 by Robert Bly. All reprinted with permission of HarperCollins Publishers.

Li-Young Lee, "A Story" from *The City In Which I Love You*. Copyright 1990 by Li-Yoiung Lee. "Early in the Morning," "Persimmons," "Eating Alone," and "Eating Together" from *Rose*. Copyright 1986 by Li-Young Lee. All reprinted with permission of BOA Editions, Ltd., www.boaeditions.org.

Karen Kovacik, "What My Father Taught Me About Sex," "Herman Kafka's Dinnertime Pantoum," "Come as You Are," and "Nixon on the Pleasure of Undressing a Woman" from *Beyond the Velvet Curtain*. Copyright 1999 by Karen Kovacik. Published by Kent State Press. "Jankowice, Poland," courtesy of Karen Kovacik. All reprinted with permission of Karen Kovacik.

# Notes

To Order Copies of Poetry Report, Book Report, Grammar Report, My Book Proposal, or DVD Copies of Mark Shaw's "How To Become A Published Author or Poet: A to Z  Seminars:"

Telephone Books For Life Foundation 970-544-3398

E-mail at help@booksforlifefoundation.com,

Visit Books For Life Foundation at 450 South Galena Street, Aspen, Colorado

Write Books For Life Foundation at P. O Box CC, Aspen, Colorado 81611

---

## Seminars, Speaking Engagements

Jim Walker, Mark Shaw and other Books For Life Foundation staff members and advisors are available to conduct seminars focusing on writing tips, publishing strategies, and storytelling ideas at high schools, colleges, universities, libraries, writer's centers, writer's groups, youth groups, senior centers, corporations, and legal organizations. For more information, visit www.booksforlifefoundation.com.

# Jim Walker

Jim Walker is a poet, photographer, writing teacher who has published his work in many national literary magazines and newspapers. His self-published chapbook, *Down*, features a cross section of his poetry written in the last ten years. A creative writing instructor at Indiana University's campus in Indianapolis, Indiana, Mr. Walker received his training in poetry at the well-regarded MFA program at Warren Wilson College in Asheville, North Carolina. He lives in Indianapolis with his wife and two young children.

# Mark Shaw

Mark Shaw is a former lawyer turned author with fourteen published books. They include *Book Report, Grammar Report, Poetry Report, From Birdies To Bunkers, Miscarriage of Justice, Let The Good Times Roll, The Jonathan Pollard Story, Larry Legend, Testament To Courage, The Perfect Yankee, Bury Me In A Pot Bunker,* and *Forever Flying.*

Mr. Shaw is a literary consultant, and creative director of Books For Life Foundation. Along with his canine pal, Black Sox, he lives in Aspen Colorado. More about Mark Shaw and contact information is available at www.markshaw.com or www.booksforlifefoundation.com

# Poetry Report

Written *by* a published poet and a published author *for* aspiring poets, Poetry Report provides practical advice for every poet who dreams of becoming published. Guaranteed to inspire, Poetry Report is the only guide you'll ever need.

---

## You'll learn:

- Alternative Forms Of Poetry So You Can Choose The Right Style For You

- How To Create Unique Themes for Your Poetry

- How To Improve Poetry Skills Through Exercises

- What Publishing Alternative Is Best For You

- Why It Is Important To Market The Poetry Book Proposal, Not The Book

- How To Choose The Right Publisher

- How To Protect Yourself With Agency And Publishing Contracts

---

# Praise For *Book Report*,
# Companion To *Poetry Report*

"Mark Shaw tells it like it is, straight and to the point."

Jodee Blanco, Author,
*The Complete Guide To Book Publicity*

"*Book Report* is a timely, welcome, and thoroughly 'user friendly' advice guide which is very highly recommended reading for aspiring authors and poets."

*Midwest Book Review*

"Your *Book Report* was just what we needed. Of the self-help books we've read, yours is the easiest to follow and implement. We love the way you push the reader toward success. We will be published."
Poet Brian Terrel, Indiana

"Chatting with you about *Book Report* increased my enthusiasm levels enormously."

Kerrie Ashcroft, Australia

Printed in the United States
15791LVS00002B/1-69

Library of Congress Control Number: 2019933612

ISBN 978-1-338-20416-2 (hardcover)
ISBN 978-1-338-20415-5 (paperback)

10 9 8 7 6 5 4 3 2          21 22 23 24

Printed in China    62
First edition, August 2020
Edited by Cassandra Pelham Fulton
Book design by Phil Falco
Publisher: David Saylor

KEBECHET WAS THE
DAUGHTER OF ANUBIS,
GUARDIAN OF THE
AFTERLIFE.

UNLIKE ANUBIS'S
HEART, WHICH HAD
LONG SINCE TURNED
TO SAND AND WAS
THEREFORE DRAINED OF
ANY COMPASSION SAVE
FOR THE LOVE OF HIS
DAUGHTER, KEBECHET'S
HEART WAS STILL
WHOLE AND PURE.

TO AVOID HER
BECOMING LIKE HIM,
ANUBIS TASKED
KEBECHET WITH THE
CLEANSING OF NEW
SOULS BEFORE THEY
WERE GRANTED
PASSAGE INTO THE
UNDERWORLD.

BEFORE MEETING ANUBIS, EVERY SOUL WAS GIVEN A SMALL VASE OF WATER; THE AMOUNT OF WATER BROUGHT BEFORE ANUBIS WOULD HELP HIM DETERMINE IF THAT SOUL WAS MEANT FOR THE AFTERLIFE OR IF THEIR TIME WAS BETTER SUITED FOR A LATER DATE.

KNOWING THAT HIS DAUGHTER COULD BE USED AS A BARGAINING CHIP FOR IMMORTALITY, ANUBIS GIFTED KEBECHET WITH A SWORD: A BLACK-BLADED KHOPESH THAT SHE WAS REQUIRED TO KEEP BY HER SIDE AT ALL TIMES.

IF EVER THREATENED OR ATTACKED, KEBECHET WAS TO USE THE SWORD TO DEFEND HERSELF, SENDING THAT SOUL DIRECTLY TO ANUBIS WITH NO WATER. ANY SOUL BROUGHT TO ANUBIS WITH A VASE AS DRY AS HIS HEART WAS DENIED PASSAGE INTO THE UNDERWORLD AND INSTEAD CAST OUT INTO THE NOTHINGNESS.

BUT ANUBIS HAD
LONG SINCE LOST HIS
UNDERSTANDING OF A
PURE HEART AND
WAS UNABLE TO SEE
THAT KEBECHET
WOULD NEVER BE
ABLE TO USE SUCH
A WEAPON.

TO PLEASE HER FATHER,
KEBECHET STILL KEPT
THE SWORD BY HER
SIDE, HOPING SHE'D
NEVER HAVE NEED OF IT.

IT HAS BEEN SAID THAT IF THE
SWORD OF KEBECHET IS EVER
FOUND, IT MEANS KEBECHET NO
LONGER CLEANSES THE SOULS OF
THE AFTERLIFE AND AN IMMORTAL
NOW WALKS AMONG THE LIVING.

LIFE SIGNS?
ZERO
EXCELLENT.
THE POWER OF THE GOLDEN LION CONTINUES TO IMPRESS.
MAKE A COURSE FOR CADA'DUUN TO REPLENISH THE PLASMA WEAPON.
WHAT DO YOU MEAN, SOMETHING IS HAPPENING ON CADA'DUUN?

# CHAPTER ONE

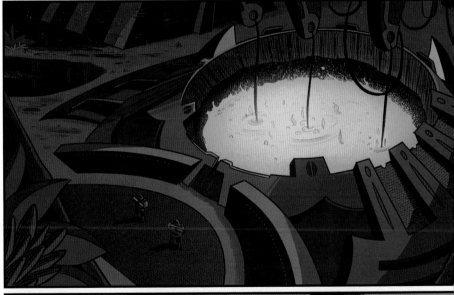

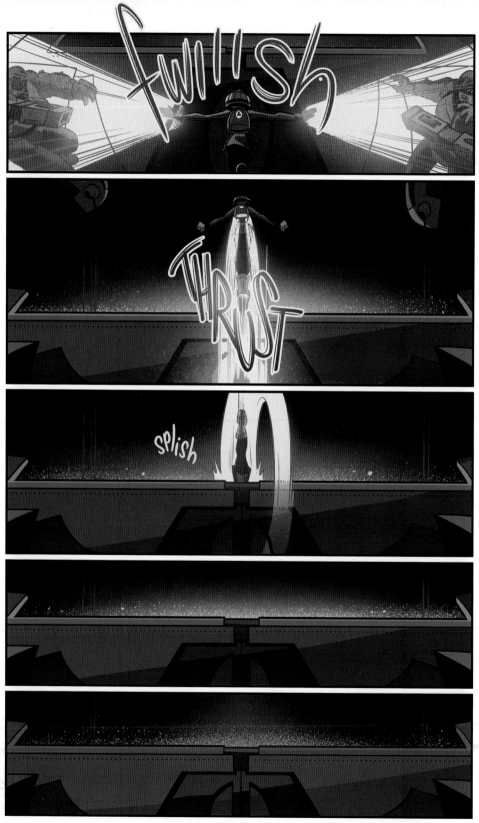

UGH.

I CAN'T BELIEVE I'M STILL GETTING TALKED INTO BEING TELEPORTED.

KI KI!

MOM!

DAD!

YOU'RE SAFE.

AH!

BLAZT!

CLEOPATRA!

WHERE'S YOUR JETPACK?

DESTROYED WHEN I COOLED THE GOLDEN LION PLASMA!

MINE IS LOW ON FUEL.

AND THIS BASIN IS CAVING IN.

CAN YOU REACH ME?

I'LL TRY!

RRUMBLE

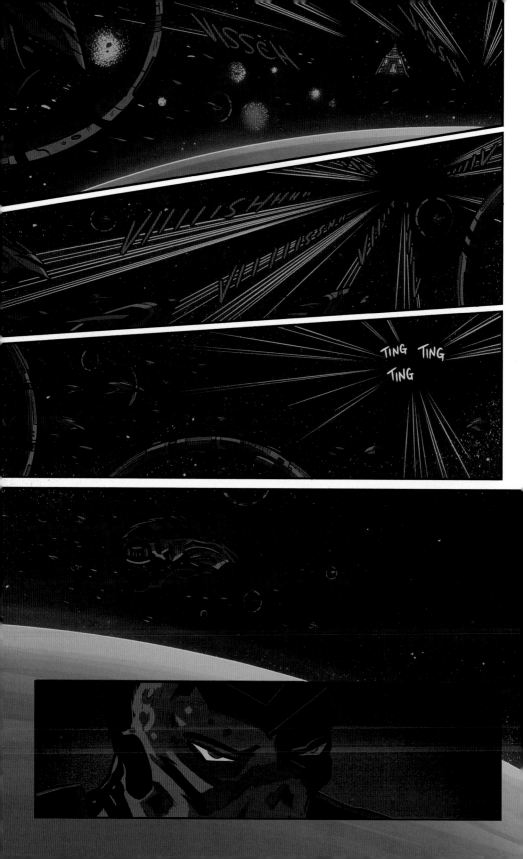

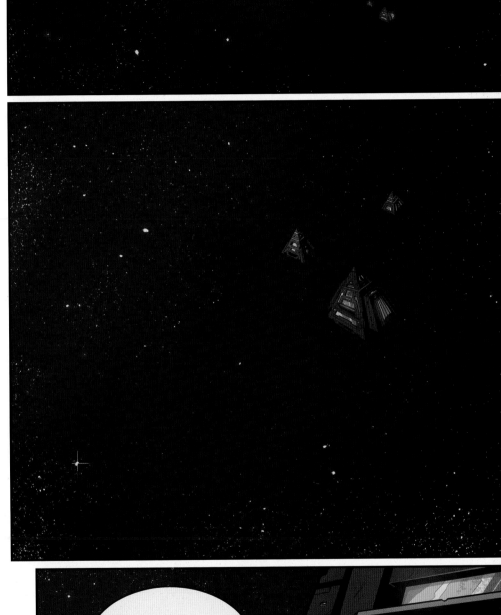

IT'S BEEN TWO WEEKS AND OUR SCIENTISTS HAVEN'T DETECTED ANY TRACE OF THE GOLDEN LION PLASMA LEFT ON CADA'DUUN.

THE PLAN WORKED. WITHOUT AN ENERGY SOURCE TO POWER IT, OCTAVIAN'S SUPER-WEAPON WILL BE ALL BUT USELESS TO HIM NOW.

IT WAS A RARE WIN. BUT THE COST...

JAVEL...

HASILRIG.

AND EVERYTHING ELSE.

I KNOW THE CADA'DUUNIANS WERE FULLY ON BOARD WITH THIS MISSION, BUT AS ADMINISTRANT, YOU CAN'T IGNORE THE TOLL IT'S TAKING ON THE GALAXY. ANOTHER CIVILIZATION WITHOUT A HOME.

ANOTHER DISPLACED TRIBE.

JUST BUILDINGS, KHENSU. THEY CAN REBUILD.

WE CAN REBUILD.

SOME THINGS AREN'T AS EASILY REPAIRABLE AS BUILDINGS, MSAMAKI.

WE AREN'T TALKING ABOUT THE MISSION ANYMORE, ARE WE?

SHE'S STILL SO YOUNG AND HAS SEEN MORE LOSS IN THIS UNENDING WAR WITH OCTAVIAN THAN WE EVER DID BEFORE SHE ARRIVED.

Sit

IT'S NOT FAIR.

LIFE'S NOT FAIR, KHENSU. ALL ANY OF US CAN DO IS FLUFF UP OUR FUR AND AWAIT THE UNIVERSE'S NEXT CHALLENGE WITH BRAVERY AND HUMILITY.

AN ATTEMPT TO CONTROL FATE ONLY INCITES DESPAIR.

YOU...UM... MISSED ANOTHER ONE OF MY HISTORY LESSONS.

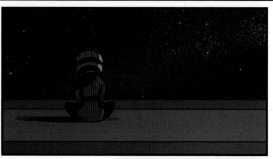

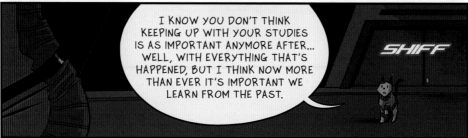

I KNOW YOU DON'T THINK KEEPING UP WITH YOUR STUDIES IS AS IMPORTANT ANYMORE AFTER... WELL, WITH EVERYTHING THAT'S HAPPENED, BUT I THINK NOW MORE THAN EVER IT'S IMPORTANT WE LEARN FROM THE PAST.

SHIFF

THERE ARE MANY OF US-- MOST OF US, ACTUALLY-- WHO FEEL WE CAN LEARN A LOT FROM YOU AS WELL.

THE PROPHECY STILL STATES THAT THE QUEEN OF THE NILE WILL LIGHT THE DARKNESS THAT--

STOP IT!

JUST...

STOP IT, KHENSU.

LOOK AT WHAT'S BECOME OF THIS GALAXY SINCE I'VE BEEN HERE. OCTAVIAN OCCUPIES THE AILUROS SYSTEM. BOTH JAVEL AND HASILRIG ARE DEAD...

YOUR MOM.

AND THE WORST PART IS NONE OF THEM EVEN LIKED ME VERY MUCH. THEY WERE THE ONES WHO KNEW BETTER.

KNEW THAT I SHOULDN'T BE HERE IN THE FIRST PLACE.

OKAY. SOMEONE NEEDS TO SHOW ME HOW LOCKS WORK ON THESE DOORS.

IT'S REALLY SIMPLE. YOU JUST HAVE TO ENTER THE DIGITS: FOUR, FIVE, THREE, TWO...

UM...

RIGHT. I'LL SHOW YOU SOMETIME.

CHIRP!

LEAP

purrr

SORRY, PROFESSOR. WE DIDN'T MEAN TO INTERRUPT.

IT'S ALL RIGHT, AKILA.

I WAS JUST ABOUT TO TAKE MY LEAVE.

YOU TOLD ME NOT TOO LONG AGO THAT YOU ARE NOT IMPORTANT. THAT THE PEOPLE OF MAYET ARE. BUT WE ARE ALL IMPORTANT, CLEO. EVEN YOU.

DON'T LOSE SIGHT OF THAT.

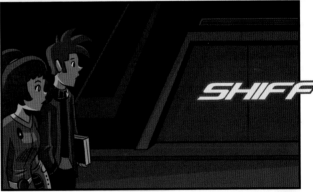

SHIFF

SPEAKING OF SOMETHING IMPORTANT, I FEEL LIKE **THAT'S** WHAT WE INTERRUPTED.

SO ARE YOU BOTH HERE TO GIVE ME SOME HORRIBLY STRAINED PEP TALK AS WELL?

UM...ACTUALLY, WE CAME TO WISH YOU A *HAPPY BIRTHDAY.*

CHIRP!

OH.

YOU FORGOT AGAIN, DIDN'T YOU?

WELL...

OKAY. YES.

BUT IT'S NOT JUST THAT.

WHERE I'M FROM, A BIRTHDAY WASN'T JUST A CELEBRATION OF ANOTHER YEAR ON EARTH.

OR IN THIS CASE, A DETACHED, FLOATING SCHOOL BUILDING.

A BIRTHDAY MEANT EXTRA RESPONSIBILITIES. PEOPLE EXPECTED MORE FROM YOU.

I WAS A REGENT BEFORE THE TIME TABLETS BROUGHT ME HERE, RULING BESIDE MY DAD. HE WAS DEALING WITH A LOT FROM OUTSIDE OF EGYPT AND WAS THROWING MORE AND MORE AT ME. JUST IN CASE HE...WELL, JUST IN CASE HE COULDN'T DO IT HIMSELF ANYMORE.

I WASN'T THE BEST-BEHAVED DAUGHTER, NOR DID I HAVE ANY EAGERNESS TO RULE EGYPT. I WASN'T EVEN SURE I WANTED TO STAY *IN* EGYPT. I DIDN'T TREAT A LOT OF MY DUTIES AS REGENT VERY SERIOUSLY. THE DAY I WAS OUT SLINGING PEBBLES AT LIZARDS--THE DAY I TOUCHED THE UTA TABLET--MY DAD WAS OUTSIDE THE KINGDOM DEALING WITH AN INVADING EMPIRE.

THAT MEANS... WHEN I ARRIVED HERE...

THERE'S A GOOD CHANCE...

I COULD HAVE BEEN A QUEEN.

THE PROPHECY!

QUEEN OF THE NILE!

I KNOW.

I KNOW.

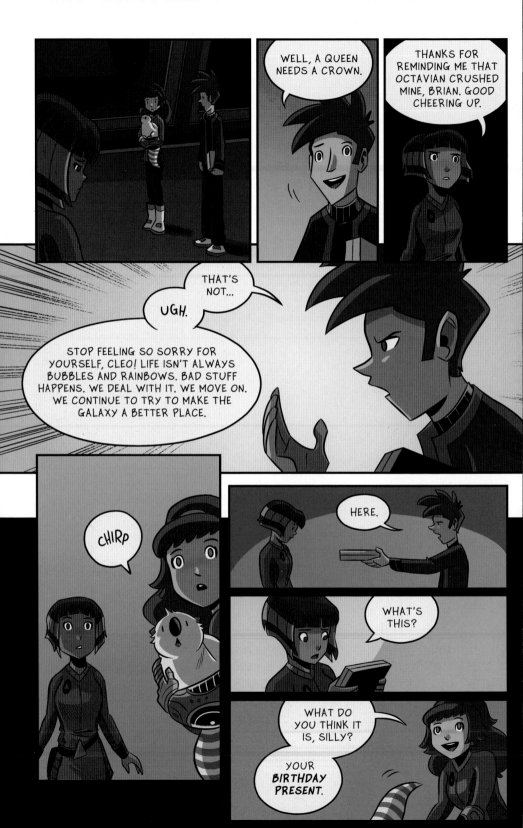

!

HOW...?

IT'S A REPLICA, OBVIOUSLY. WE BOTH KNEW HOW ATTACHED YOU WERE TO THE ORIGINAL.

YOU HARDLY EVER TOOK IT OFF.

IT...IT WAS AN HEIRLOOM.

WE WERE HOPING IT MIGHT...YOU KNOW...

UM...

GET YOU OUT OF YOUR FUNK.

WOW, YOU EVEN GOT THE IBIS JUST RIGHT.

THONIS
REMOTE, PREVIOUSLY UNPOPULATED PLANET ON
THE OUTERMOST EDGE OF THE NILE GALAXY

VRRR— CHACK

LAND!

CHIRP!

PRECIOUS NON-EXPLODING LAND! OH, HOW I MISSED YOU!

UH, CLEO?

PURRRR

53

UM...

WHY ARE THEY ALL STARING AT ME?

YOU'RE THE QUEEN OF THE NILE, CLEO. SAVIOR OF THE GALAXY. PROPHESIED DEFEATER OF OCTAVIAN.

AND YOU ARE ROLLING AROUND IN THE GRASS.

54

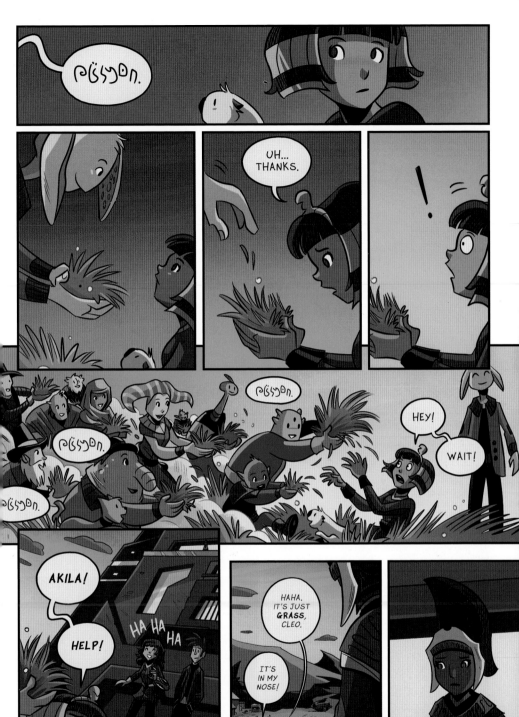

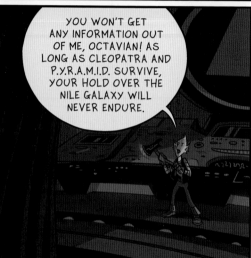

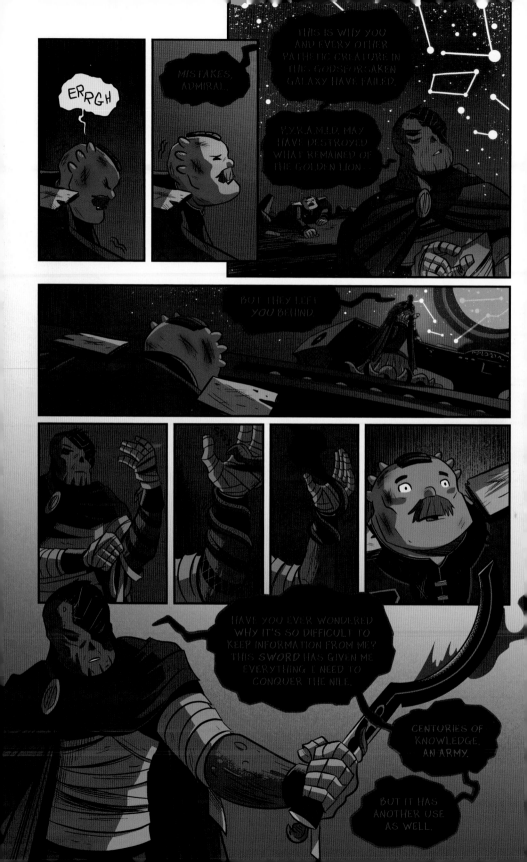

VISSSCH

SSSCH

MY VICTORY IS NOT A BELIEF, ADMIRAL.

IT IS AN EVENTUALITY.

TING

HE IS CORRECT, OCTAVIAN.

AS LONG AS THE GIRL LIVES, OUR PLANS REMAIN THREATENED.

NOT TO WORRY, MY LORD...

THERE'S NOWHERE LEFT FOR HER TO GO.

THE TECHNOLOGY IS SOMETHING I'VE BEEN THEORIZING FOR A WHILE. IT'S ONLY IN THE PAST YEAR THAT I WAS ABLE TO CRACK HOW TO INVENT IT.

A CLOAKING DEVICE THAT USES A COMPLEX ALGORITHM ORIGINATING FROM THE SAME CALCULATIONS WE USED TO FIGURE OUT THE DEFENSE SHIELD THAT SURROUNDED MAYET.

STEALTH PLANET.

*CLOAKED* PLANET.

WAIT. *THAT'S* WHY YOU DISAPPEARED DIRECTLY AFTER THE ATTACK ON MAYET.

I WAS WORKING ON IT HERE.

P.Y.R.A.M.I.D. HAS BEEN BRINGING REFUGEES TO THIS PLANET AS A SAFE HAVEN EVER SINCE.

YOU KNEW ABOUT IT, TOO?

IT HASN'T BEEN EASY TO COMMUNICATE WITH YOU THIS YEAR, CLEO. YOU'VE BEEN...

DISTANT.

I'M SORRY.

THIS...

**ALL** OF THIS...

IT'S MY...

IT'S **NOT**. IT'S NOT YOUR FAULT, CLEO. NO ONE COULD HAVE KNOWN OCTAVIAN HAD MULTIPLE PLASMA WEAPONS OVER MAYET THAT DAY.

YOU NEED TO STOP BLAMING YOURSELF.

IT'S MORE THAN THAT. I...

BLIP

HERE'S YOUR, UM...THING.

THINGS WERE BETTER ON HYKOSIS.

HYKOSIS?

HUFF
HUFF

THERE'S PEOPLE FROM HYKOSIS HERE?

SURVIVORS?

THERE'S PEOPLE FROM **EVERYWHERE** HERE.

I KNOW WHAT YOU'RE HOPING, CLEO, BUT P.Y.R.A.M.I.D. KEEPS A PRETTY THOROUGH LOG OF WHO LANDS ON THIS PLANET. NO ONE MATCHING ANTONY'S PROFILE HAS COME THROUGH THAT ATMOSPHERE.

BELIEVE ME. I'VE CHECKED.

EVERY DAY.

NOT **EVERY** DAY, BRIAN.

HE MAY NOT HAVE EVEN BEEN IN HYKOSIS CITY, YOU KNOW.

YEAH...

WHY THIS PLANET?

THAT DESERT OUT THERE MAKES **ASTEROIDS** SEEM LIKE PARADISE.

THERE HAD TO BE OTHER PLACES IN THE NILE THAT WERE, UH...

COZIER.

I ASSUMED IT HAD SOMETHING TO DO WITH LOCATION?

AT LEAST YOU GOT LUCKY FINDING THIS OASIS.

UM...YEAH. NOT SO MUCH LUCK AS IT IS **SCIENCE**.

IT'S WHAT POWERS THE PLANET'S CLOAK. BECAUSE OF THE GENERAL INSTABILITY OF ITS PROPERTIES, I COULDN'T RISK TESTING ANYWHERE WITH INDIGENOUS LIFE, SO I HAD TO FIND THE MOST REMOTE YET SUSTAINABLE PLANET IN THE NILE.

PLANET THONIS.

MOM?

YOU **KNEW** ABOUT THIS?!

HAH.

NOW YOU KNOW HOW IT FEELS.

DON'T TALK TO YOUR MOTHER LIKE THAT, KI KI.

DAD??

CHIRP!

MIHOS???

ET TU?

THIS IS PRICELESS.

HI THERE, CLEOPATRA.

HI, AKILA'S DAD.

SINA AND TULUK, DEAR.

RIGHT.

TAK TAK TAK

**YOU** DIDN'T KNOW ANYTHING ABOUT THIS, DID YOU?

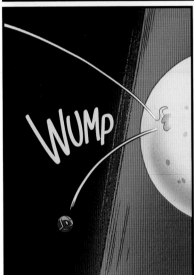

SO THAT LAKE AND ALL THE VEGETATION ABOVE IS A RESULT OF THIS BEING DOWN HERE, ISN'T IT? JUST LIKE ON CADA'DUUN.

AND A COMPLETELY UNINTENTIONAL SIDE EFFECT OF THE CLOAK TESTING. TOOK ONLY THIS SMALL AMOUNT OF PLASMA TO CREATE ALL OF THE ABOVE. THONIS WAS COMPLETELY BARREN BEFORE THAT.

THE REFUGEES HAVE EVEN BEGUN CALLING THE OASIS *FEIRAN*. SOME ANCIENT WORD HAVING TO DO WITH REBIRTH.

THEY OWE A LOT TO SINA AND TULUK FOR EXCAVATING WHAT WE HAVE HERE BEFORE OCTAVIAN SEIZED THE REST OF THE SUPPLY.

SUCH A SHAME WE HAD TO DESTROY THE SOURCE.

WE DISCUSSED THIS, SINA. THE GOLDEN LION WAS FAR TOO DANGEROUS IN OCTAVIAN'S HANDS. THANKS TO CLEOPATRA, WE NOW HAVE AN EDGE FOR THE FIRST TIME IN MONTHS.

AT THE RATE HE WAS GOING, OCTAVIAN WOULD HAVE DEPLETED THE SOURCE SUPPLY ANYWAY. AT LEAST NOW, THERE'S HOPE IN THE GALAXY AGAIN.

STILL, THE ENRICHMENT IT COULD HAVE BROUGHT US...

WHA?? WHERE?

RA, IS THAT YOU?

IT'S YOUR MOTHER, DEAR, BUT I'M FLATTERED.

GASP!

RELAX, SLEEPYHEAD. NOTHING HAPPENED.

DID YOU SERIOUSLY JUST CALL ME SLEEPYHEAD? YOU, WHO PASSES OUT EVERY THIRTEEN SECONDS?

HEY, I HAVE EXTENUATING CIRCUMSTANCES!

YEAH.

STILL WEIRD.

I'M GLAD YOU TOLD US ABOUT IT, THOUGH.

FINDING OUT ABOUT YOUR CONNECTION WITH THE PLASMA ALLOWED US TO PUT THE MISSION ON CADA'DUUN IN MOTION.

IT'S JUST NICE TO HAVE A COUNCIL THAT FINALLY TRUSTS IN CLEO.

CHIRP!

THE COUNCIL!

OH, SHOOT! WHAT TIME IS IT?

ALMOST THREE NOW.

SORRY, I FORGOT THAT WAS THIS AFTERNOON. GO ON. I NEED TO MONITOR THINGS DOWN HERE.

GOOD LUCK!

THANK YOU, AKILA'S MOM!

C'MON, MIHOS.

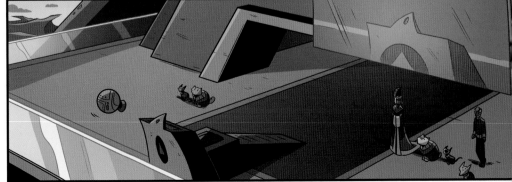

UM.

COUGH COUGH

AHEM

CITIZENS OF THE NILE GALAXY!

nod

IT HAS BEEN ALMOST SEVEN MONTHS SINCE THE UNFORTUNATE DESTRUCTION OF P.Y.R.A.M.I.D.'S BASE AND THE OCCUPATION OF MAYET. OCTAVIAN AND HIS ARMY HAVE CARVED A WOUND THROUGH THE AILUROS SYSTEM WE NEVER THOUGHT POSSIBLE. SOME OF YOU MAY EVEN FEEL THAT ALL HOPE IS LOST. THAT OCTAVIAN HAS ALREADY WON. AND LOOKING OUT AT THE BROKEN SHIPS SCATTERED BEFORE ME...

IT'S HARD TO ARGUE WITH THAT SENTIMENT.

WOW.

HE IS HORRIBLE AT THIS.

BLIP

VZCH

UM. YES. NOT...

NOT GOOD.

ᒥᑎᑊᒪᗋᗅᑎ

ᒥᑎᑊᒪᐯ

BUT! I AM HERE TO ASSURE YOU THAT THERE *IS* STILL HOPE.

THANKS TO THE EFFORTS OF P.Y.R.A.M.I.D., WE HAVE SUCCESSFULLY DESTROYED OCTAVIAN'S POWER SOURCE FOR HIS NEW WEAPON. HE CAN NO LONGER USE IT TO WREAK HAVOC ON OUR HOMES!

THIS, OF COURSE, IS ALL THANKS TO OUR PROPHESIED SAVIOR, THE QUEEN OF THE NILE, *CLEOPATRA VII!*

RAH

CLAP CLAP

ALL RIGHT, CLEO.

YOU'RE UP!

CLEO?

WHO...

UM...

WHO WILL BE HERE SHORTLY.

EVERYONE, PLEASE BE PATIENT.

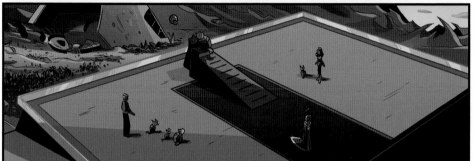

UH... OKAY.

ANY QUESTIONS?

CHIRP!

THEY THINK JUST BECAUSE OF SOME STUPID PROPHECY OR BECAUSE I CAN SNAP MY FINGERS AND CREATE A LITTLE PINK FLAME THAT I'LL SOMEHOW VANQUISH AN ENTIRE ARMY.

SNAP

I CAN'T DEFEAT OCTAVIAN, YOUR MAJESTY. I WON'T BE ABLE TO KILL HIM. I ALREADY TRIED.

AND FAILED.

IS EVERYTHING--

BLEEP BLEEP

BOOP

APOLOGIES, YOUR MAJESTY. NORMALLY I'D CONTACT MSAMAKI, BUT--

WHAT IS IT?

THERE'S A SHIP IN THE SOLAR SYSTEM. IT'S ONE OF OURS BUT...OLDER. THEY ARE RELAYING A MESSAGE ON OUR SECURE NETWORK.

ON OUR...

WHAT DOES IT SAY?

IT SAYS THEY ARE FRIENDS WITH CLEOPATRA.

IT ALSO SAYS THEY HAVE A SHIP FULL OF CHILDREN. THAT THEY ESCAPED THE DESTRUCTION OF HYKOSIS CITY.

HYKOSIS??

GIVE THEM THE COORDINATES. LET THEM IN.

PIRATES.

CHAPTER THREE

VZZZZ
BLEEP

I LIKE THE NEW ARM, RED.

BLOOP BEEP

WE WERE STRANDED ON LUX. HEARD THEY SOMEHOW ATTAINED A CHEETAH CELL, SO I BORROWED IT.

YOU BORROWED FROM *PIRATES*?

LIKE, DO YOU PLAN ON GIVING IT BACK TO THEM?

OKAY, I *STOLE* IT. BUT, I MEAN, THEY'RE PIRATES. THEY STOLE IT FIRST.

PROBABLY.

PRETTY BRAVE.

PRETTY STUPID.

SOOO YOU'VE JUST, WHAT? BEEN FLYING AROUND IN THAT BUS ALL YEAR?

WE INITIALLY WERE EN ROUTE TO MAYET, BUT AFTER WE HEARD WHAT HAPPENED...

ANYWAY, WE BRIEFLY FOUND SHELTER ON KHARTOUM UNTIL OCTAVIAN OBLITERATED THAT CITY, TOO. WE'VE ESSENTIALLY BEEN PLANET-HOPPING TILL WE CAUGHT WIND OF THIS PLACE.

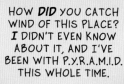

IT HASN'T BEEN EASY, BUT THOSE ARE STRONG KIDS. THEY'VE BEEN HANDLING THINGS BETTER THAN MOST OF THE TRIBES WE'VE COME ACROSS.

EVEN HELPED US GET OUT OF A TIGHT SPOT OR TWO.

HOW *DID* YOU CATCH WIND OF THIS PLACE? *I* DIDN'T EVEN KNOW ABOUT IT, AND I'VE BEEN WITH P.Y.R.A.M.I.D. THIS WHOLE TIME.

YOU DON'T FLY AROUND IN A STEALTH SHIP FOR AS LONG AS I HAVE WITHOUT PICKING UP ON CERTAIN TRAILS. STEALTH TECH LEAVES A RESIDUE.

I INVESTIGATED A FEW LOCATION RUMORS AND--

VOILÀ.

PRETTY CLEVER.

PRETTY SCARY.

IF ANTONY CAN FIND THIS PLACE...

RELAX. IT **WAS** CLEVER.

~WINK!

I WOULDN'T HAVE BROUGHT THOSE ORPHANS HERE IF I DIDN'T THINK IT WAS SAFE.

SPEAKING OF, THE TECHNOLOGY PROTECTING THIS PLANET IS REALLY IMPRESSIVE.

WOULDN'T RESIST MEETING WHOEVER DESIGNED IT.

SHUFF

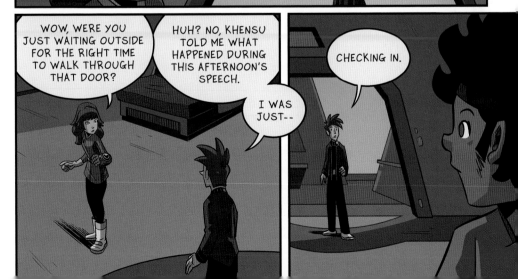

WOW, WERE YOU JUST WAITING OUTSIDE FOR THE RIGHT TIME TO WALK THROUGH THAT DOOR?

HUH? NO, KHENSU TOLD ME WHAT HAPPENED DURING THIS AFTERNOON'S SPEECH.

I WAS JUST--

CHECKING IN.

*Sigh*

THERE'S ALSO THIS.

HEY!

IT'S THAT EGYPTOLOGY BOOK!

YOU'VE SEEN THIS BOOK BEFORE?

IT WAS IN THE ALEXANDRIA LIBRARY. IT'S HOW WE FOUND OUT ABOUT THE TIME TABLETS.

I THOUGHT WE LOST IT WITH EVERYTHING ELSE.

HOW DID YOU GET IT?

ANNA FOUND IT IN HARKHEBI'S STUDY SHORTLY AFTER WE PUT HIM TO REST.

MAYBE KHENSU GAVE IT TO HIM?

WHY BRING IT HERE?

LET ME SEE THAT.

I DON'T BELIEVE IT.

WHY DIDN'T YOU SHOW THIS TO ME BEFORE, BRIAN?

I HONESTLY DON'T REMEMBER SEEING THAT BEFORE.

WHY? WHO'S BAKARI, CLEO?

HE WAS MY TEACHER. BEFORE I WAS ZAPPED HERE FROM THE PAST.

HE WAS A LOT LIKE KHENSU, ACTUALLY...

SHUFF

WHO WAS A LOT LIKE ME?

IS THERE A *MICROPHONE* IN HERE?

KHENSU. WE NEED TO SEE THE TIME TABLETS.

WHAT?

WHY?

YEAH, WHERE DID *THAT* COME FROM?

YOU READ THE INSCRIPTION.

ALL I COULD READ WAS YOUR NAME AND THAT TEACHER OF YOURS. THE REST WAS JUST...SHAPES.

DON'T LOOK AT *ME*.

I COULDN'T MAKE HEADS OR TAILS OUT OF IT, EITHER. PARTLY WHY I BROUGHT IT TO YOU.

WHAT ARE YOU ALL--

THE *SEBA*.

I HAVEN'T SEEN THIS SINCE I WAS A KITTEN.

HOW DID YOU GET THIS?

ANTONY HAD IT. BUT, I MEAN, YOU'VE SEEN IT SINCE THEN, RIGHT? WE GAVE IT TO YOU BEFORE WE LEFT THAT TIME FOR HYKOSIS.

NOT THE ORIGINAL. THE ONE YOU FOUND IN THE LIBRARY WAS A COPY.

A COPY?

MOST OF THE BOOKS THAT WERE IN THE ALEXANDRIA LIBRARY WERE COPIES.

DO YOU REALLY THINK P.Y.R.A.M.I.D. WOULD BE FOOLISH ENOUGH TO STORE ALL OF THE LAST REMAINING TEXTS IN THE GALAXY UNDER ONE ROOF?

WELL, THEY DO SEEM TO BE GATHERING THE LAST REMAINING GOOD GUYS IN THE GALAXY ON ONE PLANET.

OH, *THAT'S* WHERE CLEO GETS IT.

YOU ARE MUCH SCARIER.

ARE YOU SAYING YOU CAN READ THIS, CLEO? NO ONE HAS EVER BEEN ABLE TO DECIPHER WHAT THAT INSCRIPTION SAYS.

WELL, SURE.

WOW, IS THIS WHAT IT FEELS LIKE TO BE BRIAN?

OR AKILA?

ANTONY.

ANYONE IN THIS ROOM, I GUESS...

JUST READ IT, CLEO.

WHOA. CALM DOWN, HOT PINK.

HE'S WITH US.

SORRY ABOUT THE SCARE.

I REALLY DESPISE WHEN I HAVE TO DO THAT.

ALSO, HE TALKS.

OH!

HERE.

WASHED UP NEAR ME AND BRIAN.

SHORTLY BEFORE, UM...*HE* FOUND US.

SOME NICE FEATURES ON THAT HEADPIECE, PRINCESS.

WHAT IS GOING ON?!

127

I CAN'T BELIEVE FOD FRANZE IS HERE.

WHO IS HE?

THIS GUY WE MET WAY BACK WHEN WE CRASHED ON HYKOSIS. REAL JERK.

AND SHOULD WE ASK WHY HE HAS IT OUT FOR CLEO?

SHE SHOT HIS HAT.

SHE SHOT... HIS HAT.

IT IS SOMETHING APPARENTLY NO ONE DOES, BUT, Y'KNOW...

CLEO.

NO, NO. I GET IT.

WHY AREN'T WE ARRESTING HIM?

SO FAR HE HASN'T REALLY DONE ANYTHING WRONG. JUST SHOUTING TO SEE CLEOPATRA.

HE'S GOING TO INCITE A RIOT.

...DOESN'T **NOT** MAKE SENSE.

SHE DID SAVE THAT VILLAGE.

JUST SAYING, IF YOU'RE GOING TO USE AN AMPHIBIOUS METAPHOR TO FLY HOME YOUR POINT, MAYBE DO YOUR RESEARCH?

THIS ISN'T RIGHT.

IS HE TYPICALLY BETTER AT BIOLOGY?

WHERE ARE WE GOING?

TO MEET SOMEONE.

BUT **WHERE**?

WHERE YOU NEED TO BE.

AND YOU'RE THOTH. GOD OF KNOWLEDGE AND WISDOM.

IS THAT ANOTHER QUESTION?

I THOUGHT THOTH WAS AN IBIS? LIKE THE ONE ON MY CROWN.

THE ONE ON YOUR CROWN?

THIS.

THAT'S A SNAKE.

HAH!

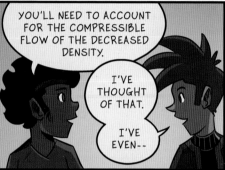

137

MAJESTY!

SHE'S ALIVE BUT FADING.

SHE NEEDS CRITICAL MEDICAL ATTENTION.

I CAN'T BELIEVE SHE SURVIVED THIS.

BLOOP BLOOP BLOOP

AKILA.

REST

OH NO.

THE OASIS.

IT'S...DYING.

MOM. MOM, IT'S AKILA.

MOM?

DAD?

WE NEED TO SEND GUARDS TO THE PLASMA CHAMBER.

THE WHAT?

THE OASIS IS THE RESULT OF GOLDEN LION PLASMA THAT POWERS THIS PLANET'S PROTECTIVE TECHNOLOGY. IF THE VEGETATION IS DYING, THAT MEANS OUR CLOAK AND SHIELD ARE COMPROMISED AS WELL.

I THINK IT'S *TOO* LATE.

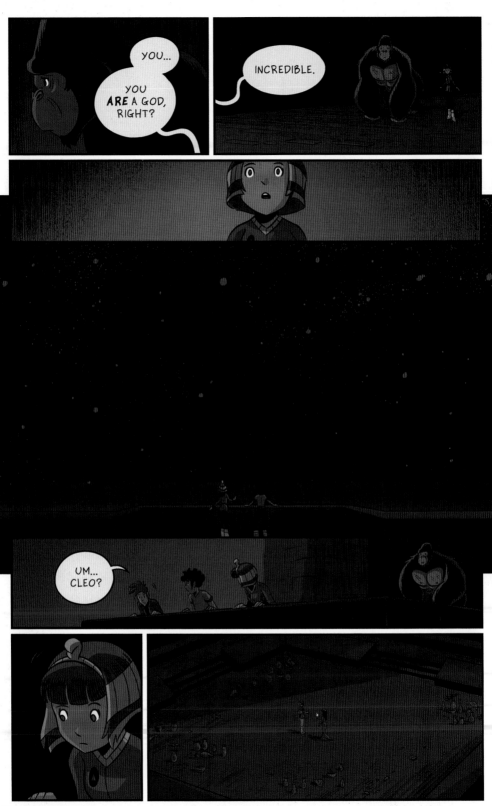

FLASH

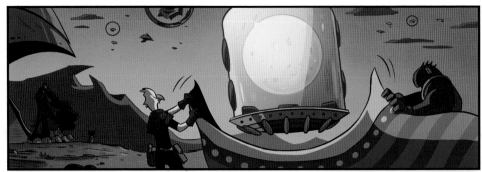

THE PHARAOH HAS ALSO BEEN TAKEN CARE OF. WE'RE ROUNDING UP THE REST OF P.Y.R.A.M.I.D.'S COUNCIL AS WE SPEAK.

I'M IMPRESSED.

HOWEVER, NONE OF THEM ARE WHO I WANT.

TH' PRINCESS, CORRECT?

CLEOPATRA?

NOT A FAN, EITHER.

FOD FRANZE. WE 'AVEN'T MET, BUT AH'M THRILLED TA BE IN BUSINESS WITH YA.

FLAP FLAP
splish
CLEOPATRA.
WELCOME TO THE END OF THE UNIVERSE.

# CHAPTER FOUR

I KNOW THEY'RE **GONE**. GONE WHERE?

ARE THEY OKAY?

THAT'S... FEIRAN.

IS THIS HAPPENING RIGHT NOW?

THE PAST.

WHAT IS IT WITH THE AMBIGUOUS ANSWERS IN THIS PLACE?

WHY AM I HERE?

TO PROTECT YOUR WORLD.

IT IS BEING SWALLOWED BY A DISTURBED ELDER ONCE STATIONED THERE TO PRESERVE IT. IT IS ALL BUT GONE NOW.

YOU ARE STANDING ON THE LAST REMNANT OF ITS EXISTENCE.

...

THE LAST...

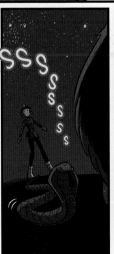

HSSSSSSS

151

SHE SEEMS DIFFERENT FROM THE OTHER CREATURES I'VE ENCOUNTERED TODAY.

YOU ARE CORRECT. SHE HAS A DEEP CONNECTION TO DUAT AS WELL AS TO ANUBIS, ITS FORMER GUARDIAN. HE KEPT THE SOULS THAT RESIDED HERE INTACT.

NOW HE INHABITS A FRIEND OF YOURS INSTEAD.

GOZI!

HE BEGAN CALLING HIMSELF BY ANOTHER NAME, BUT YES.

NONE OF OUR KIND CAN DIRECTLY INTERFERE OUTSIDE OF THIS DOMAIN, SO ANUBIS NEEDS A VESSEL ON YOUR WORLD IN ORDER TO ACT UPON IT.

ANUBIS POSSESSES OCTAVIAN?

IS THAT WHAT CAUSED HIM TO BECOMES SUCH A TYRANT?

I'M AFRAID A MILLENNIUM OF LOSS HAS DONE MORE TO SHATTER GOZI'S SOUL THAN POSSESSION EVER COULD.

THERE'S THIS SWORD.

MY FRIEND AKILA THINKS IT MAKES HIM IMMORTAL.

THAT SWORD IS AT THE ROOT OF ALL THIS. IT USED TO BELONG TO HER FAMILY.

HER FAMILY?

SO IT'S TRUE!

HASILRIG.

WE NEVER RECOVERED HIS BODY ON CADA'DUUN.

HASILRIG WOULD DIE BEFORE EVER TELLING THAT MONSTER OUR COORDINATES.

IT--

ERRGH

DOESN'T MATTER.

WE ANTICIPATED HIM FINDING US EVENTUALLY.

YOU WHAT?

HE'S BEEN ONE STEP AHEAD OUR ENTIRE LIVES. IT WAS ONLY--

OW

A MATTER OF TIME.

WE HAVE A PLAN, THOUGH.

BRIAN DISCOVERED A WAY TO USE THE PLASMA AGAINST OCTAVIAN. BUT WE NEED CLEOPATRA'S POWERS FOR IT TO BE EFFECTIVE.

WHAT IS IT?

WHERE IS CLEOPATRA?

BUT UNBEKNOWNST TO THE YOUNG PRINCE, ANUBIS HAD PLANTED A PIECE OF HIS SOUL INTO KEBECHET'S SWORD.

ANUBIS USED THE SWORD TO ENSLAVE THE PRINCE AND, FUELED BY RAGE, THREATENED TO CONSUME EVERY LIVING BEING IN THE UNIVERSE AS PUNISHMENT FOR HIS DAUGHTER'S DEATH.

IT TOOK ALL OF OUR NUMBERS TO FINALLY DEFEAT HIM, WITH RA, OUR MOST POWERFUL, TRAPPING ANUBIS'S ESSENCE WITHIN THE SAME INSTRUMENT THE MAD ELDER HAD USED TO WREAK HAVOC ON YOUR WORLD.

THE SWORD WAS BURIED, ALONG WITH THE PRINCE'S ENTIRE FORTUNE AND TWO TABLETS I INSCRIBED WITH A WARNING...

THAT ANUBIS MAY RISE AGAIN.

THAT STAR FELL ONTO A PLANET IN THE NILE GALAXY WHERE IT REMAINED HIDDEN UNTIL YOUR BATTLE WITH ANUBIS'S GENERAL, OPHOIS.

BEFORE HE DIED, RA TRANSFERRED HIS REMAINING ESSENCE INTO THAT OF A DYING STAR.

THE GOLDEN LION!

SO THAT'S THE KEY TO DEFEATING HIM!

PERHAPS.

THE THREADS BETWEEN TIME ARE PERPETUALLY WINDING.

THE WORDS THAT BAKARI WROTE TO ME-- THE ONES YOU SAID BROUGHT ME TO DUAT. HE SAID THAT I REPRESENT THE THREE POINTS OF TIME. THAT MUST HAVE BEEN WHAT HE WAS REFERRING TO.

THE PAST, THE PRESENT, AND THE FUTURE.

HOW DID HE KNOW I WOULD BE HERE?

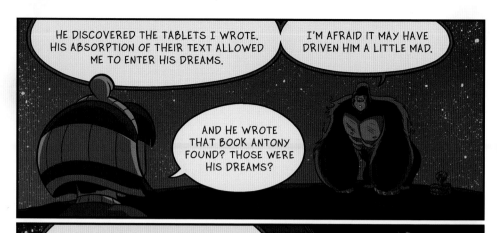

HE DISCOVERED THE TABLETS I WROTE. HIS ABSORPTION OF THEIR TEXT ALLOWED ME TO ENTER HIS DREAMS.

I'M AFRAID IT MAY HAVE DRIVEN HIM A LITTLE MAD.

AND HE WROTE THAT BOOK ANTONY FOUND? THOSE WERE HIS DREAMS?

HE DID HIS BEST TO INTERPRET WHAT I WAS TRYING TO FOREWARN HIM ABOUT. HE DECIPHERED THE MESSAGE I WROTE ON THE TABLETS. LATER HIS BOOK WAS DISCOVERED AND REINTERPRETED ON A SCROLL. THAT SCROLL WAS FOUND AND REINTERPRETED AGAIN.

THE SCROLL I WAS TOLD ABOUT THE DAY I ARRIVED AT P.Y.R.A.M.I.D.

SO BAKARI WROTE THE PROPHECY.

EVEN WITHOUT BEING HERE, HE'S STILL BEEN TEACHING ME HOW TO BE A QUEEN.

WHAT DO I NEED TO DO?

NO, NOT YOU.

THE QUEEN OF THE NILE.

BLAM
BLAM
BOOM
RUMBLLE
CCRSHH
FIND OUT IF ANY SHIPS HAVE LEFT THE PLANET.
CLEOPATRA MUST BE FOUND.

WHAT DO YOU MEAN?

I *AM* THE QUEEN OF THE NILE.

AREN'T I?

THAT CROWN ON YOUR HEAD--

THE ORIGINAL ONE--

WHERE DID IT COME FROM?

IT...WAS A GIFT FROM MY MOM.

SHE GAVE IT TO ME THE DAY SHE DIED. TOLD ME HER MOTHER HAD GIVEN IT TO HER.

THAT CROWN HAD BEEN IN YOUR FAMILY FOR GENERATIONS: A SYMBOL FOR WHAT'S IN YOUR BLOOD. IT'S HOW YOU WERE ABLE TO ACTIVATE THE TABLETS. AN ENERGY PASSED ON FROM YOUR FIRST ANCESTOR.

YOU'RE SAYING MY MOM COULD DO THIS, TOO?

SHE HAD THE POTENTIAL.

AND THIS ANCIENT ANCESTOR OF OURS?

BEFORE THE PRINCE FELL TO ANUBIS, HE AND KEBECHET HAD A DAUGHTER. THIS IS HER, A CREATURE BORN BETWEEN YOUR WORLD AND OURS AND HENCE NOT HELD CAPTIVE BY THE SHACKLES OF SPACE AND TIME. SHE HELPED ME POWER THE TABLETS THAT BROUGHT YOU TO THE NILE GALAXY.

WOW.

SO...

SO ANYONE IN MY FAMILY LINE COULD BE THE QUEEN OF THE NILE.

PAST, PRESENT, OR--

ⲡⲁⲃⲉ!

173

THIS IS SENSELESS SQUANDERING, CLEO.
WE KNOW FULL WELL THAT YOU CAN'T DEFEAT ME.
NO.
BUT I CAN DISTRACT YOU.
VRRUM
TAKE HIM OUT, DAD!

AAAAAAAAAA
FWUSH
FWOOSH
YOUR MAJESTY!
NOW!
AARRGH
YOU THINK YOU CAN DEFEAT ME?
TO FINISH WHAT EVEN TIME HAS FAILED TO ACHIEVE?
I AM STRONGER THAN LIFE ITSELF!
I AM A GO--
RRK.
FWOOM
AH!

CLEO?

YOU DID IT. YOU DEFEATED OCTAVIAN.

CLEO?

CLEO?

ARE YOU ALL RIGHT?

IT'S MINE NOW.

YOU ARE
MINE NOW.

AS IT WAS
ALWAYS MEANT
TO BE.

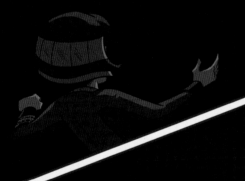

TOGETHER
WE ALONE WILL
FINISH WHAT WAS
STARTED.

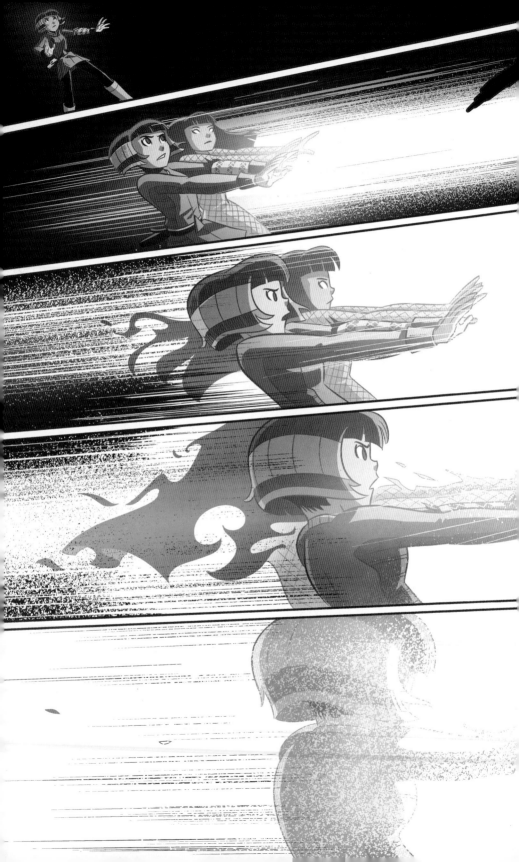

ALL HAIL PHARAOH YOSIRA!

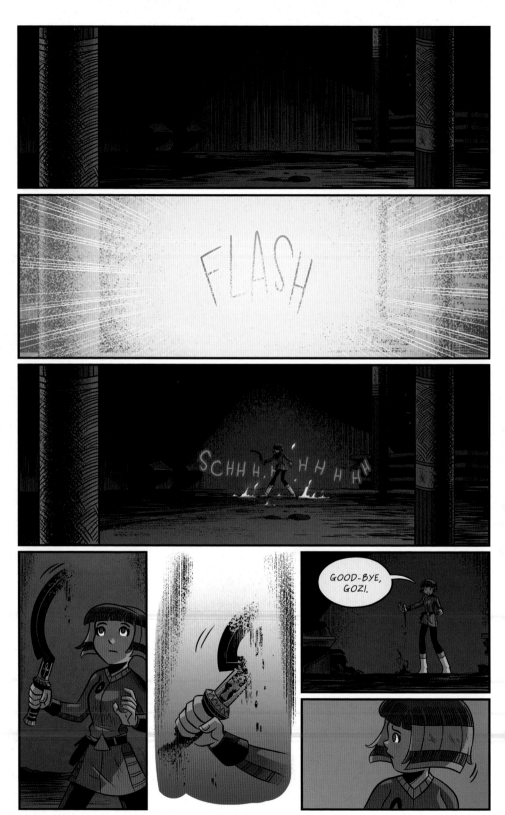

222

EGYPT?

I'M...
HOME.

YOU... YOU FOLLOWED ME!

Oof

HOW?

WELL, IT WASN'T IMMEDIATE. IT TOOK SOME TIME FOR BRIAN TO DISCERN THE PROPERTIES, AND QUEEN YOSIRA HAD TO FIGURE OUT HOW TO POWER IT, BUT--

OH.

GUESS IT WAS A ONE-WAY TICKET.

NO MATTER. WE KIND OF EXPECTED THAT TO BE THE CASE.

FIVE MONTHS AFTER THE BATTLE OF FEIRAN...

EARTH HISTORY 3

EARTH HISTORY 1

A FEW CALCULATIONS AND BRIAN WAS ABLE TO DIRECT THE JUMP TO ROUGHLY THE SAME TIME AND PLACE YOU FIRST ARRIVED HERE IN EGYPT.

WE ALL THOUGHT YOU WERE, WELL... THAT WAS, UNTIL KHENSU SAW YOUR NAME IN ONE OF HIS EARTH HISTORY BOOKS.

STILL NOT SURE WHY YOUR OLD TEACHER WAS SO INSISTENT I BE THE ONE TO COME FIND YOU.

HE NEVER SAID AND I NEVER PRESSED.

DIDN'T TAKE MUCH CONVINCING, THOUGH.

THE NILE GALAXY WAS NEVER QUITE AS EXCITING AFTER YOU LEFT.

PLUS, THINK OF THE TREASURE I'LL FIND IN **THIS** TIME PERIOD.

OH! SPEAKING OF WHICH, I BROUGHT YOU SOMETHING.

HERE YOU GO. SORRY I TOOK IT WITHOUT ASKING.

YOSIRA SAID MAYBE SHE'LL GET IT BACK ONE DAY.

AND THAT'S HOW CLEOPATRA VII, ALONG WITH HER PARTNER, ANTONY, REPELLED AN ALIEN INVASION, DEFEATED A ROMAN EMPIRE, AND MADE THE KINGDOM OF EGYPT ONE OF THE LARGEST AND MOST PEACEFUL CIVILIZATIONS OF ALL TIME, EXPANDING EVEN TO OUR OWN NILE GALAXY.

# EPILOGUE

ANY QUESTIONS?

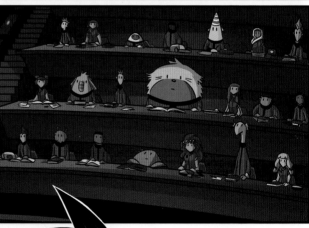

THAT **DON'T** INVOLVE PUNCHING XERX AND TAKING DOWN ROBOTIC MUMMIES?

CLASS DISMISSED.

# THE END

# ACKNOWLEDGMENTS

Thirteen years ago, I drew a picture of Cleopatra. I surrounded her with stars and planets, gave her a space helmet, a ray gun, and a space suit–wearing cat. I wrote the title *Cleopatra in Spaaaace!* above her head and then moved on to other things.

"You need to make that Cleopatra drawing into a real comic," my friend Jeremy messaged me (so, first off, thank you to Jeremy). Other friends of mine told me the same thing soon after. I didn't have any ideas, but I started drawing a comic anyhow. My wife, Jen, suggested I give Cleo a space bike that looked like a sphinx. Suddenly I had a lot of ideas. Suddenly I had a lot of drawn comic pages. Suddenly I had a story. Ed Masessa from Scholastic Book Fairs noticed this story, showed it to David Saylor (publisher of the Graphix imprint), who showed it to Cassandra Pelham Fulton (editorial director of Graphix), who thought they might like to publish this harebrained idea about a teenaged Cleopatra in space.

Suddenly I had a graphic novel series.

Those are the immediate people I need to thank for why you are holding this sixth and final Cleopatra in Space book, the culmination of nine years' worth of work. I owe a huge amount of gratitude to many who helped me during this time, as well:

My agent, Judy, for navigating me through a very different publishing world than I was used to. My two boys, Oliver and Orion — both of whom were born during the production of this series — for keeping me rooted in reality while I fell into a world of aliens and time travel. My extended family for their endless support. My Scholastic family for *their* endless support. My cats, Ash and Misty, for making sure I didn't get lost and lonely huddled up in front of my computer ten hours a day. Christ for this very same thing.

This book wouldn't look the way it does without Phil Falco's excellent art direction and my amazing team of color flatters: Mary Bellamy, Kate Carleton, Lee Cherolis, and Josh Dykstra. Thank you for all your help!

I wrote the ending to *Queen of the Nile* before I ever drew a single page of Book One. No one would have ever read Cleo's fate without the incredible number of teachers, librarians, booksellers, parents, and kids out there who recommended Cleopatra in Space to other readers. For this, I am forever in your debt.

Finally, this series literally would not exist without Cleopatra, the *actual* Cleopatra, and all of the artists who scribed her story on scrolls, stone, walls, and canvases. Thank you for those words and pictures. And, Cleopatra, if you are up in the stars looking down on this comic right now, forgive me for the artistic license. But I gotta say, you sure look radiant in pink.